Rachel

NICOLA COX ON GAME COOKERY

Nicola and Simon Cox run Farthinghoe Fine Wine & Food Ltd, their widely known Cookery School and Wine Merchant business, from their Old Rectory home near Banbury where they live with their four children.

Former *Sunday Times Cook of Britain* (which encouraged Simon to give up a successful military career in 1974 to found their joint business), Nicola's demonstrations at Farthinghoe are now recognised as both outstandingly enjoyable and popular. They run Spring and Autumn seasons and visitors come from far and wide to enjoy a day at Farthinghoe with Nicola or one of her star guest demonstrators. In addition to her days at Farthinghoe, Nicola has done some three hundred cookery demonstrations round England, Scotland and Wales and abroad in Hong Kong and California. When time allows, she hunts in the winter and gardens in the summer (their garden is open on occasion to the public). Already the author of two previous successful Victor Gollancz/Peter Crawley books, *Good Food from Farthinghoe* (1981) and *Country Cooking from Farthinghoe* (1984), and three specialist Magimix and Food Processor books, Nicola is also a well-known cookery journalist: past Cookery Editor of *Brides*, regular contributor to *Good Housekeeping* and *Decanter*, she now freelances with many recent articles in *A la Carte*, *Taste*, *The Times* and *Living*.

Simon Cox has been a wine merchant for fifteen years and a Master of Wine since 1985. He has a catholic list that attracts private customers from all over the country as well as from the Far East. Widely travelled through all the wine areas of Europe, he has also investigated the Cape, tasted widely during three visits to California and is actively planning his first visit, with Nicola, to the vineyards of New Zealand and Australia.

Travel is one of their great loves, enabling them to refresh their ideas and enhance their constantly evolving cookery programmes and wine list. Simon has shot and fished since boyhood and their three sons are equally keen. The kitchen at Farthinghoe sees many a gathering of those who know what a fresh run sea trout or a young grouse look like and their critical advice has helped to make Nicola's game recipes so stylish and authentic, all with that absolute reliability that is her hallmark.

Also by Nicola Cox

GOOD FOOD FROM FARTHINGHOE
COUNTRY COOKING FROM FARTHINGHOE

NICOLA COX
on
GAME
COOKERY

With Wine by Simon Cox MW

LONDON
VICTOR GOLLANCZ LTD
in association with
Peter Crawley
1989

"What would the world be, once bereft
of wet and of wildness? Let them be left,
O let them be left, wildness and wet;
Long live the weeds and the wilderness yet."
Inversnaid – Gerard Manley Hopkins

First published in Great Britain 1989
in association with Peter Crawley
by Victor Gollancz Ltd
14 Henrietta Street, London WC2E 8QJ

British Library Cataloguing in Publication Data
Cox, Nicola
Nicola Cox on game cookery.
1. Food: Game dishes. Recipes
641.6'81
ISBN 0-575-03923-X

Photoset in Great Britain by
Rowland Phototypesetting Ltd
Bury St Edmunds, Suffolk
and printed and bound in Great Britain by
Butler and Tanner Ltd, Frome, Somerset

ACKNOWLEDGEMENTS

Years of hunting, shooting and fishing have brought me into contact with many generous people who have shared their knowledge with me and from whom I have gleaned fascinating nuggets of information; I've also met lots of country people in the twelve years I have been demonstrating Game Cookery at the Game Fair, many of whom have also shared their knowledge with me; to all of them, my grateful thanks. I have a great debt also to all the gamekeepers I have talked to, especially Frank Holman at Wood Hall and Peter Walker at Blubberhouses, pressing them unfairly to put their deep instinctive knowledge into words for the amateur. Special thanks are due to Richard Parker for finding me some of the game I needed and to Mark Price for complying cheerfully with impossible requests; to Brian Charlesworth for giving me lots of lovely game, to Ken Fowler for turning up with the unusual birds and beasts I sometimes needed and to Edward Trotter for shooting the Pink Footed Duck in the photograph for me.

My thanks also to Richard Prior for the use of his succinct and accurate charts and to Alexander Trotter, then Chairman of The Nature Conservancy Committee for Scotland, for checking some of my facts. My thanks especially to Gollancz Managing Director Stephen Bray for the concept, design and layout, to Andrew Kay for the artwork, to Delphine MacCormick for her paintings, to Elfreda Powell for her skilful editing and, of course, to the whole production team from Gollancz who have made this such a beautiful book. My thanks particularly to Peter Myers for the pleasure of working with him and above all for the beautiful photographs which entirely capture the spirit of what we wanted. Peter Crawley my publisher has again nudged me gently and tactfully towards the completion date one is never ready for. Mrs James our secretary has grappled with the word processor on my behalf and Simon, my dear husband, has wrestled with my drafts to his eternal credit. My thanks go to them all and to my family who will be sad that such profligate use of game may now have to be moderated!

Farthinghoe   *Nicola Cox*
Spring 1989

CONTENTS

INTRODUCTION

Man has hunted game since prehistoric times and he's still at it, just as enthusiastically as ever. It may no longer be strictly a necessity but the excitement of the chase lingers on and it is still a great pleasure for us to cook the rewards. England and Scotland have a wonderful tradition of game cookery, in spite of the fact that the chase used to be the preserve of princes and a few rich landlords, with the horrific punishment of hanging often meted out for the illegal taking of game. Mercifully all this is in the past and it is now open to all of us to shoot or fish or just to buy game without having to get our feet wetter than in the pavement puddles in front of the shop. Game is widely available from butchers, fishmongers, specialist game dealers and some go-ahead supermarkets. Much of it comes from big sporting estates but plenty also from farms and rough shoots, all of which must sell to cover some of their expenses; it also now comes from an increasing number of game farms, established to provide most game from red deer to quail. Sad to say, much of our best game goes abroad because of the ease of modern distribution and the ability of our European neighbours to pay for it. I am keen to encourage my readers to a greater use of our fine home-bred game and this is one of my main reasons for writing this book. Many suppliers will be found in Henrietta Green's *British Food Finds* (Rich and Green, 1 Moorhouse Road, London W2 5DH, 01-727 9808).

One of the other reasons for my great enthusiasm for game is that it is such a wonderfully healthy food. It is naturally somewhat lean and what fat it has is *not* the saturated fat that we are now advised to avoid. It is mostly produced naturally, much of it in quite wild or certainly very rural surroundings where it has little opportunity to eat food that is full of additives and is less likely than most livestock to graze in sprayed or artificially fertilised fields. So game, particularly the really wild game – grouse from the high moors, duck from the Norfolk flight pond or partridge from the Dales – is, rather like hill and moorland lamb, one of our most natural and most delicious foods.

There are, of course, already a number of books – some of them excellent but many now out of print – which have stimulated me in the past to experiment with game. Some of these were written, as it were, by the sportsman's wife, that somewhat long-suffering body who starts out enthusiastically on her adopted pilgrimage but whom one sometimes finds beginning to look a little harassed and wild-eyed as yet another bulging game bag is flung triumphantly on to the kitchen table. These books took a robust and thoroughly down-to-earth approach; they advised on a range of subtly contrasting shepherd's pies to reduce the inevitable tedium of this worthy dish by making it from goose breasts or from the liver of roe deer.

Then there are those written by chefs in conditions that seem somewhat more detached from the real world of the muddy welly: these will only use fine specimens of exquisitely shot young game and the best cuts of prime venison, and are splendid in their way. They have a wealth of excellent ideas and technical advice, especially if you buy your game in prime condition from a good dealer at not inconsiderable cost. They sometimes seem, however, a little less appropriate for your eleven-year-old son's first, rather badly shot pheasant or a grouse the young spaniel had a bit of fun with before eventually, reluctantly, bringing it back to the butt.

Twelve years of demonstrating Game Cookery at the annual Game Fair has given me a clear idea of the sort of recipes people want and the dishes they enjoy. So I have gathered together a catholic range of some of my favourite recipes; some are classics for which I think I have found a particularly nice version; some are forgotten dishes of the past which I have rediscovered by delving into some of my old books and others have been given by friends; even more are my new and original creations which reflect our modern approach to a healthy and lighter style – the new approach to game, if I may call it that. This takes a very traditional medium and dresses it in a more modern suit of clothes: healthy, carefully cooked from the best possible ingredients and imaginatively presented. Some of the recipes are in the chef's style with a perfectly trimmed breast of this or that, bathed in a beautiful sauce and served on a plate with a pretty garnish; these are lovely for last-minute cooking, as a chef would do it, or if you are cooking for just a few. But life is not always like that and I know from long experience how difficult they are for the cook-hostess to produce perfectly. So I have thought out plenty of others that do not take too much of that last-minute preparation which so easily spoils your enjoyment of your own party, always a terrible mistake. Having said that, I must honestly say that the perfect bird often needs strict timing and close attention to produce the perfect result, especially for roasts or delicately and lightly cooked dishes. But there are plenty of other slow-cooked dishes that can be used for game no longer in the first gay flush of youth and where an hour or so, let alone split-second timing, will not much matter.

As far as the richness and presentation of the dish is concerned, some old-fashioned dishes did perhaps look and taste a bit heavy. They had powerful ingredients like clove, nutmeg and mace mixed with generous quantities of mushrooms, sweetbreads, cockscombs (where can we buy these now?) and forcemeat balls, good though all these are. Made with fresh garden vegetables, home-cured hams and well-hung meat, they must have tasted wonderful and been very suitable for those rather better exercised, uncentrally heated days. I am keen, as always, to learn and preserve the best from this tradition.

On the other hand, there is also now an easily discernible rejection of some of the bolder experiments of the nouvelle style with its carefully contrasting and undoubtedly beautiful plate pictures, especially those that leave us hungry!

My approach, and the approach I know to be popular with the cook-hostess, is a blend, if you like, of both of these somewhat polarised views. It is towards tasty, homely dishes with subtly chosen yet complex flavours, perfectly blended and knit together, carefully cooked and intelligently presented. I have had to be ruthless in rejecting anything that didn't quite merit a place, even some old friends. I have discussed different styles and techniques and I hope you will find, as I have done, that you can adapt or vary the recipes to suit yourself, the season and the ingredients you are able to find or have handy in cupboard or freezer. Because game has little natural fat, it is inclined to be a little dry unless sympathetically prepared and cooked; those of you who have been cooking game for years are probably up to all the dodges but, for new game cooks, there are a number of useful tips included.

I hope you will like some of my ideas, use the book often – perhaps even grow to love it – and that your days of wondering what to do with yet another pheasant will become but a distant memory!

THE GAME SEASONS

Game may be offered for sale up to 10 days after the end of the season

	June	Jul	Aug	Sep	Oct	Nov	Dec	Jan	Feb	Mar	Apr	May
Grouse			12--	----	----	----	--10					
Ptarmigan[1]			12--	----	----	----	--10					
Black Game			20--	----	----	----	--10					
Partridge				1 --	best		----	----	1			
Pheasant					1 --	best		----	1			
Capercaillie[1]					1 --	----	----	--31				
Snipe			12--	----	----	----	----	--31				
Wild Duck[2 & 3]				1 --	----	----	----	----	...			
Wild Geese[2 & 3]				1 --	----	----	----	----	...			
Woodcock												
England & Wales					1 --	----	----	--31				
Scotland				1 --	----	----	----	--31				
Golden Plover[1]				1 --	----	----	----	--31				
Hare[4]		1 --	----	----	----	----	----	----	--28			

1. I have not included recipes for Ptarmigan because not many are shot and I have never cooked them; nor Capercaillie for I have never had one and reports are not auspicious; nor Golden Plover which again I have never had and I am not sure I would want to shoot, though I am sure they are delicious.

2. Wild Duck and Geese may be shot until 20 February below high-tide mark.

3. Species allowed to be shot:
   Geese: Canada, Greylag, Pinkfooted, Whitefronted (England & Wales only). (Wild geese may not be offered for sale.)
   Duck: Common Pochard, Gadwall, Goldeneye, Mallard, Pintail, Shoveller, Teal, Tufted Duck and Wigeon.

4. Beware. A few more laws exist concerning where they may be shot, by whom and when. For further details, see The Wild Life and Countryside Act 1981.

NO CLOSED SEASON
Wood pigeon, Collared dove, Rabbit and Muntjac deer

THE GAME SEASONS

		June	Jul	Aug	Sep	Oct	Nov	Dec	Jan	Feb	Mar	Apr	May
DEER						England & Wales							
Red	Stag			1 --	----	----	----	----	----	----	----	--30	
	Hind						1 --	----	----	--28			
Fallow	Buck			1 --	----	----	----	----	----	----	----	--30	
	Doe						1 --	----	----	--28			
Roe	Buck	----	----	----	----	--31						1 --	----
	Doe						1 --	----	----	--28			
Sika	Stag			1 --	----	----	----	----	----	----	----	--30	
	Hind						1 --	----	----	--28			
						Scotland							
Red	Stag		1 --	----	----	--20							
	Hind					21	----	----	----	--15			
Fallow	Buck			1 --	----	----	----	----	----	----	----	--30	
	Doe					21	----	----	----	--15			
Roe	Buck	----	----	----	----	--31						1 --	----
	Doe					21	----	----	----	----	--31		
Sika	Stag		1 --	----	----	--20							
	Hind					21	----	----	----	--15			

How to Choose Game and Fish and Prepare it for the Oven

Many people will of course be getting their game prepackaged from the supermarket, so the decisions of this chapter will have been taken for them by an expert. For here we discuss the choosing and preparing of game before we even look at a recipe. Let me say at once that I appreciate from long experience that you are often left to cope with whatever your family comes back with on Saturday and you have little choice. What is then important is the right choice of recipe to make the most of the beast.

Choosing Game

Age. The first decision is whether the game is young or mature. This is more important for birds than it is, for example, for a roe deer; a second-season grouse is an old bird and is tough and difficult to cope with, while mature roe is a delight. Deciding how old a bird is, is always a problem and I have seen keeper after keeper suck their teeth in doubt or take what is obviously an arbitrary decision to please me. You will best discover the answer if you look at the bird in the feather and it's even better if you can compare a number of birds. This allows you to compare spur with spur, horny old footpad with one a little softer, beak to beak and claw against claw. Then there is the question of the relative length of some of the feathers – all quite difficult and an imprecise art. You will find further guidance on how to choose young game in the introduction to each variety. A brace of young grouse on the moor costs about two and a half times an old brace so this gives you an indication of the relative kitchen value and how important it is to get it right. If you regularly get your game from a shoot, you may be able to select your own or you may have to trust the keeper who knows it is in his interests to please you. If you buy from a dealer, he can buy where he likes, has the experience to choose the best and the sense to hang it properly. Make sure he knows what you want, that he knows you know a bit about it and that you will be in the market for plenty more if he looks after you.

We are now so used to our meat being young, easily chewed and digested, that many of us find it difficult to realise how great is the difference between young and old. Once old, no one can tell quite how old although examples of birds more than two or three years old are rare. My advice is never to roast or quickly cook anything that you even suspect of being old. Choose instead another recipe that suits better and allow plenty of margin for error for it is so difficult to defer supper till next morning! I was once caught out by a jugged hare that had still some way to go after six hours' cooking and I now try to cook that sort of dish well ahead, probably the day before, which also improves the taste; conversely, a juvenile bird will collapse if cooked too long. So choose the game you want for your menu or choose the dish to suit the game.

Quality. Assuming you want a brace of young pheasants, the next hurdle is to assess their quality and this means how they have been reared, raised and shot.

Most pheasants that come to table are reared birds and are usually good and plump, sometimes too fat. I remember a reared bird in California that was so gross that we took pounds of thick yellow fat off it before it was ready for my demonstration. Wild pheasants are smaller, leaner and I suspect they taste better – they certainly fly better. Most other birds, except reared partridges, are from the wild environments of marsh or moor and are usually leaner and fitter animals, needing careful treatment if they are not to dry out in the cooking.

The way the game is killed is also important and so is what happens to the carcass when it is shot (see hanging). A cleanly shot bird is easy to deal with, perhaps having taken only a pellet or two in the head, while a low-flying pheasant, massacred at short range by a pot-hunter, is culinarily quite useless except for soup.

Choosing Fish

Fresh fish should be firm, bright (salmon and sea trout very silvery) and sweet smelling; the gills should be red and the eye bright and gleaming. Sunken, dull eyes, soft flesh that will take a thumb indentation, brownish gills, a dried appearance and any trace of fishy smell are all telltales of lack of freshness; avoid such fish if you can.

Farmed fish will have smaller fins (they haven't had to swim anywhere!), are often damaged from the pen and they may also have a scarred nose. The flesh may be less firm but it is usually good, fresh and reliable.

Preparing Game

Hanging. This is the traditional practice of leaving game in the feather or fur to hang in a cool (36–40°F/3–5°C is ideal), dry, airy place to allow time for the meat fibres of a tough wild animal to tenderise and for its full flavour to develop. This practice is widely used in cool countries with beef, lamb and most meats though it is not always easy nowadays to get properly hung meat. The length of hanging depends on a number of variables and people have differing, strongly held views. I think that it is a waste to have game so high that you overpower the intrinsic taste of the animal and I dislike over-ripe Camembert for the same reason; yet I do not subscribe to the idea of eating under-hung game because it lacks flavour and can be very tough, except perhaps where game is being first introduced in restaurants or a supermarket and where the full flavour of a well-hung grouse may be something of a surprise to their customers!

The main considerations are where you are going to hang it, temperature, humidity and the size and type of the game. You need a clean, fly-free place because fly eggs will hatch to maggots on hanging game if flies can get in to lay them. An airy larder is ideal but for much of the year a cool back room or shed will suffice. In winter, when the cold keeps the flies away, a draughty passage will suit. Bacteria need heat and moisture to develop so the hanging time depends on conditions; game that will develop in a few mild autumn days can hang in the winter wind for four weeks with little sign of decomposition. Small birds like snipe or woodcock hang quickly (and are easily missed at the perfect moment) while a pheasant will take about a week in normal autumn conditions. Those who frequently eat game like it well hung and noticeably gamy in the same way that connoisseurs like well-hung beef. You must expect quite a pronounced gamy smell, especially when you start to draw the birds, but this does *not* mean that the game is 'off' or that the *cooked* bird will be too powerfully flavoured; so don't panic, it's just the smell of well hung game. On the other hand, bad game has a distinctly 'off' smell which is quite different. In general, do *not* wash game because water speeds up decomposition and diminishes the flavour but, if you are worried that your hanging might have been for just too long, the prepared game can be dunked with one added drop of Domestos or a capful of Milton, then dried thoroughly and cooked at once.

An important point that is frequently overlooked is the treatment of game before it gets to the larder. Good keepers will collect the game as it is shot and hang it in an air current (perhaps on hooks in the back of the Land-Rover) to cool rapidly. Too frequently game will stay packed in a game bag or tucked deep in a warm pocket, or cast on to a handsome-looking but heat-retaining pile, or in the airless boot of a car, all of which starts the decomposition process.

Once in the larder, attach a date tag to each creature with the date shot or you will forget which day it was shot, or which bird arrived first. Birds should hang individually by the head from a loop of string round the neck, ungutted and separated from each other, preferably with air circulating all around them. Do not hang badly shot birds, birds shot on a wet day or those that have landed in water too near perfect ones for they will taint far sooner. Rabbits and hares hang head down with a container (a yoghurt pot or some such) tied under the head to catch the blood. Do this whether you intend to use the blood or not because dried drips on the floor take a lot of removing and encourage flies. Rabbits are gutted in the field when shot, but hares are only drawn when ready to skin and eat. Venison also hangs head down, having been gralloched (gutted) immediately after it was shot. If venison is in fine fat condition, it won't need as much hanging as a lean old beast after rutting. In January I usually give our pricket fallow deer twelve days to two and a half weeks if it is cold, inspecting frequently. The aim is to get a really dry, dark coating, even with a little mould which will help to preserve it; if it is damp, pat dry and rub with flour and ground pepper.

Look carefully and frequently at your hanging game, especially in the autumn. Check that there is no fly spoil and, if there is, clean and use at once or discard. If game is damp or has a slight whiffiness but has not hung long enough to tenderise, it can be improved by rubbing with sawdust or preservatives such as equal parts of sugar and ground pepper. Game should arrive at a tender state without decomposition, and careful management produces delicious game. A greenish skin colour around a pheasant's vent indicates it is correctly hung (though some like to leave birds until a larger area is affected).

It is impossible to be precise about the length of time you will hang game which depends on the factors I have already mentioned. It may be helpful to give the usual autumn hanging times with an outside bracket for when it's very cold.

Plucking. Plucking can only be avoided by skinning birds (p. 94), very handy for some dishes if the flesh is not allowed to dry out. To pluck well and quickly you need patience, practice and dexterity, but anyone can do it given time. He who shoots it, plucks it, is my not very successful motto but as the boys start to shoot, they pluck their own birds. But they often get a day's shooting and return to school before the bag is ready to pluck, leaving me to find, usually at midnight, birds that must be plucked immediately. Sit on a stool, a large apron or

HANGING TIMES
Likely times from mild weather to cold weather

Pheasant	5 days to 3 weeks
Quail	3–5 days
Guineafowl	3–5 days
Grouse	2–3 days to 2 weeks
Partridge	2–3 days to 2 weeks
Woodcock	2–3 days to 10 days
Snipe	2 days to 5 days
Mallard, Widgeon etc.	4–5 days to 10 days
Teal	3–4 days to 1 week
Goose	7 days to 3 weeks
Capercaillie	for ever – then throw away!
Pigeon	3–5 days to 10 days
Leveret	2–3 days (probably in early autumn weather)
Hare	up to 1 week or as long as 3 weeks, if properly managed; seldom fit to roast under 8 days (old hares never)
Rabbit	3 days to 5 days
Roe and other small deer	5 days to 2 weeks
Fallow deer	1–3 weeks
Red Deer	1–3 weeks
Wild Boar	4–12 days

sack over your knees and a wide bin in front of you. Preferably pluck in an outhouse or back room for the feathers get everywhere. Heavy birds like geese which slide off your knee are best rested on an upside-down tray, set on the edge of your bin. Start plucking up one leg, against the way the feathers grow, keeping thumb and finger close to the skin; pull several feathers with a brisk tug and let go; pull and let go, keeping your fingers close to the skin. Work systematically, clearing one area before tackling the next. Pluck well up the neck and make sure the legs are completely feather-free. Grouse and pheasants have tender skin which must be plucked carefully so as not to rip it. Pheasants have patches of long feathers on each side of the breast and on the outside of the thigh; beware, for these areas rip easily so take only a couple of feathers at a time. We only pluck to one wing joint then cut off the last two. Tail and wing feathers need pulling out one at a time.

Duck and geese have firmer skin that can be attacked more robustly but as they also have a layer of down under their feathers, there is no saving on plucking time. I pluck them in the direction their feathers grow because feather and down can thus be removed in one; otherwise you virtually pluck them twice. Pigeon skin is robust so they are good birds to learn on. Birds, fresh or frozen in the feather, can be wet plucked. Allow frozen birds to semi-thaw slowly (pheasant take 6–8 hours); then, having plunged them into a sink of cold water to wet the feathers, dip them six to eight times into water at 180°F/80°C. The feathers come out pretty easily, it is definitely quicker and fewer feathers fly. If the bird was frozen, it will be safely cold again before you have finished but fresh birds for the freezer need chilling quickly after this treatment.

Singeing. Having plucked, light a gas ring or candle and, stretching the bird by holding it by legs and head, turn it over the flame until all the wispy hairs and down are burned off.

Skinning. Instructions for skinning pheasant are under Speedy Spatchcock Pheasant (p. 94) and for skinning rabbit or hare are on p. 165.

Drawing. Lay the bird on several thicknesses of newspaper. Take a pair of good kitchen scissors or game shears, a knife and plenty of kitchen paper. First remove the head (not from woodcock or snipe whose head should be skinned and left on) then pull out the neck and cut off at the base. Roll back the neck skin and carefully remove the crop which may be full of food or can be just an empty flap of skin, easy to miss; pull out the windpipe. Slip your index finger into the breast or lung cavity from the front and loosen the internal organs by turning your finger round, especially detaching anything from against the backbone. Cut round the back vent and I also snip off the ends of the two sharp protruding bones which always catch your fingers as you draw the bird.

'The Two-Fingered Draw'. I am indebted to William Chatham Jr from the States, a keen hunting man and cook who coined this great phrase for me. He believes, and I so agree with him, that one of the secrets of succulent roasted game is keeping the drawing aperture as small as possible. No ham-handed poulterer's fist, thrust deep into the bird and splitting it from leg to leg, but two careful fingers slipped in at the vent end, up under the breastbone, hooked over the heart and the entrails and neatly withdrawn (large birds like geese take a bit more than two fingers but be as neat as you can). Woodcock and snipe are usually left undrawn, as their innards or trail add flavour to the dish – but the crop is removed.

You should not break the bag of bile which lies beside the liver nor squash the liver. If the bile bag bursts, clean it off and cut off any parts it touched for even a little horribly bitter drop can spoil a bird. Pick out the heart and liver, detach the bile bag and discard; also cut off any greenish portion of the liver that has been discoloured by bile and remove the gizzard. Split the gizzard open, peel off the lining and discard the contents; scrape off the lining under running water if it does not peel off cleanly, and wash well. Set the neck, heart and gizzard aside to use to make stock. (If I have several birds I usually keep all the livers together for pâté, the hearts and gizzards together to make spiced confit and the necks for stock.) Make sure that the bird really is empty, especially of lung, and wipe out with kitchen paper, removing all internal blood. Do not forget to remove oil preen glands from duck (p. 138); they lie on either side of the tail and, if left in, give an unpleasant musky flavour to duck or stock.

Feet. These should be removed from pheasant, guineafowl, grouse, duck and goose. Cut, just through the bone from the front, below the drumstick joint, then pull off the foot and lower leg, drawing out the tendons from the drumstick. If hard to pull out, pull one tendon at a time. This careful attention makes the drumstick far better eating and is so often neglected by game dealers.

Trussing. If the bird is going to be roasted and carved, it's a good tip to remove the wish bone before trussing to simplify the carving. Fold back the neck skin to expose the breast meat, locate the breast bone and detach it with a small sharp knife, pulling the tip down and out to detach the two ends.

Trussing can be done with a trussing needle; the string passes right through the body, first through the wings and breast then back through the thigh and body, tying the ends off. Alternatively, the string can be wrapped round the bird in figure-of-eight fashion and tied to hold it neatly together. I prefer this as it is easier to wiggle the legs in their sockets when you want to see if the bird is done.

Barding. The classic practice of the past was to bard (wrap around) the breast with a sheet or strips of pork fat or salt pork; it gradually became the practice to use bacon but nowadays our bacon, even streaky bacon, is so lean it really does not do the job. As well as that, who wants all their game tasting of bacon and which of us often bothers to blanch our bacon? The best answer, one always used by good gamemongers in the past, is to bard with thin sheets of pork back-fat as is the custom in France. But nowadays even these are quite a problem to obtain. Back fat is best, for it melts slowly, does not shrivel up and does not spoil the flavour; chat up your good butcher in the autumn and ask him to get some back fat for you when a fat porker is killed. If he will almost-freeze this, then cut on the bacon slicer into thin sheets, you can keep these in your freezer, interleaved with paper and remove as required. Life being what it is, you may not be able to achieve this perfect counsel; but perhaps I can encourage you to get some back fat and cut it yourself as you need it to see if I am not right. You can also buy smoked or plain *spek* from good delicatessens; it is a solid lump of fat bacon and keeps in the fridge for ages to be used for barding or larding. Failing that, try spreading the breast of the bird with soft butter and tying a strip of Bakewell paper over the breast which also has a moisturising and lubricating effect.

To bard a bird, season and lay a thin sheet of back fat or substitute over the breast and tie on with string. This bard is usually removed for the last 5–15 minutes of roasting time so the breast may brown.

Larding. You also need some back fat or *spek* for larding (sticking into meat in small pieces). Cut this into thin strips, lay straight and freeze. Then stab holes in the game meat with a slim-bladed knife or flat skewer, running with the grain, and you can easily insert the frozen strips. Alternatively, using a larding needle, attach short lengths of fat to the needle and lard the meat by taking a stitch into it, drawing the fat through and cutting off the ends. When larding a haunch or saddle of venison, or saddle of hare, alternate the position of the stitches in each row to distribute the fat more evenly. Should you find, by some mischance in this funny modern world, some fat on your bacon, you could use that providing it was mild.

Preparing Fish

Scaling, gutting and preparing salmon is included in Cold Salmon with Green Mousseline Sauce (p. 71).

To Fillet a Salmon or Trout. If filleting a whole fish, it is best done before gutting. Take a sharp filleting knife, press the fish with your fingers on the stomach side to firm the skin along the back and cut down the back of the fish, keeping the knife horizontal and above the backbone. Remove the flesh from the backbone, sliding your knife sideways towards the tail. Cut round the head and lift off the top fillet. Remove the backbone from the bottom fillet, discard the guts, and remove all the fins from the fillets. Use the head (without gills), bones and skin for stock (see Salmon, Fennel and Sorrel Soup, p. 38).

Trout can be filleted in the same way or the backbone can be removed, leaving the head and tail in place. Start in the same way but having loosened the fish fillet from the backbone, snip the backbone behind the head and before the tail and remove with the guts, leaving the fish intact.

Some Useful Equipment

Game can be cooked with the same equipment as everything else, however sparse or comprehensive your kitchen. At its simplest a stick to spear it on and a match to light the fire will do. Trout fried on a little camping stove on the shore of the loch – what better?

But I am really talking about the kitchen and those little bits and bobs that make the job so much easier and save time and anguish on the cook's part, not to mention the specialist equipment you may feel you want and only need half an excuse to go out and buy.

Knives. Knives always come *top* of my list of priorities in the kitchen. Top-quality professional stainless-steel knives will be good friends for many years. (Don't buy carbon steel knives however good – professionals mostly use stainless steel.) Have some or all of these:
- large 8–10 inch (22–26 cm) cook's knife with heavy blade and balanced handle.
- 5 inch (12 cm) boning knife, also useful for breaking down carcasses and serviceable for filleting.
- 6 inch (15 cm) flexible knife for fine slicing and fish skinning.
- 10 inch (25 cm) smoked salmon knife (but only if you are lucky enough to need this often).
- small 4–5 inch (10–13 cm) general purpose knife, always in use.
- a good pair of poultry shears or Wilkinson's kitchen scissors with a notch for bone cutting.
- a small saw for splitting carcasses, chining loins and general bone-cutting.
- a heavy chopper to break bones and carcasses for stock; used sideways, it flattens escalopes and garlic cloves.
- a medium sized 7–8 inch (18–20 cm) stainless steel.
- an oilstone to take the shoulder off your knives and keep them really sharp. Your butcher can do this by appointment.

I have had German Giesser knives for about twenty years now. They are top quality and it is worth spoiling yourself. All I said about knives in *Good Food from Farthinghoe*, and the method of sharpening them, still holds good.

Freezer. This is hardly a piece of equipment; most of us now have it in one form or another and in some ways we might be better off without it, though few people with quantities of game would like that. I like fresh game, so all winter I try to use it as I get it. I do not really enjoy it out of season and prefer to look forward to it, rather than having the chore of finally clearing out the last of last season's pheasants in September! But it is a good idea, for instance, to gather enough mallard so you have 8–10 breasts for a party and to freeze all the legs for some future dish. I also like to keep ingredients in the freezer to enhance my cooking: frozen herbs like basil and sweet marjoram; pork back-fat for larding or barding; stock, bread-crumbs, zampona and much besides.

Food Processor. I would hate to be without a food processor because so many really time-consuming tasks like pâtés, quenelles and stuffings can now be done in moments.

Ovens. I love my Aga which is excellent for roasting and slow cooking. Modern convection ovens keep roasts moist but a true roast should have crusty brown caramelised outsides with tender centres and so much of today's slow roasting does not achieve that. My Gaggenau oven will get very hot, will brown superbly, still has convection heat and top and bottom elements that can be used independently to brown a gratin or cook the bottom pastry of a pie. The best of all possible worlds, you might say, but don't forget it is not great gadgets that make great cooks!

Turnspit – Rôtisserie. Italy and France still use the fireplace to cook, spitted birds being especially good cooked over vines. How sad that we have largely lost this tradition of open-fire cooking (except in barbecues), for food cooked thus is so tasty and the sharp heat is ideal for roasting. I use my barbecue in summer and have been experimenting with a gas rôtisserie; the only problem I have found is that the electric turnspit cannot hold a heavy bird steady, so it climbs slowly up and crashes down the other side with very uneven cooking. But for snipe, quail, partridge and grouse it is excellent and keeps them moist and succulent with a proper crispy brown skin.

Smokers. The small box, hot smokers for trout, salmon and pheasant are useful if you use decent oak sawdust. For really serious smoking you will either have to construct yourself a simple cold smoker (which is not difficult and which I have seen in Kenya but you may need advice) or buy a small commercial smoker.

A Fish Kettle. This long slim pan, with an inner tray to lift out the fish, is a great boon, especially for extra large fish if they come your way often enough. They are expensive, especially in stainless steel; you rarely see enamelled ones, the price of copper ones is astronomic but aluminium ones can be used, though it should be said that wine and vinegar, as used in a court-bouillon, do react with aluminium. If you are about to buy one, I would advise getting a pretty long one of about 24 inches (60 cms) or more because smaller fish can be done in a ham pan or roasting dish in the oven or be parcelled and baked in tinfoil or poached in a boil-in-bag. Don't forget it's nicest to leave the head on, but fish can be cut in half to cook.

Earthenware and Casseroles. I am a firm believer that earthenware gives an exceptional flavour to casseroles, stews and all slow-cooked dishes, tempering the heat for gentle cooking.

A Chicken Brick. Unglazed pottery, shaped to take a bird; it gives a succulent effect and is a healthy way of cooking game.

Cast-Iron Pans and Enamelled Casseroles. A heavy cast-iron pan is essential for browning and allowing the meat juices to caramelise properly; it must be large enough to take a couple of pheasants without being cramped; the gentle browning of game is such a vital process. An oval frying pan can also be a boon if you have plenty of fish to fry. Casseroles like Le Creuset are less good for frying but are invaluable for top of the stove and oven cooking and, like earthenware, are handsome enough for the table. The oval shape is especially good for birds and acts as a pot-roasting pan. A large oval continental pot-roaster is also an invaluable piece of equipment for covered roasting and braising long joints.

Sauté Pans and Saucepans. I have a selection of heavy French copper pans which are a joy to use and make cooking a pure pleasure. I also like quality stainless steel with a heavy sandwich base which could be copper, if thick enough not merely to be cosmetic; otherwise an aluminium sandwich can be very effective. A heavy-quality sauté pan and lid is one of the less usual but most invaluable pans in any kitchen.

Roasting Pans. You need various sizes of good heat-holding pans to fit whatever you are cooking. Sauté pans and frying pans can also double as roasting pans for small birds.

A Double Boiler or Bain-Marie. A deep thick china upper pan over a saucepan base. Delicate sauces take, make and hold so much better. The cook-entertainer will bless them a thousand times.

Fat and Lean Gravy boat. A double-lipped boat with a spout effect on one side to pour lean gravy from under the surface fat. A handsome, useful and time-saving bit of equipment.

Game Pie Moulds. The traditional waisted, fluted shape is very handsome and can be set on a baking sheet for the base to cook well; they are expensive. Removable-base cake tins, especially the continental variety with expanding sides, are a useful and modestly priced alternative and so are Pullman's pans: heavy, non-stick, removable-base tins for tortes and pies; I also often make free standing pies and pâtés.

Pestle and Mortar. Generous size and preferably pottery or stone, which will not pick up flavours, though I also have a good cheap teak one that I like.

String. Not too thick for trussing and *not* nylon which will melt in the oven!

Muslin. Buy butter muslin; cut large squares for straining stocks and sauces etc. then wash and use again; use small squares for bouquets garnis (also handy for decanting wine).

Bakewell Paper. Not unimportant because it makes an excellent substitute for pork back-fat for barding birds, keeping them moist and succulent. It is also useful in the base of terrines and timbales so they turn out easily.

Skewers. Long flat skewers are needed for barbecuing; I set quail on them for easy turning in the oven or under the grill. Wooden satay skewers also have their uses for pan-fried kebabs and generally holding things together and so do little wooden cocktail sticks.

Needles. Rather more specialist are trussing and larding needles. The trussing needle is long enough to go right through the bird and strong enough to be threaded with fine string. The larding needle holds a piece of fat to stitch into the meat (but see also my cunning method for larding on p. 17). There is a much larger tool with a channel in it which you load with a lardon, push right through the meat then draw back, leaving the lardon of fat in the meat; this is excellent for big venison joints which need to be kept well larded but is usually only owned by butchers. I have only used it in Germany.

Note All the recipes have been based on imperial measurements, though metric equivalents are shown. It is important to work each complete recipe either in imperial or metric and not in a mixture of both.

A conversion chart and oven temperature guide appears on page 218.

All spoon measurements are made using measuring spoons filled level, unless otherwise stated.

Useful Ingredients and Basic Recipes

The real ingredients are the game and fish themselves, well chosen, carefully prepared and sympathetically cooked and the simpler the better. But there are some ingredients which particularly seem to suit and others which are necessary for its successful cooking.

Stocks and Fumets

I like to start with stocks and fumets for any chef will tell you that good cooking depends on good stocks. I do not rely on them nearly as much as a chef does, knowing that many people do not always have stock available, but I must tell you how to make good stock and I can assure you your dishes will benefit from it. A freezer, though taking the edge off the finest stocks, will allow you to use stock when you want it; it melts quickly in a saucepan or microwave, so stock-up! Raw or cooked carcasses can be tossed into a bag in the freezer until you have enough to brew up; boned-out game frequently marinates for a day, giving you time to make a little stock with the bones, and the microwave makes small quantities of stock quite well.

Brown Game Stock

Chopping the carcass small to release the marrow, frying or roasting to a good brown, adding wine and reducing it right away – these are all points that will give you good tasty stock, best of course from raw carcasses. Don't be frightened to reduce it considerably once strained because it started off very lightly salted. Game does not have a lot of gelatine so include veal bones, the ideal answer, or something else that does. Pig's trotters are best boiled in plenty of water for 20–30 minutes then rinsed to remove impurities before using.

Ingredients

about 2 lb (1 kg) mixed game carcasses including wing tips, feet etc.
1½–2 lb (675–900 g) veal bones, blanched pig's trotters, pork skin or chicken wings
1 tbs oil
1 small onion, diced
1 carrot, diced
1 stick celery, diced
a few slices leek

4–6 fl oz (100–175 ml) white or red wine
2–3 juniper berries
1 clove
1 clove garlic
6 peppercorns
4–6 parsley stalks, sprig fresh thyme, ½ bay leaf
about 4 pt (2.25 l) water, to cover
¼ teasp salt

Break the bones and carcass to release the flavour from the marrow. Brown in the fat in a large pan, or roast in the oven, adding the diced vegetables to brown well; then tip into your stock pan and deglaze the roasting pan well. Add wine and reduce completely until everything is frying again. Repeat the process with water (or even better with more wine or some stock) for a strong colour and good flavour. Add water to cover and the remaining ingredients, bring to the simmer and skim; then cook in a very slow oven (225°F/110°C/ Gas ¼) for 4–6 hours, or simmer for 3–6 hours on top of the stove. Strain through a double layer of muslin (game often has a lot of sediment) and cool. For concentrated stock, remove any fat when cold and reboil to reduce the quantity; then season further (if using for reduction sauces, leave unseasoned). Cool and chill.

Fish Fumet

Made from white fish bones and skins, this is also a great joy to have in the freezer. Chat up the fishmonger and make plenty, perhaps with a hint of prawn in it, and you will reap the rewards. For a tasty salmon head stock for soups see p. 38.

Ingredients

Makes approx. 2 pt (1.2 l)

2 lbs (900 g) white fish skins and bones (turbot or sole are best)
1 small onion, sliced
6–8 parsley stalks
1 thin slice lemon
½ bay leaf
1 tiny sprig thyme and fennel
4–6 peppercorns
¼–½ pt (150–300 ml) dry white wine
a few mushroom stalks (optional)
about 2½ pt (1.5 l) cold water to cover
¼ teasp salt

Place the washed fish bones and skin with the gills removed in a pan on top of all the other ingredients (if you put the other ingredients on top, they all float up and get skimmed off). Bring to the boil, skim well and simmer for 30–40 minutes (never longer). Strain through muslin and reduce further for flavour if necessary.

Court-Bouillon for Poaching Fish

Ingredients

4½ pt (2.5 l) water
½ pt (300 ml) dry white wine, more if you wish
1 onion, sliced
3 carrots, sliced
1 small leek, sliced
1 stick celery, sliced
bouquet garni of 5–6 stalks parsley, small branch fennel or a few fennel seeds, good sprig lemon or ordinary thyme, 1 bay leaf and sprig tarragon (optional)
12 peppercorns and 2 allspice berries
juice of 1 lemon or 2–3 tbs wine vinegar
2 teasp salt

Place all the ingredients in a pan (not aluminium which reacts with wine and vinegar) and simmer for 15 minutes or so. Cool before straining, if practical.

Marinades – The Tenderisers

These acidic preparations help to break down tough meat fibres or add flavours and lubrication to tender cuts. I think the oil is as important as the wine and, for any real tenderising effect, allow from 2–10 days marinating. I have given a suitable one for most recipes and, as I don't like or use very old or strong venison and don't like to mask the flavour of good game, I don't use strong marinades frequently. Here is a delicate one for fine meats for a few hours and another standard one for venison, hare or wild boar to save you looking elsewhere; there is also a pungent, heavy cooked one if you have something really growly to deal with. Don't forget yoghurt, buttermilk, lemon juice, kiwi or pawpaw purée can all be used to tenderise meats and dry marinades of salt, garlic, herbs and spices can be rubbed into meats for flavouring.

Delicate White Wine Marinade

Use this for young pigeon, rabbit or hare and for young roe or fallow deer.

Ingredients

1 shallot or sweet onion, diced
1 carrot, diced
1 sprig celery leaf, chopped
1 bay leaf, sprig thyme, 2 parsley stalks and
   2–4 juniper berries

2 tbs olive oil
¼–½ pt (150–300 ml) dry white wine
   (or half dry vermouth and half wine)
1 slice lemon

Mix all the ingredients and pour over the game in a china or glass bowl; or use in a plastic bag which allows less marinade to cover the surface of more meat and makes it easy to turn by just turning the bag over! Leave for 2–3 hours or overnight.

Red Wine Marinade

Another uncooked marinade but stronger in flavour. Use this for hare, older roe or fallow deer, red deer, pigeon and grouse, and don't be frightened of marinading meats for 3–5 days or more for heightened flavour and greater tenderising effect.

Ingredients

4 fl oz (100 ml) port ⎫ use more if needed
4 fl oz (100 ml) red ⎬ to cover the meat
   wine ⎭
1 onion, diced
2 carrots, diced
1 stick celery, diced
2–3 cloves garlic, crushed

6 juniper berries
8 peppercorns, crushed
2–3 parsley stalks
2 bay leaves
2 sprigs thyme ⎫ or 1 teasp herbes
1 sprig rosemary ⎬ de Provence
2 tbs olive oil

Crush the garlic, juniper and pepper, bruise the herbs and mix with the port, wine and vegetables. Massage the oil into the meat and pour over the rest to cover. Leave for 2–3 or even 4–5 days for older meats. Keep in a cool larder or fridge.

Powerful Cooked Marinade

Use this for older red deer, other venison, wild boar, hare and pigeon to be braised. Being a cooked marinade, meat can lie in it for 3–10 days in a cool larder or fridge for maximum effect.

Ingredients

2 fl oz (50 ml) oil
2 onions, diced
2 carrots, diced
2 sticks celery, diced
3–4 cloves garlic, sliced
1 stick cinnamon
4 cloves
2 blades mace
6 allspice berries
6 juniper berries

2–3 slices fresh or ½ teasp dried root
  ginger
2 bay leaves, sprigs lemon thyme and 4–6
  parsley stalks
8 peppercorns
4 fl oz (100 ml) spiced or wine vinegar
1 bottle red or white wine
2 tbs redcurrant or other fruit jelly, or 2–4
  fl oz (50–100 ml) mushroom ketchup or
  1–2 tbs Worcestershire sauce (optional)

Fry the vegetables in the oil until softened, add the spices and fry for several minutes; then add vinegar and wine and simmer, covered, for 20 minutes; cool before using. You can melt jelly into the marinade or add mushroom ketchup or Worcestershire sauce for a sweet touch or additional flavour if you wish.

Other marinades. These can be found from the index in individual recipes.

Spiced Flavouring Oil for Meats and Marinades

Use this in marinades or to brush over birds and steaks before roasting or grilling.

Ingredients

10 fl oz (300 ml) good fruity olive oil
1 clove garlic
1 branch fresh rosemary
1 branch sweet marjoram

6–8 black or dried green peppercorns
4–6 grains lavender (optional)
1 chilli (optional)

Flatten the clove of garlic and bruise the herbs between your hands. Bruise but don't crush the peppercorns, lavender and chilli (if used). Warm the oil gently and add all the ingredients to it in the bottle. Close and leave to stand in a warm place for several days or ideally a week before using. Keep in the cupboard and use as required.

The Lubricants

The most important items after the stocks and marinades are the fats and lubricants used to keep naturally dryish game meats from drying out. I have already discussed barding and larding on p. 17. In stews and braises the lubricant can be lardons (little oblongs) of fat smoked streaky bacon or belly of pork. Don't neglect to add them for they ooze their lubricating fat slowly into the meat as it cooks, keeping lean game meat moist; try to find someone to cut decent streaky bacon in almost ½ inch (1 cm) thick slices for you. I prefer smoked bacon as it is lightly flavoured these days. Don't worry, you do not have to eat the fat for it can be blotted off the top of the casserole, when its job is done.

Extra lubricants I have used are zampona, the stuffed pig's trotter from Italy, which will hang in its box for months until opened, then can be frozen in chunks if you don't use it all at once. It adds a lovely gelatinous quality to sauces, something that game does not have of itself. Ordinary pig's trotter and pork skin, cheap enough and stored in the freezer, can also add this syrupy rich element to dishes. Marrow, scraped from the centre of the bone, is another marvellous enricher, rarely used nowadays but easily obtainable from your friendly butcher. Cream cheese is another great lubricant; if used in stuffings or popped inside roasting birds, it's delicate enough not to jar the flavour but does its job well. Cream and crème fraîche are the great sauce finishers, the latter adding just that much more flavour and depth. Always use good butter in fine sauces, olive oil where it counts (especially in continental dishes) and a delicate healthy sunflower oil on other occasions. I also use small amounts of walnut, hazelnut, almond and sesame oils as flavourings for their wonderful aroma. Other fats which add savour are goose fat, duck fat, pork and chicken fat so, if you ever have any, do not discard them for they all add so much taste to certain dishes.

Enhancers

Herbs. Use fresh herbs where you can; frozen are next best, keeping their aroma well when stored in the freezer. Dried herbs can be just as successful in some dishes provided they are of a good quality and freshly dried; I usually dry a variety in the microwave for winter use and freeze some. The herbs I use most are parsley, thyme, lemon thyme and wild thyme, chervil, tarragon, basil, lovage and marjoram. All these seem to have an affinity with game but be adventurous and try others when you can and don't forget fennel, dill and chives with fish.

Spices. Juniper has always been associated with game, but try new ones like the Peruvian pink pepper berry (*Shinus molle*), sold often as *baies roses* or 'pink peppercorns' though they are not peppery at all, but have a junipery hint that marries well with game. Allspice, cloves, nutmeg and coriander, as well as mace, are all classic game spices so use them for their warm notes. Green peppercorns and the French mix of quatre-épices are also especially nice with game.

Vinegars. Often used with game for their acid balance or for their tenderising effects in marinades. Effectively they range from delicate lemon juice through quality white wine, to fruit-flavoured vinegars as well as red-wine vinegars and sherry, tarragon and herbed vinegars; it is easy to make your own. The strong shallot, spiced or garlic vinegars are also useful and finally you must not forget the superlative and wildly expensive balsamic vinegar, used only as a flavouring, drop by parsimonious drop, in salads, on steaks and in sauces.

Spiced Vinegar

I like to make a bottle of this particularly fragrant spiced vinegar for the winter. Look for a quality wine or cider vinegar base because the run-of-the-mill Dufrais or such like is very ordinary.

Ingredients

15 fl oz (450 ml) bottle white wine or cider vinegar	2–3 leaves celery
3 juniper berries	2 young leaves blackcurrant
1 sprig tarragon	1–2 sprigs salad burnet
1 sprig hyssop (optional)	1–2 sprigs marjoram, preferable the annual
2 sprigs lemon thyme or thyme	sweet marjoram (*Origanum Majorana* or
2–3 leaves chervil	*Marjorana hortensis*)

Bruise the juniper berries and herbs and stick them all into the bottle of vinegar. Close tightly, label and keep in the warm for 3–4 days; use any time after three weeks, and it will keep the winter long. You can change the variety of herbs you use depending on what you grow or can get.

Shallot and garlic vinegar. 2 oz (50 g) peeled, bruised shallots and 1 oz (25 g) garlic, added to a bottle of wine vinegar, are also useful for adding to marinades.

Dried Mushrooms and Other Flavourings. All mushrooms, including dried Chinese and especially the dried *cèpe* (*Boletus edulis*) add a wonderful depth to game; they were formerly used here and are still much used on the continent so buy them abroad or from Italian grocers in little packets (where they will probably be called *porcini*). Since bringing a huge bag back from Florence market which then hatched its quota of little white wrigglers that turned to moths and flew away, leaving me with mere dust and powder, I now keep them in the freezer where they stay fresh and eggs can't hatch (I suspect many packets sold here have already been sterilised so don't worry). Do be generous in using them though I think I'm always a little bit on the mean side. Glynn Christian taught me to soak them in plenty of water then simmer vigorously, adding a little sherry, until the water has almost gone. It seems to bring out their flavour greatly. Strain off carefully for there is usually sand in the bottom.

Peppermill Mix. This is our own mixure of black and white peppercorns with the addition of coriander, allspice and sometimes green peppercorns. It can be used in cooking or at the table. A wide range of herbs and spices including pink pepper berries and peppermill mixture are available by post from Farthinghoe Fine Wine & Food Ltd, Old Lane, Farthinghoe, Brackley, Northants NN13 5NZ.

Anchovy. Another useful flavour heightener was used a great deal in the old days (a leftover from Roman times?) and is well worth including. Sharwoods have a useful little tube of anchovy paste that can live in the fridge and be squirted into things, but anchovy essence or tinned anchovies will both do well.

Shallots. I also include them here; I know onion can always be used but shallot has a much more delicate flavour and should be available all through the year from Brittany; use the pinky variety when you can get them or grow your own from a few small bought ones.

Drink for Game. Looking at my recipes I see what a wide range of booze can be used. Obviously red and white wine and cider, then Madeira, Marsala, vermouth and port which, all being fortified, keep well for cooking (and are not *so* likely to be drunk by the cook!) and add lovely complex flavours to sauces. The spirits respond well with Cognac, Armagnac, whisky, Calvados, and rum heading the list. Some liqueurs work well, notably Drambuie but only with full-flavoured game, and so sometimes do the eaux-de-vie and liqueur de cassis; so the cry is, if you like the idea, try it.

Two Last Thoughts

First the sweet accompaniments: game has a great affinity with and need for the sweet touch. So often that spoonful of redcurrant jelly, honey or treacle just brings a sauce into focus or the grapes, prunes, kumquats, apples, Seville oranges or pineapple add that sweet note and final flourish that just makes the dish. Almonds, hazelnuts, walnuts or pecan also add a sweet finishing touch and chestnuts have a distinct sweetness. Secondly, the final figure in the equation or piece in the jigsaw that completes a fine dish, is the bland accompaniment. It can be the background or frame that successfully points up and shows off the other combined ingredients. This important group includes brown, white or Basmati rice; all the noodles you care to think of — wheaten, home-made, spätzle or buckwheat; then there is burghal, the bland cracked wheat of the Middle East which also makes an excellent stuffing, maize-meal polenta from Italy, couscous from North Africa, sweet potatoes and pumpkin from the Americas and of course potatoes, cooked in so many ways. Use these accompaniments to complete the balance of the course.

Roast Game Birds

Possibly the best way to serve good game, unless you have it very often, is just plain but perfectly roasted. It is an art to roast well and the bird needs careful watching and basting to keep it succulent, tender and perfectly cooked. Roasting is done in a hot oven with dry heat, originally on a spit, to get crisp skin and tender moist flesh. I am going to talk about roasting generally then give a chart for timing and tips for each bird and any variations.

First, know your oven. My Aga roasts beautifully and so does my new Gaggenau convection oven that will get very hot with even, all-round heat. Good roasting needs a really hot oven. Too many birds in the oven at once will cool it, lengthen the cooking times and birds will tend to stew, rather than roast. Pre-heat the oven, usually to hot (450°F/230°C/Gas 8). If roasting frequently, make clarified butter which heats much hotter without burning. Bring the birds to room temperature; this is most important or they will cool the oven. Stuff if you are going to or season inside and slip in a nob of butter, sliced apple, onion, potato or orange to keep the bird moist (a small back end aperture is important, see the two-fingered draw, p. 16).

Barding is also of great importance: use a sheet of pork back-fat or alternatives such as soft butter and Bakewell paper. Use bacon only infrequently or all your game tastes of bacon (see barding p. 17) and truss (p. 17). Heat your chosen fat – usually about 2–4 oz (50–100 g) – butter, oil or dripping in a shallow-sided heavy roasting tin that will let the heat in and hold it well and, once hot, add the birds. They should have space around them for steam to evaporate but not be lost in a huge tin or the fat will burn; so choose your roasting pan to fit the birds; omelette pans or sauté pans can be used. Roast, basting and turning every 10 minutes or so and lowering the temperature if necessary. A little marinade, wine or stock is sometimes used for basting but the aim is always not to allow the fat to burn but to allow pan drippings to become brown, sticky and tasty (well-caramelised pan juices make wonderful tasty gravy); too brown and they turn to cinders and burn, too much liquid in the pan and they never caramelise. Birds with red meat such as grouse, duck and goose, to be served rare, should have a breast that has just stopped feeling soft and spongy under your finger; birds with white meat that should be just cooked should have a little more resilience to the touch on the breast, and legs that no longer feel elasticy and tight in the socket: well-cooked birds should have legs that feel slightly looser. It is all a bit of an art but by using careful timings, your perceptions and a little experience, you will soon master it. Depending on size of bird, 5–10 minutes before the end of the cooking time, remove the bard and return the birds to the oven to brown and finish cooking.

Resting Roasts. Once cooked, remove them to rest in a turned-off oven or Belling warming cupboard where they cannot go on cooking; in any event, somewhere with a temperature below 170°F/75°C. Small birds need 10 minutes or so while larger ones are happy for up to ¾ hour. In this time the tissues and fibres relax, juices re-enter the tissue and pinkness spreads evenly; so do not neglect this very important step of resting roasts before serving. Pour off the fat and finish the gravy or sauce; game birds usually have thin gravy which is just good stock used to deglaze the pan juices and reduced. More elaborate sauces will be found in the recipes. Old English cooking served butter gravy with fine birds, fresh butter melted into the pan juices, perhaps with a squeeze of lemon and a pinch of cayenne, wonderful and not intrusive to the flavour of the game. Serve up the birds on croûtes if used and with garnish and sauce or gravy.

Roasting Chart

PHEASANT

Oven Very hot 450°F/230°C/Gas 8	*Time* 30–45 min
Prep Bard; stuff.	

Tips Rest. Use Chatham two-fingered draw (p. 16). Serve just cooked. *Serves* 2–4 people.	*Accompaniments* Plain or butter gravy, fried bread croûtes, fried breadcrumbs, bread sauce or Herb and Onion Dressing as for goose (p. 145), whisky-soaked stale bread stuffing (p. 145).

PIGEON

Oven Very hot 475°F/240°C/Gas 9	*Time* 15–20 mins
Prep Bard with fat or bacon.	

Tips Rest; serve rare. *Serves* 1 person.	*Accompaniments* See Spatchcock Grilled Pigeon (p. 126), butter gravy, croûtes, watercress.

QUAIL

Oven Hot 425°F/220°C/Gas 7	*Time* 18–20 mins
Prep Bard; wrap in vine leaf.	

Tips Rest; a little bit of butter inside during roasting helps to keep moist and tender; serve completely cooked, but not overcooked. Allow 1–2 birds per person.	*Accompaniments* See Quail chapter (p. 115).

WOODCOCK

Oven Very hot 475°F/240°C/Gas 9	*Time* 15–18 mins
Prep Bard; remove gizzard but do not draw.	

Tips Rest; serve rare; flame with brandy or eau-de-vie. *Serves* 1 person.	*Accompaniments* Trail (innards) spread on croûtes; breadcrumbs; thin or butter gravy.

SNIPE

Oven   Very hot 475°F/240°C/Gas 9   *Time*   10–15 mins
Prep   Remove gizzard but do not draw; bard.

Tip Rest. *Serves* 1–3 per person.	*Accompaniments* Trail (innards) spread on croûtes; breadcrumbs; thin or butter gravy.

GROUSE

Oven   Very hot 450°F/230°C/Gas 8   *Time*   20–30 mins
Prep   Bard.

Tips Rest; pop butter and/or fruit (autumn raspberry) inside; serve quite rare; leg can be removed for separate dish and breasts served very rare; deal with Blackcock and Grey Hen as for Grouse but inclined to be dry. *Serves* 1 person (large grouse can be halved).	*Accompaniments* Bread sauce, fried breadcrumbs, croûtes, thin gravy or butter gravy, watercress, fruit.

PARTRIDGE

English (Grey) and French (Red-legged).

Oven   Very hot 475°F/240°C/Gas 9   *Time*   15–20 mins for English and 18–25 mins for French.
Prep   Bard; wrap in vine leaf.

Tips Rest; cook with a nut of butter or vine leaf inside; serve barely pink. *Serves* 1 person (the larger, Red-legged Partridge can be halved).	*Accompaniments* Thin gravy, butter gravy, fried breadcrumbs, fruit, Noisette Sauce (p. 113).

GOOSE

Canada, Greylag, Pinkfooted and Whitefronted Goose
Oven and Prep   See Pot-Roast Goose (p. 145).

Tips Rest; stuff with apple, onion, orange or bread soaked in whisky; serve rare. *Serves* 6–8 people.	*Accompaniments* Orange sauce (p. 202), Wild Goose Sauce (p. 145), Marquis' Sauce (p. 140), Canadian Roast Apple Sauce (p. 204), Wild Rice (p. 209), Herb and Onion Dressing (p. 145), Sweet Potato Purée (p. 208), Green Herb Pudding (p. 210).

MALLARD

Oven Very Hot 475°F/240°C/Gas 9	Time 20–25 mins
Prep Bard.	

| Tips   Rest; best off stubble in autumn; fruit stuffings; serve very rare; just serve breast; legs need more cooking so keep and devil or continue roasting for second helpings. *Serves* 2–4 people. | *Accompaniments*   Thin gravy, orange sauce, Marquis' Sauce (p. 140), Wild Goose Sauce (p. 145), Wild Rice (p. 209), Herb and Onion Dressing (p. 145), Canadian Roast Apple Sauce, Cranberry Sauce (p. 204). |

TEAL

Oven Very hot 450°F/230°C/Gas 8	Time 15–18 mins
Prep Bard.	

| *Tips*   Rest; serve rare. *Serves* 1 person. | *Accompaniments*   Usual duck accompaniments. |

WIDGEON

Oven Very hot 450°F/230°C/Gas 8	Time 18–20 mins
Prep Bard.	

| *Tips*   Good flavour, depending what they have eaten; rest; serve rare *Serves* 2–3 people. | *Accompaniments*   Usual duck accompaniments. |

POCHARD, TUFTED AND PINTAIL

Oven Very hot 450°F/230°C/Gas 8	Time 15–25 mins according to size.
Prep Bard.	

| *Tips*   Rest. Have not the cachet of other duck but, depending on feeding, can be good. *Serves* 1–3 people. | *Accompaniments*   Usual duck accompaniments. |

GUINEAFOWL

Oven Very hot 450°F/230°C/Gas 8	Time 25–30 mins
Prep Bard; wrap in vine leaf.	

| *Tips*   Rest; dry meat so try marinating, as a further preparation, in flavoured oil; serve just cooked. *Serves* 2–4 people. | *Accompaniments*   Bread sauce, cream-cheese stuffing. |

Roast Venison, Hare, Rabbit and Wild Boar will be found in the appropriate chapters.

GAME SOUPS AND STARTERS

Light soups for summer, warming winter soups, soups that are almost stews like Meg Merrilees' Poacher's Soup (p. 34) are all included here, together with fishy first courses, pâtés and some dishes that can be as easily offered for light lunches.

Some are relatively expensive, others are just little ways of using up any spare bits of fish and game you might have handy. I have included one or two recipes using pheasant eggs, for game farms are practically giving away unsuitable eggs in the spring and they are tasty and delicious.

Some of the pâtés, such as Rillettes de Lapin (p. 51) and Tuddenham Potted Pheasant (p. 55), will keep well for some time and are ideal for digging into when it suits you. Potted Pigeon (p. 56) and Game Pâté with Peppercorns (p. 49) are made from good cooked game and make an excellent starter or lunch with a salad. I like to use Confit of Pheasant (p. 100) – or any game – to make delicious and original salads, perhaps with the addition of fried croûtons or smoked bacon lardons and herbs. All sorts of oils and vinegars including our own Spiced Vinegar (p. 27) can be used for the dressings.

Soups

Game Avgolemono

Any good stock, game stock especially, can be used for this simple Greek soup, but it really must be good and tasty or the soup will be dull. Sometimes I add some soaked *cèpe* mushrooms for the rich, meaty flavour they impart which contrasts well with the sharp lemony tang of the soup.

Ingredients   *Serves 4*

2 pt (1.2 l) very good game (or chicken)   2 eggs
   stock   1 lemon
2 tbs long grain rice   a little parsley, very finely chopped

Bring the stock to the boil and add the rice. Simmer until the rice is well cooked then season. Beat two eggs well in a bowl, add 1 tbs cold water and gradually the juice of half a lemon. Slowly, slowly, drop by drop beat at least half of the soup into the eggs then pour this into the remaining soup. Stir over low heat for a minute or two to thicken slightly. *But do not let it boil.* Correct the seasoning and lemon and serve with very finely chopped parsley.

Suggested Wine. Dry sherry or Sercial Madeira.

Chinese Style Game Soup

This is another soup that calls for good stock. It is based on a Chinese hot-sour soup and should have a nice balance between hot, sweet and sour so adjust the flavouring to achieve this. Everything to make it can be stored dry or frozen and it takes only moments to make; only add the prawns and herbs as you serve it so they remain tender and fresh.

Ingredients   *Serves 4–6*

2 pt (1.2 l) good reduced game stock	2 tbs soy sauce
2–3 spring onions or a very little finely shredded onion	2 tbs vinegar
	a few shreds fresh chilli or ½ teasp chilli sauce
2 oz (50 g) button mushrooms or several soaked dried Chinese mushrooms	2–3 teasp potato flour or cornflour
1 teasp ginger shreds	2 oz (50 g) frozen prawns
3 oz (75 g) green peas	finely chopped chives, parsley or coriander
1–2 teasps sugar	salt and pepper only if necessary

Slice the spring onion and mushrooms finely and add to the stock with ginger, peas, sugar, soy, vinegar and chilli. Bring to the boil. Mix potato flour with a little water and add it; then boil for 1–2 minutes until clear; add prawns, chopped herbs, seasoning if needed and serve at once.

Suggested Wine. Hot Chinese rice wine or Sercial Madeira.

Poacher's Soup (after Meg Merrilees)

This is adapted from one of my favourite authors, Meg Dods, who published her *Dods on Cookery* in Scotland in 1826. Her fastidious attention to detail delights any keen cook. She says 'This savoury and highly-relishing new stew soup may be made of any and everything known by the name of game' – and so it can. The debate in our family is whether to leave the joints of game as they are and serve it in large bowls with plenty of bread as a main course knife and fork soup or, as the soup itself is so delicious, to serve a bowl of the soup, followed by a ladleful of the stew. It makes a great shooting lunch served either way, depending on your soup bowls and taste. It can also be thickened by making a purée of some of the meat and vegetables. However you use it or make it, and it is a bit of an undertaking, it is useful for using up odd birds and beasts of uncertain age, or for clearing the freezer of old inhabitants!

illustrated opposite: Chinese Style Game Soup (see above), Salmon Rillettes with Lemon and Dill (see page 46)

Skin and discard the fat of wild duck if they have been long in the freezer. Sometimes I make it with game stock from the freezer, sometimes I make the stock first from the animals' carcasses, augmented by a bag of necks and gizzards from the freezer and perhaps the remnants of a leg of lamb.

Ingredients

Serves 10–12

½–1 pheasant (I tend to use carcass and
    legs only)
1 old grouse }
1 old partridge } or brace of either
½ hare or 1 rabbit
1 wild duck
a little oil or dripping
4–6 large onions
good pinch sugar
½ teasp mixed spice
flour
6–12 oz (175–350 g) carrots
4–8 sticks celery
6 small potatoes, peeled
1 small white cabbage (optional)

Stock
Use 6 pt (3.6 l) good game stock or make it
    as follows:
scraps and carcasses from the game
2 carrots, cut up
1 turnip, cut up (optional)
3–4 onions, quartered
1 tbs whole allspice
2 teasp black peppercorns
bunch parsley stalks
bay leaf (optional)
8 pt (4.8 l) cold water

To Finish and Thicken

1 tbs mushroom ketchup (optional)
1–1½ oz (25–35 g) butter }
1–1½ oz (25–35 g) flour } for thickening (optional)
¼ teasp ground mace
⅛ teasp ground allspice
dash Spiced Vinegar (p. 27) or sherry
    vinegar
1 glass port (optional)

To Make Stock. Take the breasts and legs off the birds and joint the rabbit or hare. Put the scraps and carcasses, washed, in a pot, setting the good joints aside for the soup. To the pot add any bones, scraps, necks and gizzards you may have and all the remaining ingredients. Simmer, skimming as necessary, for a good 3 hours or cook overnight in a slow oven. Strain the stock through muslin, de-grease and you should have about 6 pt (3.6 l) left.

To Make the Soup. Slice the onions and fry with a good pinch of sugar to a really good dark brown in a little oil or fat in a heavy frying pan; remove to the soup pan. Sprinkle the reserved game joints with mixed spice, roll in a little flour, shake off the surplus and brown the bits in hot oil or fat (you can add them un-fried if you prefer, it is a matter of taste and colour). Add the fried game to the soup pan, cover with 6 pts (3.6 l) good game stock (see above) and add the carrots in large dice, the celery in slices and the potatoes in chunks. Bring to the boil and simmer, skimming from time to time. Add the cabbage, cut into quarters, after about 1 hour and cook for a further 1–2 hours until the game is all tender but not overdone. Taste and add 1 tbs of mushroom ketchup for colour and flavour if desired. This soup can be served as it is with final flavourings or thickened with a brown roux which is how I prefer it.

To Make a Brown Roux. Melt the butter in a small heavy frying pan. Add the flour and cook, stirring all the time, over moderate heat until the flour darkens to a good hazelnut colour; allow about 10 minutes for this and do not burn the flour by cooking too fast. Once it is a good colour, whisk this mixture into your soup by spoonfuls until it is thickened to your satisfaction. Simmer for a little longer, skimming as necessary. Season with ground allspice and mace, plenty of ground black pepper and salt if necessary; add perhaps a shake of chilli sherry or a flavoured vinegar (I like shallot, spiced, raspberry, tarragon or sherry vinegar) and, if necessary, a pinch of sugar or a touch of redcurrant jelly.

It should be a good rich brown, medium thick and very tasty with all the bits in it. Serve, stirring a little port into the soup tureen or into individual bowls.

Suggested Wine. Medium dry sherry.

Chestnut and Game Soup

The late autumn is the moment for plump fresh chestnuts and I freeze them then for later use, for by Christmas they are often shrivelled. They are beasts to shell but I think I really have found the best way to prepare them so follow my instructions on p. 207 carefully.

You can of course use a tin of unsweetened purée for the soup and I certainly would do so for a large shooting lunch or some such; for a special occasion, however, I use fresh chestnuts.

Combined with a generous amount of cooked game meat as well as good stock, you will have an excellent and tasty soup. Pheasant, partridge and grouse are my favourites for this soup though any game can be used alone or in combination or a joint of Confit of Pheasant (p. 100) can be added for flavour. I also find it very useful to use up the carcass and scraps after having roast game.

Ingredients *Serves 4–6*

1 lb (450 g) chestnuts or ¾ lb (350 g) unsweetened chestnut purée	1 onion, sliced
2½ pt (1.5 l) good game stock	1 stick celery, sliced
any scraps cooked game meat	1 medium-sized potato, diced
1½ oz (35 g) duck fat, bacon fat, butter or oil	1 bay leaf
1 carrot, sliced	sprig thyme
	salt and pepper
	croûtons of fried bread

Melt the fat in a pan and add the carrot, onion and celery and potato. Sauté gently until softened a little then add the peeled chestnuts, or purée, and any cooked game. Cover with the stock and add the bay leaf and a sprig of thyme. Simmer together for about 40 minutes or so until the chestnuts and vegetables are very tender then remove the bay leaf, thyme and any bones. Purée and sieve, correct the seasoning and serve with hot croûtons of fried bread.

Suggested Wine. Medium dry sherry.

Salmon Fennel and Sorrel Soup

If you have filleted a salmon to make Kippered Salmon (p. 39) or one of the other dishes, you will be left with the head, tail, backbone and fins, ideal to simmer down for soups. This one is delicate and creamy with a hint of fennel (if you have no fresh fennel, add some fennel seed to the fumet) which I flavour discreetly with Chinese curry powder, with its flavour of anise, and finish with fine sorrel shreds.

Ingredients   *Serves 6–8*

Salmon Head Fumet

head, tail, backbone, fins and generous scraps from a good-sized salmon	1 slice lemon
4 pt (2.3 l) water	1 teasp coriander seeds
¼ pt (150 ml) dry white wine	several stalks fresh fennel or ¼ teasp fennel seeds
1 onion, sliced	½ teasp peppercorns
1 carrot, sliced	3–4 parsley stalks, sprig thyme, bay leaf
1 stick celery, sliced	and tiny piece lovage if available
1 clove garlic, slightly flattened	1 teasp salt

Soup

2 oz (50 g) butter	1–2 teasp delicate curry powder
1½ oz (35 g) plain flour	(Sharwood's Chinese for preference)
2 shallots, finely diced	½ pt (300 ml) milk
3 tender fennel stalks or ¼–½ bulb	5–6 good sorrel leaves
Florence fennel	a little cream (optional)
3 pt (1.8 l) of the salmon fumet	salt and pepper

Salmon Head Fumet. Wash the salmon head really well, removing the gills and running water through the head to remove any traces of blood. Place the head, bones and bits in a large pan, cover with the water and bring to the boil. Skim off the copious froth and scum until the fumet is clear then add all the other ingredients. Simmer for 40 minutes, reducing to 3 pts (1.8 l), skimming if necessary, then strain through muslin or a fine sieve.

Soup. Melt the butter in a large heavy pan. Slice or dice the fennel and soften gently with the shallot in the butter without browning. Add the curry powder, fry for a moment then add the flour and cook over moderate heat for several minutes.

Draw the pan off the stove, wait for the sizzling to cease then add the salmon fumet. Bring to the simmer, whisking all the time, and simmer for about 10 minutes before adding the milk.

To Finish. Remove any tough midribs from the sorrel; lay the leaves one on another, roll up tightly and cut across into tiny shreds. Add a handful of shreds to the soup with the cream, if used, adjust the seasoning and heat until the sorrel shreds wilt – merely a moment in spring but a little longer later on. Serve at once.

Suggested Wine. Modest white.

Starters

Kippered Salmon and Variations and Sweet Mustard Sauce

All forms of gravadlax, pickled salmon or pressed salmon are deservedly popular these days but I would also like to show you this old Scottish way of preserving fish. I make no apology for repeating this dish which I previously published in *Good Food from Farthinghoe* because it is such a treasure, but I am now suggesting some ideas for new variations. Arguably better than smoked salmon, I found the recipe in my great-great-grandmother's manuscript cooking book from Perthshire in the 1840s. It was originally used to preserve salmon which was then hung up for what could be called a long time to become very dry and hard; for use, it would be soaked and grilled. But never mind these ways of long preservation because we now have our freezers; what we are after is an easy short-term kippering or pickling to achieve a texture and flavour like smoked salmon.

I used to think you needed a whole salmon, or at least a whole side, but have since discovered that a pound or so piece or tail end will be just as easy to prepare to use as nibbles for a drinks party or for several people as a dinner-party first course.

Kippered salmon deserves fresh-run wild salmon and is best served in complete simplicity with nothing but lemon and nutty brown bread and butter. Lesser quality fish – not so fresh run, farmed or frozen salmon – are ideal for the variations which have added flavoursome ingredients like dill, lemon or lime rind, whisky or Pernod. They can be served with Sweet

Mustard Sauce or used in little Glazed Salmon Tartlets (p. 43). Any little bits that are left over can be added to scrambled eggs or whizzed up to make a tasty spread.

All these recipes can be adapted to use sea trout (always finer than salmon anyway), large brown or rainbow trout, or herring.

Ingredients	*allow 3–4 oz (75–100g)* *sliced kippered salmon per person*
a whole fresh salmon or a fine side or a centre cut or tail piece, cleaned and scaled	
per pound boned fish weight	
1½ tbs coarse sea salt	a pinch saltpetre (available from decent chemists)
1½ tbs Barbados or soft dark brown sugar	1 teasp brandy

Fillet the side of salmon off the bone and trim off the fins. Run your finger down the flesh from head end to tail to lift the bones to show you where they are; remove all possible bones with tweezers.

Mix the salt, sugar and saltpetre together; sprinkle a little of this mixture on a large plate (use only china, glass, enamel or stainless steel for this) and lay the salmon on it, skin-side down. Cover with another layer of the mixture and sprinkle brandy over it. If you are doing a whole salmon, prepare the second side as the first and lay it skin-side up on top of the first side. Sprinkle with more of the mixture and cover with a large flat dish (for one side, I cover with greaseproof paper first) and a heavy weight (a couple of old irons or several large tins of food). Keep in a cool larder or the fridge and let it lie for 24 hours to 3 days or even up to 6 days. Turn over and baste with the juices which run out of it if you can.

Remove from the juices and wipe down with kitchen paper (the juices can be incorporated in a sauce for the salmon if you wish). Slice the salmon thinly as smoked salmon or more thickly on a steeper diagonal cut as for gravadlax. Serve with lemon and brown bread and butter and Sweet Mustard Sauce if you wish.

A small piece of salmon or sea trout only needs sprinkling with the mixture and wrapping in cling film and keeping in the fridge. The prepared fish, carefully wrapped, will keep for a week or so in the fridge.

A bit of advice from Meg Dods is that if the fish is very large and rich, it may be better if rubbed with salt and drained of excess moisture for a day before it gets the final salting.

Variations. Try white or light brown sugar instead of dark Barbados sugar. Use whisky, rum or Pernod instead of brandy. Omit the preservative saltpetre, which is now considered somewhat undesirable, because we don't now intend to keep the prepared salmon for long. Include herbs, crushed peppers, lemon or lime rind if you wish. Dice the fish instead of slicing it and serve it in a little mound with a little diced cucumber, dill and sour cream salad or scatter the dice over the top of a fish mousse. Or serve it sliced with sour cream, blinis and all the trimmings or in any other way that strikes your fancy – it will always be delicious.

Suggested Wine. Best white.

Gravadlax

This Scandinavian way of preparing fish has become, deservedly, very popular.

Ingredients
a side or middle cut of salmon
fresh dill
coarse sea salt
caster sugar
white or black peppercorns

All sorts of proportions are recommended from ½–2½ oz (12–65 g) salt per pound of fish with usually rather less sugar and sometimes mustard and brandy. I favour a heaped tablespoon of salt per pound of prepared fish with a tablespoon of caster sugar and 2 teaspoons crushed peppercorns. The amount of dill depends on its strength. Commercially greenhouse-grown dill needs chopping and scattering thickly over the salmon. Garden dill, with its intense flavour, can just be laid whole on the salmon.

Otherwise prepare the dish in exactly the same way as Kippered Salmon.

To Serve. Cut in quite thick, slightly slanting slices down to the skin and allow 2–3 slices, depending on the size of the fish, approx. 3–4 oz (75–100 g) per person. Serve with lemon wedges, brown bread and butter and hand Sweet Mustard Sauce (see below) separately.

Suggested Wine. Best white.

Sweet Mustard Sauce

To get just the right flavour you need a sweet Scandinavian mustard like Slotts, though a French mustard like Savora, mild Dijon or a good German mustard will give you a delicious sauce. It's so good you can just dip bread in and eat it! It's also a very good sauce with avocado.

Ingredients   *Serves 6–8*

about 4 tbs mustard
2 tbs caster sugar (or vary by using soft
   brown sugar)
egg yolk (optional)
1–2 tbs white wine vinegar

5–6 tbs sunflower oil
4–5 tbs liquid from fish (optional)
2 tbs finely chopped dill (though I have
   made it without and it is still quite
   delicious)

Mix the mustard and sugar (you can start with an egg yolk as if making mayonnaise if you wish) and gradually whisk in the vinegar, oil, fish liquid and dill, balancing the flavours. Serve in a sauceboat with Gravadlax or Kippered Salmon.

Piquant Salmon Fingers

A little leftover kippered or smoked salmon is delicious pounded up with about half its weight of butter, a good shake of Tabasco, a little paprika, a squeeze of lemon and seasoning. Spread this on to hot toast, pressing in well; cut into fingers and serve hot with the apéritif or to accompany a dish like Cold Scrambled Eggs with Kippered Salmon and Sorrel or the Salmon, Fennel and Sorrel Soup (p. 38). It can also be spread on cold toast or biscuits for canapés or be used to make delicious stuffed eggs.

Suggested Wine. Crisp white.

Cold Scrambled Eggs with Kippered (or Smoked) Salmon and Sorrel

If you have kippered yourself a side of salmon (p. 39) you can use up any remnants in several delightful ways and this is probably my favourite. Pheasant eggs can be used if available.

Ingredients   *Serves 4–6*

2–3 oz (50–75 g) kippered or smoked
   salmon, cut into fine batons
4–6 new eggs (or 12 pheasant eggs or
   2–3 duck eggs)
1 tbs cream or milk
a shake of Tabasco

1–1½ oz (25–35 g) butter
1 tbs finely scissored chives or a little lemon
   thyme (optional)
a small handful of finely shredded sorrel
salt and pepper

Whisk the eggs with the cream and a shake of Tabasco and very light seasoning. Melt the butter in a heavy pan, add the eggs, chives and sorrel and cook carefully, scraping the curls of cooked eggs from the bottom of the pan with a wooden spoon.

Cook neither so fast that the egg cooks into coarse tough curls nor so gently that it thickens without texture; to my mind scrambled eggs should have generous tender curls of egg just holding together in a creamy mass. Do not over-cook but stop before they reach the point of perfection for they will continue to cook in the pan and while they cool.

Now fold in the shreds of salmon, turn into a serving dish and leave to cool though it is, of course, also delicious served hot. Serve with toast fingers, either plain or spread with Piquant Salmon Spread.

Suggested Wine. Not ideally suited to wine. Finish your apéritif or modest white.

Glazed Salmon Tartlets

Crisp cream-cheese pastry tartlets are filled with pressed salmon on a limy mayonnaise and yoghurt base and topped with lime aspic. You can serve the pressed salmon on its own, sliced like smoked salmon, or you can vary the tartlets by filling them with blanched summer vegetables to make a light and pretty dish. The glaze allows you to prepare them ahead without their getting tired but is not essential to the dish.

Ingredients *Serves 4–6*

Pressed Salmon (variation of Kippered Salmon, p. 39)
12 oz (350 g) middle cut of salmon
1 tbs sea salt
1 teasp white sugar
grated rind of ½ lime
pepper

Cream-Cheese Pastry
4 oz (100 g) soft butter
4 oz (100 g) cream cheese such as Eden Vale
   Somerset soft cream cheese
6 oz (175 g) plain flour
¼ teasp salt

Lime Glaze
½ pt (300 ml) good aspic (Haco)
lime juice to taste

Filling
5 fl oz (150 ml) mayonnaise
5 fl oz (150 ml) natural thick yoghurt
lime juice to taste
salt and pepper

Decoration
strips cucumber skin
sprigs dill, parsley or chervil

Pressed Salmon. Fillet and skin the salmon. Mix the salt and sugar with a little grated lime rind and pepper. Sprinkle some on a plate, lay a piece of salmon on this and sprinkle over some more salt and sugar: lay the second piece of salmon on top and sprinkle with the remaining salt and sugar mixture. Cover and press lightly and leave for 12–48 hours in the fridge. Remove, pat dry and slice thinly.

Cream-Cheese Pastry. Cream the butter until really soft, work in the cream cheese, then sift and add the flour and salt; work lightly together and form into 4–6 flattened discs. Chill, wrapped, for 1–2 hours in the fridge. Roll thinly and line 4–6 individual tartlet tins of about 4–5 inches (9–12 cm) diameter, or of course you can make 1 large one. Prick the bases, line with tinfoil, fill with baking beans and cook in a hot oven (400°F/200°C/Gas 6) for about

8–10 minutes until set. Remove the beans and tinfoil, turn down the oven to moderately hot (375°F/190°C/Gas 5) and continue to cook until light golden brown and completely cooked. Cool on a rack.

Lime Glaze. Prepare the aspic according to the packet and flavour generously with lime juice. Cool until syrupy.

Filling. Fold the yoghurt into the mayonnaise, adjust seasoning and add lime juice to taste.

Decoration. Blanch and refresh some wide strips of cucumber skin. Cut into narrow strips.

To Assemble. Spread a little mayonnaise filling in the base of the tartlets, arrange thin slices of pressed salmon over this, decorate with cucumber strips and sprigs of herb and cover with a very thin layer of lime glaze. Chill until the glaze sets and the decoration is stuck down then run over another thin layer of glaze and leave to set. Serve on individual plates with a sprig of herb and a slice of lime.

Suggested Wine. Best white.

Smoked Salmon Pâté

Any trimmings from a side of kippered or smoked salmon (or inexpensive bought trimmings) can be made up into this delicate pâté. The trick for a particularly light finish is to fold whipped cream into the mixture before it firms up. Serve soft and creamy at room temperature for, if served straight from the fridge, it will crumble.

Ingredients *Serves 4*
4 oz (100 g) smoked salmon bits
3 oz (75 g) butter
2½ fl oz (65 ml) cream
a little lemon juice
paprika
salt and pepper

Just melt the butter. Place the roughly chopped smoked salmon in the food processor or liquidiser, process and add the butter in a thin stream until the mixture is very smooth; season and cool. Whip the cream and fold into the cold salmon mixture before it gets too firm, adding lemon juice to taste. Check the seasoning and turn into a pot. Serve with melba toast, brioches, fresh bread, or in a salad for which I find Florence fennel particularly good.

Suggested Wine. Crisp white.

Little Salmon Creams with Sorrel Sauce

A very elegant way to use up just a little bit of leftover salmon. I use the spinach leaves in spring when they are tender and just need holding by the stalk in boiling water for a moment.

Ingredients   *Serves 4–6*

4–5 oz (100–125 g) cooked salmon
2 eggs
2 yolks
2 tbs dry vermouth
mace
8 fl oz (225 ml) whipping cream
salt and pepper
spinach and sorrel leaves, about 4 each per
   cocotte (optional)

Sorrel Sauce

2 oz (50 g) butter	6–8 tender sorrel leaves
1 tbs very finely chopped shallot	squeeze lemon juice
7 fl oz (200 ml) whipping cream	salt and pepper
½ teasp fresh or good pinch dried tarragon	

Turn the boned, skinned salmon into the food processor bowl and process for several minutes until completely smooth. Add eggs, yolks, vermouth, mace, and seasoning; process again until smooth, stirring down if necessary (in a liquidiser process salmon and eggs together), then gradually pour in the cream. Sieve if necessary but it should now be completely smooth. If using spinach and sorrel leaves, blanch them for a moment in boiling salt water with a few drops of oil added then refresh in cold water for a moment to cool. Drain and pat dry on kitchen paper.

Line out the well-buttered cocottes with a mixture of the leaves, spinach on the outside for colour and strength, sorrel inside for flavour, leaving the leaves over-hanging the edge. Pour the salmon mixture into the cocottes and fold the leaves over the top; cover with tin foil or the leaves may dry out. Otherwise just turn the mixture into well-buttered cocottes. Set the cocottes in a bain-marie (a roasting pan with boiling water to come half way up the outside of the cocottes). Bake in a moderate oven (350°F/180°C/Gas 4) for about 20–30 minutes until just firm and set. Those in spinach will take longer.

Leave to stand for 5 minutes then turn out a cream on to each plate (easier when leaf enveloped) and spoon round a little sauce. Serve at once.

Sorrel Sauce. Melt the butter, add the shallot and soften for a moment; then add the cream and tarragon and boil, uncovered, until reduced a little. Remove any tough midribs and pile the sorrel leaves together, cut into fine shreds. Add 2–3 tbs of these shreds to the sauce and simmer for a moment or two more until the sorrel is tender but still in shreds; correct seasoning and add a squeeze of lemon juice which will thicken the sauce.

Suggested Wine. Best white.

Salmon Rillettes with Lemon and Dill

The word rillettes denotes the thready texture (as in a meat rillette de Tours) that one is looking for in this simple but excellent pâté. I poach the salmon inside a boil-in-bag so none of the flavour is lost but of course it's an ideal recipe for using up all the scraps which look so unpromising amongst the debris on the plate after you have served a whole poached salmon. You can easily substitute smoked haddock for the salmon, just poaching it in the water, rather than the bag, to draw out some salt if you think it is too salty.

Ingredients   *Serves 4–6*
8 oz (225 g) uncooked salmon steaks
6 oz (175 g) cream cheese
pinch mace
a little grated lemon rind
a little chopped fresh dill (or fennel)
1–2 fl oz (25–50 ml) whipping cream or
    yoghurt
salt and pepper

Place the fish in a boil-in-bag (lesser fish could have herbs and flavouring added in the bag), with all the air removed, in a saucepan and cover with cold water; bring gently to the boil and then draw off the stove and leave for 5–10 minutes, by which time the fish will be cooked. Drain and cool, remove the bones and skin and flake the fish roughly. Place the flaked fish, cream cheese, mace, lemon rind and dill in a bowl and crush with a fork (but don't overmix for it should not be too broken down or too smooth), adding in the cream until you have a thready mixture. If the fish was warm (the best moment to do it), the mixture should be fairly soft at this stage; it will firm up in the fridge. Correct the seasoning and turn into a pot. Serve with an interesting bread, packed into celery sticks or half avocados or in baps with lettuce for special picnics.

Suggested Wine. Full bodied modest white.

Smoked Trout Pâté

So simple, so easy, but you do need really good smoked trout and a fresh cheese to get the fine summery flavour of this delicate pâté. Serve it simply with hot toast or in a cone or timbale lined with smoked or kippered salmon. Or try it spread lavishly on firm German bread, latticed with smoked or kippered salmon or a couple of asparagus spears and lightened with several bright lettuce leaves for a lovely open sandwich lunch treat. Or combine it with hard-boiled egg yolks and use it to stuff the whites. It makes a good contribution to a mixed hors d'oeuvre or can be used as a dip with crudités, particularly with Florence fennel. Home Hot Smoked Trout (p. 66) can, of course, also be used but never seems to have quite the quality of fine cold smoked fish.

Ingredients *Serves 4*
8–10 oz (225–275 g) smoked trout (about
   1 fish)
4 oz (100 g) cream or ½ fat curd cheese,
   demi-sel or cottage cheese
¼ pt (150 ml) cream
juice of ½–1 lemon
salt and pepper

Skin, bone and roughly flake the trout into the food processor or liquidiser; add the cheese (cottage cheese needs sieving) and cream and process until smooth. Season with salt, pepper and add lemon juice to taste. Place in little pots and chill before serving with hot toast and lemon wedges or in any of the ways mentioned above.

Suggested Wine. Crisp white.

Smoked Trout Mousse

This light and delicate mousse is already in *Good Food from Farthinghoe* but I have never bettered it and simply have to include it here.

Ingredients *Serves 4–6*
8 oz (225 g) smoked trout
2 teasp gelatine
2 tbs white wine
6 oz (175 g) cream cheese (Eden Vale
   Somerset soft cream cheese for choice)
¼ pt (150 ml) plain yoghurt
nutmeg

½ teasp horseradish sauce
a squeeze of lemon juice
¼ pt (150 ml) cream
salt and pepper

Garnish
¼ cucumber

Sprinkle the gelatine on to the white wine in a cup, soak for several minutes, then stand in a saucepan of hot water to dissolve. Skin and bone the smoked trout and flake into a food processor or liquidiser. Process until finely chopped, then add the cream cheese and yoghurt. Season with salt, pepper and nutmeg and add the horseradish, the melted gelatine and lemon juice to taste and process until smooth. Turn into a bowl. Fold in the cream, whipped until just holding its shape. Put in a 1 pt (600 ml) soufflé dish and chill.

    Decorate with sliced cucumber and serve with thin brown bread and butter.

Suggested Wine. Modest white.

Marinated Trout in Dill Cream

Raw trout makes a wonderful starter when filleted, skinned, cut into strips and mixed with a sweetish cream and dill dressing. It can be eaten within a couple of hours of making or will keep for 24–48 hours in the fridge; this makes it a very useful dish for summer dinner parties. The chopped dill takes a while to flavour the cream so don't add too much to start with. Good dried dill must be sought out carefully if you have not got any fresh (though fresh can be preserved, chopped, with oil in the freezer or microwave-dried for winter use).

I prefer to make this without pepper; we are inclined to add pepper to everything without thinking but of course it is a matter of personal taste.

Ingredients *Serves 4–6*

2–3 fine trout
juice of 1 lemon
2 tbs finely chopped shallot or mild onion
1½ teasp caster sugar
8 fl oz (225 ml) double cream

2 teasp oil
1–2 tbs fresh chopped dill
salt
pepper (optional)

Fillet and skin the trout and remove any bones; this is best done by running your finger over the fillet from head end to tail to raise the bones; they can then be picked out with sharp nails or tweezers. Cut into crossways strips and season heavily with salt (you can add pepper too if you wish).

Mix the lemon juice, shallot, sugar and cream in a bowl with the oil and whisk until very lightly thickened; stir in the chopped dill and the seasoned trout strips. Cover and leave to marinade in the fridge for 2–24 hours. Serve on lettuce leaves with brown bread and butter or dark rye bread.

Suggested Wine. Iced vodka or best white.

Fresh Pickled Trout Fillets

This is a very fresh and healthy way to prepare trout fillets. It is not so rich as Marinated Trout in Dill Cream, but it too can be prepared a day or so ahead.

Ingredients *Serves 4–6*

¾ lb (350 g) filleted trout from 2–4 fish, depending on size

3 fl oz (75 ml) wine vinegar
6 fl oz (175 ml) water

Sauce

1–2 shallots, finely sliced
2 bay leaves
1 teasp sugar
plenty of peppermill mixture or pepper
good pinch ground cardamom

5–6 tbs drained yoghurt
1 tbs oil
½ teasp fresh basil, basil in oil or dried basil
1–1½ teasp sea salt

Carefully scale and fillet the fish and remove all possible bones. Soak in the vinegar and water for 6–12 hours then drain, pat dry and cut into strips. Combine the strips with all the sauce ingredients and leave to marinate for a further 6–48 hours. Serve with thin slices of nutty, dense German-style brown bread (but not quite Pumpernickel) and butter.

Suggested Wine. Iced vodka or crisp white.

Game Pâté with Green Peppercorns and Pink Pepper Berries

Any leftover game (but not scraggy, tough scraps) like mallard, pheasant, venison or grouse can be made into this delicate pâté, lightened with whipped cream and studded with green peppercorns and pink pepper berries (known as pink peppercorns or *baies roses*). Make sure you serve it at room temperature so it is soft and spreading like butter. The seasoning will go with all game but you could tie it to your game a bit more with, say, the addition of orange rind and juice with mallard, gin and juniper with venison, tarragon with pheasant and so on.

Ingredients		*Serves 4–6*
6–8 oz (175–225 g) cooked game meat, diced	1 teasp brandy	
1 small finely chopped onion	4 fl oz (100 ml) cream	
1 bay leaf	2 teasp green peppercorns	
1 clove garlic, finely chopped	½–1 teasp pink pepper berries	
4 oz (100 g) butter	salt, pepper and mace	

Gently fry the onion with the whole bay leaf in half the butter until golden; add the finely chopped garlic and brandy and cook for a moment before removing the bay leaf and scraping into the food processor or liquidiser bowl. Add the diced game meat with no skin or sinews and process until very smooth. Add seasoning and the remaining unmelted but soft butter (if you add all the butter melted, the mixture will curdle), and process until you have a smooth purée. Stir the whole green peppercorns and pink pepper berries into the cooled pâté. Whip the cream until it is just holding its shape, then fold in. The purée should be cold but not setting when you fold in the cream. If it's warm, the cream will thin out, but if it's set too much you won't be able to fold it in.

Pack into pots and serve at room temperature with hot toast or melba toast and lemon quarters. It is also nice scooped into an egg-shaped quenelle, using a dessertspoon that has been stood in warm water, and set on individual plates with some pretty salad leaves, garnished with a few pink pepper berries and green peppercorns.

Suggested Wine. Modest white or light red or medium dry sherry.

Game Terrine

Pork back-fat (off the back of the pig) is the secret of all good terrines because it melts gently into the terrine, keeping lean game lubricated and succulent. It is not always easy to get, especially now that pork is bred so lean, and butchers are inclined to fob you off with belly fat: but do search it out and you will taste the difference; we keep some in the freezer where it has a 4–6 months' life.

The other secret of terrines is a food processor which cuts and chops the meat, rather than a mincer which squeezes and presses it dry. Any game can be used for this terrine; its flavour is best if made several days ahead.

Serves 4–6

Ingredients

½ lb (225 g) lean pork
½ lb (225 g) pork back-fat
½ lb (225 g) lean trimmed raw game,
    venison, wild duck, pheasant, hare or
    grouse or any mixture
1 onion, very finely chopped
1 clove garlic, crushed
6–8 juniper berries

¼ teasp ground mace
¼ teasp ground allspice
4 tbs red wine
2 tbs brandy
2 eggs
½ lb (225 g) streaky bacon, cut very thin
1–1½ teasp salt
plenty of pepper

Keep some nice pieces of game and cut into dice. Dice half the pork fat. Trim the remaining lean pork and game of all sinew and gristle then chop, with the pork fat in the food processor, or mince. Add the diced pork fat and game, the onion, garlic, crushed juniper berries, mace, allspice and seasoning; stir in the wine and brandy and leave in a cool place for 3–12 hours for the flavours to penetrate. Beat in the eggs and cook a little bit of the mixture to taste the seasoning.

Line a terrine with streaky bacon and fill with pâté mixture. Cover and place in a roasting tin with boiling water to come halfway up the terrine. Cook in a slow oven (300–325°F/150–170°C/Gas 2–3) for about 1½–2 hours. The pâté is cooked when it begins to come away from the sides of the dish or when a skewer stuck in it produces no pink juices.

Set the terrine to cool, weight it and preferably keep for a day or two before eating to allow the flavour to mature and mellow. This can freeze but allow to thaw very slowly or it will be wet-textured.

Suggested Wine. Big white.

Rillettes de Lapin

The traditional thready pork pâté of Touraine can be adapted to use various game meats. It is one of the quickest and easiest pâtés to make and keeps well in the fridge though it does need a long slow cook. In fact, prepared carefully with no meat juices remaining in it, and packed into sterile jars, it will keep for up to a year on the shelf though as it freezes so well (one of the few pâtés to freeze really well), I doubt it's worth the slight risk always attached to home-made and preserved meat products. Anyway as well as rabbit, a speciality of Orléans, try incorporating pheasant, grouse, partridge, woodcock or wild duck; older birds can be used and will add great flavour. It is essential to use enough fat, preferably back-fat, to prevent the rillettes from becoming dry and boring.

Ingredients

1 prepared rabbit, pheasant or a variety of mixed game
⅔ of the weight of the rabbit in fatty belly of pork
⅓ of the weight of the rabbit in pork back-fat (or flair fat)
1–2 teasp coarse sea salt for each pound/½ kg of meat
¼ pt (150 ml) dry white wine
1 small onion, stuck with 1 clove
½–1 clove garlic
sprig thyme (wild thyme is good with rabbit)
good pinch quatre-épices or allspice
pepper

Cut the back-fat into cubes and put in a heavy casserole with half the wine; cook gently until the fat renders out and the wine has gone. Meanwhile, cut the rabbit and the de-rinded belly of pork into little pieces and add to the casserole with the rest of the wine, the salt, pepper, cloved onion, garlic, thyme and quatre-épices. Cover close and cook in a slow oven (300°F/150°C/Gas 2) for about 4–5 hours, stirring with a wooden spoon from time to time, until completely tender and falling from the bones. Drain the meat into a sieve. Cool until you can handle then pick out all the bones and pound the meat in a mortar or process very briefly in a food processor with plastic blade, working in the drained fat but no meat juices to make a thready pâté.

Correct the seasoning and pack into jars or containers (sterile stoneware jars if proposing to keep long unfrozen). Top with remaining fat or melted lard (to a depth of about ½ inch (2–3 cm) if proposing to keep on the shelf). Serve at room temperature so that it's not too firm with fresh bread and or gherkins.

Alternatively you can take ½ lb (225 g) boned out rabbit meat (roughly the back legs), ½ lb (225 g) belly pork and ½ lb (225 g) pork fat and proceed as above.

Suggested Wine. Modest white or light red or medium dry sherry.

My Rich Smooth Pâté

If you find yourself with a number of pheasant, grouse, wild duck or rabbit livers, take the chance to make this pâté which is based on the classic French foie-gras technique. It is *very* important to pick the livers over most carefully to remove any green tinged flesh or taint of bile to which game livers are more prone, due to the longer hanging period. The flavour of game livers is strong and, to enjoy it to the full, it is necessary to dilute it rather more than with other livers and in this recipe I use double cream for the purpose. The pâté can be scooped from the terrine or it can be carefully turned out and served in slices like foie gras. It is an exceptionally luxurious dish.

Ingredients
Serves 12–16

½ lb (225 g) fine game (or poultry) livers
milk
2 tbs port
1 tbs Cognac (or Armagnac is often used)
¼ teasp caster sugar
pinch quatre-épices or allspice
scrap garlic (optional)
tiny pinch thyme (optional)
1 teasp chopped parsley (optional)
½ oz (12 g) butter
2 teasp shallot, finely chopped
1–2 oz (25–50 g) diced streaky bacon
10 fl oz (300 ml) double cream
salt and pepper

Pick over the livers, very carefully removing threads and any sacks of green bile; also cut off any green-tinged flesh (this is very bitter and even a little bit can spoil a whole dish). Soak the livers for 1 hour in milk or water at blood heat. Drain and dry before marinating with the port, Cognac, quatre-épices, sugar, garlic, thyme and parsley (if used) and salt and pepper. Leave to marinate for 12–24 hours.

Melt the butter in a small pan and gently cook the shallot and bacon until soft and golden. Scrape into a food processor or liquidiser and process until smooth. Add the livers and the marinade, reduce to a smooth purée then add the cream and switch off at once.

Pass the mixture through a fine sieve into a terrine in a layer no deeper than 2 inches (5 cm). You can cook a little, to taste the seasoning, in the bottom of a cocotte standing in a pan of boiling water. Place the terrine in a roasting pan with hot, not boiling, water nearly to the full depth of the pâté. Cook in a slow oven (250–300°F/120–150°C/Gas ½–2) for about 45–60 minutes until the mixture sets (the water in the bain-marie should never rise above 170°F/75°C for a really delicate pâté). Leave to cool and keep in a cool larder for 1–2 days.

Suggested Wine. Medium dry sherry or big white.

Rosemary Smoked Pheasant Breast Salad

The Chinese smoke food in their woks using tea, sugar and various other flavourings; this is a wonderful way of simply and quickly adding flavour to various meats and fishes. Any heavy frying pan or roasting tin lined with tinfoil can be used and I favour herbs with the sugar for smoking. You will find this a good method for cooking pheasant or chicken breasts, even if you are not going to smoke them and of course the salad and dressing can be varied as much as you like.

Ingredients

Serves 4–6

2–3 pheasant breasts, depending on size
1–2 avocados
various salad leaves, red pepper strips and
    slices of tomato

To Smoke the Pheasant

1 tbs Demerara sugar
3–4 good sprigs rosemary or other herbs

Dressing

1½–2 teasp Dijon mustard
1–2 teasp sugar
3 tbs peach or flavoured vinegar
8 tbs oil, mixed olive and sunflower
salt and pepper

Stock to Cook Pheasant Breasts

1 pt (600 ml) chicken stock
1 sliced carrot
1 stick celery
2–3 slices fresh root ginger
1 tbs sherry
2 sliced spring onions
1 teasp peppercorns
bouquet garni
salt

Boil up the stock ingredients in a heavy lidded pan. Slip in the pheasant breasts, bring to the boil and switch off. Take off the stove and leave for 2–3 hours until cooked.

To Smoke. Line a wok or large frying pan with tinfoil; sprinkle with the sugar and lay the rosemary on top. Set the drained and dried pheasant breasts on a rack over it. Set the pan over medium heat and once it starts to smoke, cover with tinfoil and a lid and seal the joint with damp cloth or wet kitchen paper. 'Smoke' over low heat for about 10 minutes; leave unopened until ready to use.

To Serve. Whisk the dressing ingredients together. Thinly slice the smoked pheasant breast and arrange attractively on a plate with salad leaves, thinly sliced avocado and tomato; garnish and spoon over the dressing.

Variations. Use chicken, duck or turkey breast or fish fillets instead of pheasant. Use various oils, vinegars, mustards or herbs. Use different vegetables and salad for garnish or toss all together in a big bowl.

Suggested Wine. Modest white or light red.

Pickled Pheasant (or Quail) Eggs

In May or June game breeders are almost giving away pheasant eggs that are not commercially suitable. They may be double-yolkers or infertile or show a hairline crack when candled. This short seasonal glut should be taken advantage of by anyone near enough to a game farm. I have devised this pickled egg recipe, not remotely throat-searing and pungent as pub pickled eggs often are, but as gentle as possible with flavourings suitable for these delicate eggs. Use them as an apéritif or in salads, perhaps with red lettuce, watercress, sorrel, salad potatoes or croûtons of bread fried in butter and good olive oil and a creamy dressing, flavoured with a herbed or spiced vinegar. They can also be used to add a little zest to sauces such as Gribiche, Mayonnaise or an old-fashioned egg sauce with chervil on fish.

Ingredients
15–20 pheasant (or quail) eggs
2–3 slices fresh root ginger
2 small chillies
2–3 sprigs fresh tarragon
2–3 cloves garlic
12 whole peppercorns
¼ teasp celery seed or a few sprigs of celery
    leaf
2–3 sprigs thyme or sweet marjoram
1 bay leaf
up to 1 pt (600 ml) tarragon or wine
    vinegar
an equal quantity cold water
¼ teasp salt

Before boiling the eggs, carefully pack them into your jars then pour on water to cover and measure it, to test how much vinegar and water you will need. Now place equal quantities of vinegar and water in a pan to give you this same measurement or a bit more; add all the spices and bring to the boil, covered. Leave to steep and cool, covered.

In another pan boil the eggs in water for 6–7 minutes (quail eggs need only 5 minutes) then cool under running water, peel and pack into perfectly clean jars. Pour the cooled vinegar preparation over them, packing in the spices and herbs, to cover completely then seal tightly with vinegar-proof lids (jars which had chutney and such-like are fine; they have a plastic seal and coating inside the lid which does not corrode with vinegar). Keep eggs for 2–3 weeks before using.

Pheasant Eggs with Basil Mayonnaise. It may be that some of these delicate little eggs from the game farms have a tiny crack and won't boil, so I poach them for a nice little salad starter. Just poach them for 3–4 minutes until still soft, slip into cold water until ready to use then dry on kitchen paper and serve with mixed salad leaves and perhaps courgette or cucumber strips. Dress with a lightly curried mayonnaise, mixed with thick yoghurt and shreds of basil. Sprinkle a little cayenne over the dish.

Tuddenham Potted Pheasant

Neil Alston, a great host and good friend for whom I have done a number of cooking demonstrations in Norfolk, gave us a smooth pheasant terrine which was delicious and I thought it such a good way of using up badly shot or rather mauled birds (I don't mean to imply that Neil's a bad shot!). I have based this recipe on his and think it is one that many will find useful. If you cover it carefully with clarified butter, it will also keep as a great standby for up to a month.

Ingredients

Serves 6–10

1 large pheasant
¼ teasp mace
⅛ teasp ground cloves
sprig thyme
1 bay leaf
4–6 oz (100–175 g) streaky bacon rashers
2 tbs port
1 tbs wine vinegar
6–8 oz (175–225 g) butter (you could use a
    proportion of ham fat)
½ lemon
½ teasp salt
plenty of pepper

Rub the pheasant all over, inside and out, with the mixed salt, pepper, mace and cloves; leave for several hours if possible. Place the thyme and bay leaf in a heavy casserole and set the pheasant on its side on top. Cover with the bacon and add the port, vinegar and 2 oz (50 g) or so of the butter. Cover closely and cook in a very moderate oven (325°F/170°C/Gas 3) for 1½–2 hours or until tender. Leave to cool in the pan. Then remove the pheasant, pick off all the meat, discarding skin and gristle and process with the bacon and any fat from the casserole. Do not use any juices or jelly if you wish to keep the potted pheasant for it would cause it to go off. Once really smooth, add the remaining butter (you need about ⅓ of the weight of pheasant meat and a good cock bird will give you about 1 lb (500 g) picked meat) to make a smooth paste. Correct the seasoning and add lemon juice to taste.

Pack into small clean pots and run clarified butter over the top. Keep for a day or so before eating for the flavour to mature. It will keep for a month in the fridge as long as no juices were included and a generous layer of clarified butter (or ghee) covers it.

Suggested Wine. Modest white or light red.

Potted Pigeon with Cream Cheese

I especially like to use pigeon left over from Marinated Pigeon with Mediaeval Flavours (p. 127) because it is so tasty and the cooked garlic cloves can go into the pâté and give it such flavour. When cooking, it's always best to pack your casserole tightly so I usually add an extra pigeon or two so as to be able to make this pâté afterwards. But any leftover game could be used in this way. It is much lighter than old-fashioned potted meat which was pounded with butter and spices and kept under a layer of clarified butter. Of course it won't keep so long – but doesn't usually get a chance to. It also makes a great sandwich filling.

Serves 3–4

Ingredients
flesh from 1 cooked pigeon, partridge,
    grouse or about ⅓ of a pheasant (about
    6–8 oz (175–225 g) meat)
2–4 oz (50–100 g) cream cheese
any number of cooked garlic cloves from
    Mediaeval Pigeon recipe or ½ clove fresh
    garlic
½ teasp anchovy paste or ½ anchovy fillet
pinch mace
cayenne pepper or Tabasco sauce to taste
squeeze lemon juice
salt and pepper

Process the meat, garlic and anchovy until smoothish; add in the cream cheese, mace and add salt, cayenne and lemon juice to taste and process until smooth. Pack into pots and serve at room temperature with hot toast and lemon quarters or use as sandwich filling or heighten the seasoning and spread on fried bread croûtes and top with capers or gherkins as a savoury.

Suggested Wine. Modest white or light red.

FISH

Trout

Trout (*Salmo trutta*) has been eaten almost for ever. The caveman of the Dordogne enjoyed it under his river bank, pre-Palaeolithic Hebrideans kept their potassium, phosphorus and sulphur levels up with it (albeit unknowingly!) and many recorded feasts and banquets down the ages have featured trout on the menu.

Nowadays the word trout can conjure up all sorts of totally different images. There are those tiny speckled fellows, tails wavering, head to current in a bright clear burn; the ghostly shapes dimly seen in the weedy water of a chalk stream or perhaps the lazy rise and ring on a Highland loch of a still evening as the midges start to bite. Or again the bracing slap, slap of waves against the wooden boat as the line is kept tight and the net is positioned by the ghillie as everyone holds their breath. Another image is of hot sultry days on the local gravel pit with heavy and somewhat lifeless two pounders being lugged barely protesting from the water. To our son Andrew, till graduating to an Argyllshire river, trout was the fish farm in rural France where with pole, line, maggot and hook he could fish his own supper from the well-stocked woodland lake. Ten minutes there sufficed for everyone to catch their own and great self-control had to be exercised not to end up with far more expensive fish than were required!

For many others, trout is rainbow-hued and lies on the fishmonger's slab, perhaps pink-fleshed from the addition of permitted carotenoids to its pelleted food, instead of eating the fresh water shrimp in which carotenoids naturally occur. With luck it may have been 'exercised' against an artificially strong current of running water to build a little condition, texture and muscle before it meets the stunner or is 'harvested', as the trout farmer euphemistically puts it! But don't get me wrong; farmed fish can be very good, especially picked up fresh from a good farm or from your reliable fishmonger but it is not quite the same as the little wild fellow.

The fish produced from all these visions are all a little bit different and need to be treated in their own way. The half pounder from loch or burn is best straight into the frying pan with a little butter while the rainbow from the fishmonger perhaps needs a little light cooking, to keep him firm, and a nice tasty sauce to add flavour. I've included recipes for all these and it is for you to choose which you will find best suits your fish.

Trout with My Mother's Herb Sauce

My mother, a creative and very good natural cook, makes this sauce to go with trout, sea trout or salmon. She adjusts and varies the herbs, depending on the fish and the time of year, using just one or a nice mixture of garden herbs or bought watercress, fennel fronds or celery leaves. The important thing is to make the sauce ahead, the work of a moment with the food processor, then leave it to rest in a bain-marie or on the back of the Aga for the flavour to mellow and develop.

Ingredients
Serves 4–6

4–6 good trout of about 11 oz (300 g) each
½–1 oz (12–25 g) butter
1 lime or lemon
salt and pepper
parsley or watercress to garnish

Herb Sauce

2 egg yolks
6–8 oz (175–225 g) best unsalted butter
1 tbs lemon juice to taste
1 tbs wine vinegar

1–2 tbs finely chopped herbs like fennel, watercress, sorrel, parsley or any nice mixture
salt and pepper

To Cook the Trout. Wipe the trout with kitchen paper, gut and wipe out inside. Season inside and out with salt and pepper and a few drops of lime or lemon juice and lay in a generously buttered shallow baking dish; cover loosely with very well greased paper or tinfoil. Cook in a hot oven (425°F/220°C/Gas 7) for about 14–18 minutes until the eye has gone white and the flesh at the thickest part no longer feels soft and 'squishy' but just resilient. Remove the paper for the last few minutes if they are not already going a nice golden brown.

Herb Sauce. Chop up and melt the butter gently. Process the egg yolks in a food processor and add the lemon juice then the vinegar. With the engine running, gradually pour in the melted butter, rather like making mayonnaise. Add herbs and seasoning and turn into a serving dish or jug. Stand this container in a warm place like the side of the Aga or in a pan of warm water; in about 20–30 minutes it will have thickened nicely and the flavour will have developed. It will keep happily for an hour or so. Serve with trout, sea trout or salmon. It can also be used cold if you prefer.

Suggested Wine. German Kabinett.

Truite Farcie en Papillote

By removing the backbone and gutting the fish by cutting along the back rather than the belly, you can pack the stuffing into the belly cavity and none will escape.

Any edible mushrooms you may find as you fish such as chanterelles, trompettes de la mort, *cèpes* or any such can be included in the stuffing for flavour. Do take the trouble to squeeze the juice from the mushrooms (it can be added to stocks or soups) because, if you don't, they take so long to cook down that their flavour spoils. Chefs can manage because they have such fierce heat and wide pans.

Ingredients   *Serves 4*
4 trout
a few almonds
2 oz (50 g) butter or oil
a small quantity of white wine

Stuffing
¾ lb (350 g) button mushrooms
1 tbs very finely chopped shallot
a little lemon juice
1 tbs double cream
salt, pepper and cayenne

For un-gutted trout, open along the back and remove the backbone, cutting the bone near the head and tail and also removing the guts. Ready gutted fish have to be stuffed in the stomach cavity. Season the fish with salt, pepper, cayenne and squeeze of lemon.

Stuffing. Chop the mushrooms finely and squeeze out in a piece of muslin to expel the moisture. Melt 1½ oz (35 g) butter in a frying pan and cook the mushrooms with a good squeeze of lemon and the shallot; season with salt, pepper and cayenne; when completely dry, add 1 tbs of cream and cook for a moment more.

To Cook the Trout. Stuff the trout with this mixture and lay each trout on an oval of buttered tinfoil. Scatter with chopped almonds, moisten with a few drops of white wine and close up into parcels.

Bake for 12–14 minutes in a hot oven (450°F/230°C/Gas 8) and serve at once. Each guest opens their parcel on to their plate, losing none of the juice or savour. An Hollandaise or cream sauce can be served separately with this but it is not essential.

Suggested Wine. German Kabinett or Spätlese.

Trout with Braised Lettuce and Pink Tarragon Sauce

illustrated opposite

I don't often advocate red wine with fish but this good light Hollandaise style of sauce makes a pretty pink contrast with the green of the braised lettuce, a much underrated cooked vegetable. The boiled-down red wine and herb reduction will keep happily in the fridge for weeks; it is then very quick to make the sauce when you want it.

Ingredients *Serves 4–6*

4–6 trout
4–6 sprigs tarragon (optional)

Pink Tarragon Sauce

8 fl oz (225 ml) red wine
2–3 tbs red wine vinegar
3 tbs finely chopped shallot
a small bunch fresh or 1–2 teasp dried
  tarragon
4–6 black peppercorns
1 egg yolk
6–8 oz (175–225 g) good butter,
  preferably unsalted
1–2 teasp pink pepper berries
salt, if necessary

Braised Lettuce

4 smallish hearts of lettuce or 1–2 large
  ones
2 oz (50 g) butter
salt and pepper

Pink Tarragon Sauce. Place the wine, vinegar, shallots, some tarragon (keeping back about 1 teasp very finely chopped tarragon) in a non-aluminium saucepan and simmer until the shallot is cooked and only about 3–4 tbs of syrupy liquid remain. Strain, pressing well the debris in the sieve, and cool. Melt all but 1 oz (25 g) of the butter. Place the yolk in a double boiler or bowl, whisk well, add the wine and vinegar reduction and set over a pan of hot, not boiling water, so the bowl does not touch the water. Add half the cold butter and stir well until the yolk thickens. Remove the bowl quickly from the heat and stir in the remaining cold butter, to check the cooking and stop the yolk from curdling. Now gradually whisk in the melted butter, leaving out some of its white salty milky residue, to make a thick but flowing sauce. Stir in finely chopped tarragon to taste, correct seasoning and add most of the pink pepper berries. Set the bowl, covered with clingfilm, in a pan of tepid water and leave in a warm place like the back of the stove where it will keep quite happily for several hours before serving.

Braised Lettuce. Cut the lettuce into halves or quarters and blanch in a large pan of boiling salted water for 1–2 minutes. Drain, refresh under cold water then drain and squeeze out well. Melt the butter in a heavy wide casserole, add the lettuce in one layer and braise, covered, for about 5 minutes on each side, boiling away any spare liquid at the end.

To Cook the Fish. Place the gutted, wiped and lightly seasoned trout with a sprig of tarragon, if available, in the stomach cavity, in a steamer or buttered dish and steam or bake until just

cooked and feeling firm. Steaming will take about 8–10 minutes and baking about 14–18 minutes.

Dish up the trout on a large plate, arrange the braised lettuce at each end, spoon a little of the sauce over the trout, serving the rest in a sauceboat, and scatter with a few pink pepper berries.

Suggested Wine. Modest white.

Chinese Steamed Fish

You need a steamer that will hold your fish set in a dish, or an oval pot roaster with a trivet will do well if your steamer is not large enough. A good fresh fish has the most delicate sweet flavour cooked this way and the sauce a most authentic Chinese taste. Dried Chinese mushrooms (available from Chinese stores and with a shelf life of a year or more) give it the real flavour. You can use this for a couple of fine half pounders or one big trout and it is also excellent for whittling (first year sea trout) or larger sea trout. Watch the steaming very carefully to catch the moment when the fish is just done (but you don't want to keep taking the lid off the steamer!).

Ingredients

Serves 2–4

1–1½ lb (450–675 g) whole trout, sea trout or sea bass
2–3 spring onions
2–3 slices fresh root ginger
2–3 teasp light soy sauce
2 teasp Chinese wine or sherry
2–4 dried Chinese mushrooms soaked in tepid water for ½–¾ hour

1–2 slices ham or lean bacon
1 tbs chicken fat or oil
1 teasp cornflour
4 tbs chicken stock or mushroom-soaking water
½ teasp salt

Wipe the whole fish and slash three times on each side. Cut the spring onions and ginger slices into thin strips. Place all the onion and half the ginger on a dish and season the fish by rubbing with salt, soy and sherry. Lay on top of the onion and ginger. Cut the drained mushrooms and the ham into thin slices and scatter over the fish with the remaining ginger and a dribble of chicken fat or oil.

Place the fish, lightly covered in tinfoil, in a steamer over fast boiling water and steam for about 15–20 minutes, or until cooked (the moment the thickest part just stops feeling squidgy when you press it). Remove. Mix the cornflour with the chicken stock or mushroom water in a small saucepan, add in the sauce from the fish, boil up to thicken and correct seasoning. Pour over the fish and serve.

Suggested Wine. Crisp white (preferably Muscat d'Alsace or German Kabinett).

Trout en Papillote with Fennel and Tomato

The trout can either be stuffed with this nice burghal, herb and pine nut stuffing or left unstuffed. If stuffing it, it is easier if the trout is gutted and deboned from the back to leave the stomach cavity intact. The lovely flavours of fennel, tomato and a touch of Pernod go wonderfully with trout and you could just pour the sauce over a dish of trout and bake them like that, rather than parcel them. Personally I feel that parcelling them keeps the lovely fresh flavours intact.

Ingredients   *Serves 4*
4 good trout
2–3 tbs olive oil
2 shallots, finely chopped
2 heads Florence fennel
4 good tomatoes, skinned, de-seeded and
    roughly chopped
1 tbs tomato purée
¼ teasp fennel seeds
½–1 teasp Pernod (optional)
1 lemon or lime
salt and pepper

Stuffing (optional)
6 tbs burghal (cracked wheat)
1–2 tbs pine nuts
2 tbs finely chopped fennel leaf or parsley
1 egg yolk
a little grated lemon rind
salt and pepper

Stuffing. Soak the burghal in cold water for 20 minutes then drain and press dry in a cloth. Lightly brown the pine nuts in a little oil. Combine the soaked burghal, chopped herb, pine nuts, yolk, lemon rind and seasoning.

To Cook the Trout. If stuffing the trout, de-bone and gut from the back, snipping out the backbone at the head and tail ends. Season and stuff with the stuffing and reform.

Soften the shallot in the oil in a frying pan or casserole, add the finely sliced fennel and soften gently; then add the chopped de-seeded tomato, the tomato purée, fennel seeds, Pernod and seasoning; cook gently together until tender and full flavoured.

Lightly oil four sheets of tinfoil, lay a trout on each and on each lay two thin half slices of lemon or lime; then spoon over some tomato-fennel mixture. Parcel tightly and bake in a moderately hot oven (375°F/190°C/Gas 5) for about 15 minutes or until just done.

If preparing ahead, let the tomato-fennel mixture get quite cold before assembling.

Suggested Wine. Modest white.

Butter Fried Trout with Pine Nuts and Florence Fennel

There is hardly a better way of cooking a firm fresh trout than by cooking it in butter. Add a few nuts at the end and if you have no pine nuts, which have a luscious delicate flavour, then use flaked almonds, hazelnuts or a mixture of both. The fennel, fried until browning then braised until tender, perfectly complements the trout.

Serves 4

Ingredients

4 fine trout
1½–2 oz (35–50 g) best butter
4–6 tbs pine nuts (or use flaked almonds or
    hazelnuts)
a little more butter to finish
2–3 tbs torn fennel leaves, leaf watercress
    or parsley heads
½ lemon
salt and pepper
    milk and seasoned flour (optional)

Fennel
2–3 heads Florence fennel
1 oz (25 g) butter or olive oil
squeeze lemon juice
salt and pepper

Fennel. Start with the fennel which takes longer to cook and choose a wide heavy pan with a lid. Cut the fennel into quarters or eighths, keeping attached at the core, to fit in one layer in the pan. Heat the butter, add the fennel in one layer and fry gently until just browning at the edges, turning once. Now add 2–3 tablespoons water, season, cover and braise gently for 20 minutes or so until completely tender, adding a few drops of water if they dry out before they are ready. Turn again and, once ready to serve, take off the lid, turn up the heat and cook until all the liquid has gone and the fennel are again frying and browning at the edges. Squeeze over a little lemon and serve with the fish. It is this contrast of crisping brown edges and tender middles that is so appealing.

To Cook the Trout. Wipe the trout clean and season inside with salt and pepper; if you wish for a crisper skin you can dip in milk and seasoned flour before frying. Heat the butter in a heavy pan (oval pans for fish are especially useful). When the butter is frothing, lay in the fish and, adjusting the heat to moderate so the butter does not burn, fry the fish for 6–8 minutes on each side until crisp and brown. I find it easiest to fry the nuts separately in a small pan in a little fresh butter whilst the fish are cooking, but you can pop them in the pan with the fish. Fry the nuts gently until they are an even golden brown.

Set the fish on a serving dish and scatter over the nuts. Now here's the classic trick that makes it really taste good; discard the frying butter and carefully wipe out the pan; add a generous ounce or so of fresh, good butter and swirl around until frothing, then browning and smelling nutty; at once add the torn fennel leaves, watercress or parsley heads, fry for a moment, then add a good squeeze of lemon juice and pour over the fish. Serve at once. You could do the initial frying in oil though the flavour is not so good (olive oil excepted) or you could finish the fish with hazelnut oil or almond oil. Parsley and herbs fried in this way have a wonderful flavour.

Suggested Wine. Best white.

Trout Fillets in Ginger and Leek Sauce

This is a lovely fresh modern dish; it is useful in that you can prepare the leeks, fillets and sauce then just cook for 4–6 minutes when you are ready. Some people do like not to have to grapple with heads and bones.

Ingredients   *Serves 4–6*

4 good fresh trout, filleted
1 lb (450 g) tender leeks, white and some
    green part
2 tbs oil or butter
2 teasp fresh ginger cut into fine shreds
3 fl oz (75 ml) dry vermouth, such as Noilly
    Prat
8 fl oz (225 ml) fish fumet (reduced to 2–3
    tbs) or ½ fish or chicken stock cube
½ pt (300 ml) double cream
2–3 tbs shredded watercress
½ lime or lemon
salt and pepper

Cut the cleaned leeks into fine lengthways shreds about 2–3 inches (8 cm) long. Heat the oil in a wok or wide frying pan and cook the leeks, stirring all the time, until wilted and almost cooked; season lightly and remove to a gratin dish which will take the trout fillets in one layer. Lay seasoned trout fillets on the leeks in one layer, cover the dish and cook in a moderately hot oven (375°F/190°C/Gas 5) for 4–6 minutes until the fish is just done. Meanwhile, add the ginger, vermouth, reduced fish fumet or stock cube to the pan in which you wilted the leeks and reduce over high flame until just 3–4 tbs of syrupy juices remain. Now add the cream and boil down until of a nice coating sauce consistency. Add the watercress shreds, seasoning and a squeeze of lime or lemon if necessary and pour over the cooked fish. Serve at once. The leeks and sauce (without the watercress) can both be prepared ahead, then the fish cooked and the dish assembled when ready to eat.

Suggested Wine. Crisp white.

Hot Smoked Trout and Iced Horseradish Sauce

Smoking fish in a little home smoker is a very good way to give them an attractive extra flavour. They will cook as they smoke and are therefore hot smoked, as opposed to cold smoked where they very gently smoke well away from any direct heat source. I usually remove the head and split the fish from the back, removing the backbone and guts but leaving the tail, like a kipper. I salt it quite heavily and leave for an hour then blot off the moisture that is drawn out. I also sometimes add a seasoning of coarse crushed peppermill mixture or chopped herbs and find lemon thyme particularly successful. Make only a thin layer of oak sawdust in the bottom of the smoker and lay the fish on a rack, well above the sawdust. Close the tin and light a fire in a couple of little tins of meths-soaked wadding, underneath the smoker. I find 8–10 minutes will do a couple of 10–12 oz (275–350 g) split trout, less time for subsequent batches; get to know your smoker and check and turn off or remove fish the moment they stop feeling squidgy.

Serve whilst still hot or warm or leave until cold. Serve with the Iced Horseradish Sauce or a herb vinaigrette made with a little chopped shallot and basil and good olive oil. Any fish can be smoked then used in recipes such as Salmon Rillettes (p. 46), Salmon and Spinach Pie (p. 79) or Scrambled eggs and smoked fish (p. 42).

Ingredients   *Serves 4–6*
4–6 smoked trout

Iced Horseradish Sauce
4 fl oz (100 ml) whipping cream
1 tbs olive, walnut or hazelnut oil
2–3 teasp finely grated fresh horseradish or
    rather more of a horseradish sauce
    (to taste)
good squeeze lemon juice
a little chopped fresh, frozen or dried dill
    (optional)
salt

Sauce. Whip the cream, beating in the oil, horseradish, lemon, dill and salt. Once stiff, pile into a bowl and ice well before serving with smoked fish.

You can also use it on top of soups, with smoked sausage, roast beef or venison.

Salmon and Sea Trout

Who does not gasp to see the vigorous silver salmon (*Salmo salar*), mighty king of the river and sea, driving itself up a waterfall? Its power and strength as well as its cussed contrariness when it comes to our trying to catch it cannot but grip the sportsman's imagination.

Once so common (an unsubstantiated but generally accepted anecdote tells of servants begging not to be made to eat it more than three times a week), the formerly prolific salmon of the rivers of Northern Europe now has so many enemies conspiring to his downfall. The building of locks and weirs, the factory and domestic pollution of rivers, over-fishing and netting and more recently the sea fishing off the coast of Greenland and elsewhere have diminished Salar's number. To his defence has come the salmon farmer, rearing salmon for the table in northern sea tanks. This has taken the pressure off wild fish and with the ever-rising cost of rods on salmon rivers, great efforts are being made to protect him.

Salmon alevins emerge from the gravel in the small clear headwaters, their parents having made their way back by some mysterious migratory process from the sea to the river of their own birth to breed. Two or even three years are spent in the river, growing and developing through the stages of fry and parr until they become silvery, adapt for salt-water life and head for the sea as smolts. They then cover huge distances of up to two and a half thousand miles to feeding grounds, once unknown but now unfortunately discovered by modern fishing fleets. They may return to their river in one year as a grilse (tender, sweet flavoured and weighing from 2–8 lbs (900–3.6 kg)) but are more likely to return after two to three years as fully fledged salmon, weighing from 8 lbs to 30 lbs or even more. Having worked their way upriver to the narrow clear stream of their birth and laid their eggs in a redd or hollow in the gravel, the thin tired kelt usually die but occasionally make it back to the sea to renew strength to repeat the cycle.

Sea trout (*Salmo trutta*), generally smaller and even better for the table, do not go nearly so far afield and go upriver each year to spawn, sometimes living to around twenty years. Fish enter their rivers at different times; some like the Tay open in January, when the fish will be superb, but others are not at their best until summer or early autumn. We fish in Argyllshire in July for sea trout and in mid-October for some exciting, fresh-run tail-end salmon. But whenever they enter the river, they do not breed until late autumn, surviving on their fat till then.

Salmon is a fat fish and its flavour is superb. The quotable Major Pollard says: 'There is one plain and simple rule about salmon which should be remembered by every cook. Salmon has a particular and specific virtue of its own. It is best plain so do not attempt to better it'. Hear, hear, Major Pollard! I love it really fresh and when we lived at the mouth of the Doon in 1963, I ran out whenever I saw the netters (and whenever I could afford it at 4/– a pound!) to buy a fish, fresh from the sea pool with the sea lice still on it. It was my saviour when, as a young bride, we had our friend, the noted Hong Kong gourmet Ossie Cheung, and his bride Pauline to stay on their honeymoon and wanted to give them something rather special. For really fresh salmon has a creamy 'curd' between the flakes and a wonderful texture and flavour that impressed them greatly and we had great discussions about flying fish to Hong Kong (now Hong Kong has some of the finest ingredients from all over the world – including wild Scottish salmon as I found out recently). I also found splendid fresh farmed Scottish salmon on sale in California at a wholesaler in Napa; the Scandinavian fish on sale had a produce guarantee metal tab (like poulet de Bresse) and I wish we had the same pride in our fish as this remarkable export finds favour around the world.

The largest salmon, especially those not of the first quality, are best smoked. May I point you at Julia Drysdale's excellent *Classic Game Cookery*, published by Papermac, for clear instructions on home-smoking salmon, though you may feel safer sending your fish to a good smoker. These, to my mind, are few and far between, so many fish coming out either too salty and smoky or, nowadays, with dry salting and fast smoking, being rather soft and moist with less depth of flavour.

B. Portch, Cornish Sea Products, Portleven Harbour, Cornwall TR13 9JU (0736-763218) do a good, very delicate smoke and so do Strathaird Ltd, 21 Longman Drive, Inverness (0463-225959); Hamish Wilson, on the other hand, of Teviot Smokery, Kirkbank House, Eckford, Kelso, Roxburghshire (08355-253) does a more traditional slow smoke which gives a wonderful complex depth of flavours and rather better keeping quality. It really depends what smoker you can get your fish to in time, but freezing before smoking is not disastrous; Pinneys, another good firm, buy when the price is right and freeze their fish before smoking to ensure steady prices.

While keeping the recipes simple, I have tried to incorporate some useful techniques such as classic Chinese salt-baking, modern cooking of wafer slices on a plate or the grilling of trimmed tronçons. All these techniques can be adapted to your own ideas and style, giving you a wealth of new dishes whilst retaining the maxim of keeping it simple. There are a few more in the chapters on First Courses and on Eatups.

When catering for large occasions, we allow ½–¾ lb (450–675 g) of salmon per head. By the time the fish has been gutted, cooked and the head, tail, skin and fins have been removed, you will have about 6 oz (175 g) per person which is a nice generous portion. If just buying middle-cut steaks, 6–8 oz (175–225 g) is generous because salmon is a rich fish. Farmed salmon is decidedly softer than wild fish that have swum many miles, though a lot depends on which fish farm they have come from and what their diet was, so trust your fishmonger; realise also that their flesh has been coloured pink only towards the end of their time by the addition of a colourant in their diet; the fish you buy will be fresh, beautifully presented and of very consistent quality.

Cold Salmon Mousse

Almost a cold soufflé though we usually call this a mousse, which is much firmer in texture. This is very light and the flavour of the salmon comes through. Serve in a soufflé dish or glass bowl or turn out from a ring mould, individual timbales or moulds. It is pretty decorated with salmon caviar and sprigs of dill or mint, cucumber or watercress and a few prawns. A few chopped prawns folded in also make an interesting change of texture.

Ingredients
Serves 4–6

12 oz (350 g) salmon steak or
   8 oz (225 g) poached boneless, skinless
   salmon
2 tbs shallot, finely chopped
2–3 sprigs fresh or
   1 teasp dried tarragon or use other herbs
2–3 parsley stalks
4 tbs dry white vermouth (Noilly Prat)

2½ teasp gelatine
4 oz (100 g) cream cheese
good squeeze lemon juice, to taste
a little grated nutmeg or pinch mace
salt and pepper
¼ pt (150 ml) whipping cream
2 egg whites

Garnish

cucumber, or
salmon caviar and dill, or some prawns in
   shell and watercress

Season the salmon piece and slip into a boil-in or roast-in bag (or small covered container) with the shallot, herbs and vermouth. Poach or steam (or microwave) until just done and leave to cool. If using already poached salmon, just simmer the shallots, herbs, vermouth and a little water gently for about 10 minutes then strain; or strain the cooking liquid from the salmon you have cooked. In either case make up to 5 fl oz (150 ml) with water (or fish fumet or liquid you have boiled prawn shells in etc). Soak the gelatine in 2 tbs cold water in a small bowl then stand the bowl in a pan of hot water to melt (or microwave).

Place the skinned, boned and flaked salmon in the food processor and process until smooth, adding in the reserved cooking liquid. Once smooth, add the cream cheese, lemon juice, mace or nutmeg and seasoning and process; then add the gelatine. Fold in the cream, whipped until just softly holding its shape, then finally the egg whites, whipped until they just hold a peak. Turn into a 1½ pt (900 ml) ring mould, rinsed in cold water or a soufflé dish. Leave to set in the fridge. Turn out and decorate and garnish before serving.

Suggested Wine. Best white.

Cold Salmon with Green Mousseline Sauce

Decorated cold salmon – what more handsome dish for a summer party? Salmon needs simplicity to enjoy its unique flavour. Luckily, poaching salmon is the easiest thing in the world – if you have the pan for it! Place the cleaned fish in cold water (spring water, says Meg Dods) or court-bouillon, bring gently to the boil and switch off to cook and cool in the water. This infallible guide works whatever the size of the fish; small fish come quickly to the boil and cool quickly and large ones take longer and I love the beautiful simplicity and logic of this method.

My problems start with any salmon over about 8 lbs (3.6 kg). I have to use my huge ham pan (much too wasteful in which to use a court-bouillon) and, once brought to the boil, this huge pan (that lost its handles years ago before I ever owned it) is almost immovable from the stove, taking danger money and a husband lured from his wine store to help remove it to the larder! I cannot think how we catered for weddings and parties and never had a dreadful accident. Years ago, catering for one such huge wedding, in my innocence I allowed my fishmonger to get me several really large salmon, 12 pounders or so. On collecting them, I realised, at once, that they would fit into no pan of mine; panic followed by a call to my friend, the chef of The Queen's College, Oxford and soon they were cooking in his huge bain-marie. Lesson, only buy salmon you can cope with and send large fish you have caught to the smokers (or cut them in half to cook, as Prue Leith suggests, glueing the two halves back together with piped mayonnaise and concealing garnishes!).

Back to the recipe; I am no great believer in court-bouillon, feeling little flavour is going to get through the impervious mackintosh of the salmon's skin. Once your salmon (or of course sea trout for that matter) is cold and has discarded its mackintosh, it lies pink and glistening on the plate with a lustrous sheen (if it has not cracked, broken, the skin refused to come off cleanly or any of the other minor vicissitudes that visit one on unrobing a salmon). Garnish it simply and serve it quickly because it is lovely if not completely cold. Layers of cucumber, coatings of aspic, frills and furbelows of dill are time-consuming to apply and essential for the caterer who has to cook the fish well ahead and transport them for miles. But if it is just going on to your table, let the fish show its beauty.

The sauce can just be a perfect mayonnaise; this is preferably made by hand for its flavour and firm, glistening translucence or you might like to try this quite ravishing Green Mousseline Sauce that I have from my Great-Great-Grandmother's manuscript cookery book. It is little trouble now to do all the pounding and puréeing in a food processor but it must then have been quite a labour. The flavour is delicate, light and perfectly balanced, as 'modern' as you could wish and as good with trout as it is with salmon. It is this sort of dish that shows me what excellent cooks these nineteenth-century ladies were and makes me a little perturbed at the arrogance of our modern 'inventiveness', always looking for something new and different. I took this sauce to California and it really 'wowed' my audience – I do hope you will try it. Other sauces to serve with salmon, when you tire of this or cannot get the herbs, might be Sorrel (p. 45), Pink Tarragon (p. 60) or My Mother's Herb Sauce (p. 58).

Ingredients   *Allow a 2–3 lb (900 g–1.35 kg) fish for 4–6 people*

a fine salmon or sea trout
water or court-bouillon to cover
salt
herbs and cucumber to garnish

Green Mousseline Sauce   *Serves only 4–6*

2–3 sprigs fresh tarragon

3–4 good sprigs chervil

bunch parsley

1 shallot, finely chopped

1 teasp capers

½–1 small dill cucumber or 3 gherkins,
   rinsed of strong brine

4 anchovy fillets

1 hard-boiled egg yolk

a few drops sap-green colouring (optional)

1–2 tbs oil

3 fl oz (75 ml) made up and set aspic (Haco
   is a good Swiss brand)

2–3 tbs mayonnaise

3–4 tbs whipped cream

salt and pepper only if necessary

To Cook the Salmon. If not already done, set the fish on the draining board and scale carefully, working from tail to head (the back of a knife or a scallop shell is a good instrument to use); the scales get everywhere and block the drain! Now rinse off all the scales, set the fish on newspaper and gut carefully, cutting from vent to gills and withdrawing all innards; remove the gills too, if possible, for they go brownish in cooking and do not look pretty. Do not remove the head for this spoils the beauty of the fish and people could think you had bought frozen Canadian salmon! Wipe out the stomach cavity, taking great care to get the blood out, especially between the knobbles of the backbone; use kitchen paper and a skewer or knife tip. Of course, if the fishmonger has prepared the fish, you only need to check it has been done properly. Lay the salmon on the lift-out tray of the fish kettle. If you are having to 'Heath Robinson', set the salmon on a strip of wood (the side of a fruit box) on a generous piece of muslin or boiled stockinette or dish cloth and set it on upturned saucers or plates to keep it off the bottom in your pan. You lift out the fish by the generous ends of cloth.

Set in the pan with cold water to cover, with a handful of coarse salt added, or court-bouillon; cover and bring gently to the boil on the stove. Once it has reached a quite definite boil, remove from the stove to a cool spot and leave until cold; do not remove the lid as it cools. Once cold, lift the fish from the liquid, drain carefully then slide off the drainer on to a cloth. Then with a very sharp knife (a Stanley knife is good) cut the skin all around the salmon's head and gills, then cut the skin along the back. Peel off the skin carefully, removing the fins and little bones along the back and belly as you go. Remove the brown fat from the centre line only if you wish. Once skinned, carefully roll over on the cloth and remove the skin on the other side. Now, with the aid of the cloth, roll the fish on to your serving platter, wooden board or tray. The side that was top in the pan is usually the most rounded and handsome. Garnish with herbs like dill, fennel, chervil or parsley or a row of wafer-thin cucumber slices, salted for 15 minutes, rinsed and dried, set down the centre line of the fish. Serve with Green Mousseline Sauce. If you need to prepare it ahead, coat with several layers of aspic, applied whilst syrupy and let set before the next layer is applied.

Green Mousseline Sauce. Throw the tarragon, chervil and parsley, without any tough stalks, into boiling water with the shallot; blanch for a moment or two, drain, refresh with cold water and pat dry. Pound together, or process in a food processor, the blanched herbs and shallots, the capers, dill cucumber or gherkins, anchovies and hard-boiled egg yolk until bright green and smooth, adding 1–2 drops sap-green colouring only if necessary. Once smooth, work or process in the oil and aspic then sieve the mixture. Now mix with the mayonnaise and lastly fold in the cream. Keep chilled until ready to serve with the salmon.

Suggested Wine. Best white (preferably fine Burgundy).

Salmon Quenelles with Prawn Mousseline

This is a glorious, rich dish with wonderful flavours so keep the rest of the meal simple. Although it is in the realms of haute cuisine, the hard work is all done so quickly with the aid of our modern food processors. Do trim the salmon very carefully so the mixture will come smooth because it is no fun trying to sieve it later if you decide it is not smooth enough. If quenelles or the sauce daunt you, the mixture can be baked in little pots in a bain-marie in a moderate oven until just set and served with a number of sauces such as My Mother's Herb Sauce (p. 58), the Sorrel Sauce (p. 45) or the Pink Tarragon Sauce (p. 60) spooned on top. A slightly bolder move might be to steam (or bake in a bain-marie) in a well-buttered ring mould or timbale moulds, turn out and mask with the Classic (p. 77) or any other appropriate sauce.

Ingredients

Serves 4–6

Quenelles
9 oz (250 g) fillet of salmon, trimmed and
   skinned
3 egg whites
a little ground mace
10–12 fl oz (200–350 ml) double cream
salt and pepper

Prawn Mousseline
8 oz (225 g) prawns, unshelled
5½ oz (150 g) unsalted or lightly salted
   butter
½ pt (300 ml) fish fumet or ½ fish stock
   cube and water
2 egg yolks
½–1 lemon
salt and pepper

Quenelles. Pick over the salmon, removing all bones. Process the fish in the food processor using the metal blade until finely chopped, adding the egg whites and, when absolutely smooth, and you have decided you don't need to sieve it, season lightly with salt (which tightens the mixture making it harder to sieve), pepper and a tiny bit of mace. With the machine running, add the cream quickly but do not process for more than 20 seconds or the mixture might curdle. The mixture must still be firm enough to sit up on a spoon. Chill for 30 minutes or so before cooking. You can cook a little in a cocotte dish standing in a pan of boiling water if you wish to test seasoning and consistency.

Prawn Mousseline. Set 6–8 prawns aside for garnish. Shell and dice the rest, reserving the shells. Melt 3 oz (75 g) of the butter in a frying pan, add the reserved prawn shells and toss over the heat for 1 minute until heated through. Scrape the prawn-shell mixture into the food processor bowl and with the metal blade process until well chopped; then turn into a sieve, lined with a generous piece of muslin, and wring out all the prawn butter. Cool. Place the prawn shells in a saucepan with the fish fumet or stock cube and water and simmer for 10 minutes, skimming if any scum forms. Strain through muslin then reduce the prawn fumet until strongly flavoured and only 5–6 tablespoons (3 fl oz/75 ml) remains.

Using the metal blade, pour the hot prawn fumet into the processor bowl and process whilst adding dice of the remaining butter and prawn butter. Once it is all emulsified, turn it into a small pan and set aside until ready to serve. The butter could be whisked in by hand if you prefer.

To Cook the Quenelles. Bring a wide, shallow pan of salted water to the simmer. Dip a dessertspoon in warm water and take a good rounded spoonful of the quenelle mixture; shape if necessary with another wet spoon and lower into the water (tap the spoon on the bottom until the quenelle detaches). Form all the quenelles and poach for about 8–10 minutes, carefully turning once with a slotted spoon, until just firm. Remove with a slotted spoon, drain on absorbent kitchen paper and keep warm, well covered and spaced a little apart in a buttered shallow serving dish. Put the reserved prawns to heat as well.

Meanwhile, place the egg yolks with 2 teasp (10 ml) of lemon juice and 2 tbs (30 ml) of cold water in a double boiler or a bowl over hot water. Cook, whisking all the time, until the mixture doubles in bulk, becomes moussy and just holds a trail. Reboil the butter mixture, adding the diced prawns to heat through, and gradually whisk it into the egg mousseline. Continue whisking over hot water until it is a light coating consistency; adjust the seasoning and add lemon juice to taste. The sauce can be kept warm over tepid water. To serve, spoon the sauce over the quenelles and decorate with the heated unpeeled prawns. Serve at once.

Suggested Wine. Best white.

Poached Salmon with Sorrel Sauce

Gentle poaching and leaving it to stand ensures a moist and succulent fish. This simple but excellent sauce, an amalgamation of butter and cream, is very versatile as you can use lime or add other herbs or blanched watercress or even green peppercorns in place of the sorrel.

Ingredients   *Serves 4–6*

4–6 lb (1.8–2.7 kg) sea trout or salmon
1 bunch watercress or parsley
or
butter
½ glass white wine
2–3 spring onions
herbs, tarragon, parsley, lemon thyme, dill
   or chervil
2–3 slices of lemon
salt
6–8 peppercorns

Chiffonnade of Sorrel

10–20 sorrel leaves
½ oz (12 g) butter

Sorrel Sauce

5 oz (125 g) lightly salted best butter
¼ pt (150 ml) double cream
squeeze lemon juice
salt and pepper

Poach the salmon in gently simmering salt water for 4–6 minutes to the pound. Draw the pan off the stove and leave for ½ hour before removing from the water. Alternatively, you can parcel the salmon in buttered tinfoil with the white wine, salt, peppercorns, spring onions and herbs and several slices of lemon and bake in a moderate oven (350°F/180°C/Gas 4) for 30–45 minutes; don't unwrap for 10–30 minutes or so after removing from the oven or you can switch off the oven after about 25 minutes and leave it for 1–1½ hours to finish cooking and rest; it will be well relaxed and easy to deal with.

Skin the salmon, dish up on a large plate and decorate with a fine bunch of fresh parsley or watercress.

Chiffonnade of Sorrel. Take a handful of sorrel leaves, wash, shake, remove the tough midribs and shred finely. Melt the butter in a small saucepan (not aluminium) and add the sorrel. Cook gently until the sorrel is soft but still in strips and the moisture has gone.

Sorrel Sauce. Chop the butter and heat gently to melt (it must oil but not separate), add the cream and heat, but not to boiling. Draw off the stove and beat in a good squeeze of lemon (this thickens and binds it), a teaspoon or so of sorrel chiffonnade and seasoning. Serve hot.

Suggested Wine. Best white.

Salmon Sauce Louise

I invented this sauce for my daughter who is allergic to dairy products but wanted hot salmon with a luscious sauce for her 21st birthday party. The sauce is basically a mayonnaise, made over hot water like an Hollandaise so it is warm, then lightened with a little whipped white of egg and flavoured with chopped herbs and tiny dice of tomato. It was a wild success and all my greedy food-conscious family loved it. I think it really is a new idea for I have come across nothing like it anywhere, it is luscious yet healthy and light, and you can of course vary the flavourings.

Ingredients   *Serves 4–6*
a whole 4–6 lb (1.8–2.7 kg) salmon
    poached (as p. 70), or 4–6 generous
    6–8 oz (175–225 g) salmon steaks
2–3 oz (50–75 g) butter or good olive oil

Sauce Louise

½ pt (300 ml) mixed good olive oil and   salt and pepper
    sunflower oil or sunflower oil with a little   2–3 tbs chopped fresh mixed tarragon,
    walnut or hazelnut oil to taste   chervil and chives
2 egg yolks   whisked white of ½–1 egg
1 teasp Dijon mustard   1–2 deep red tomatoes, skinned, seeded
2–3 teasp tarragon or wine vinegar or   and cut in tiny neat dice
    lemon juice   salt and pepper

Sauce Louise. Warm the oil. Whisk the egg yolks for about a minute in a bowl with the mustard, 2 teasp vinegar, plenty of salt and some pepper. Set the bowl over hot water and, just like making mayonnaise, whisk in the warmed oil gradually to make a thick emulsified sauce that should be quite warm to the touch. Beat in the herbs to taste then fold in the whisked egg white and the diced tomato. Correct the seasoning and acidity and set to keep warm over tepid water only, set beside the stove but away from direct heat. I like the sauce thickly flowing like a well made Hollandaise. Serve in a sauceboat with whole hot salmon or with salmon steaks.

Salmon Steaks. If using butter, melt it gently. Brush the prepared steaks with the melted butter or oil on both sides. Steam for 7–10 minutes until just cooked then skin and serve with the sauce. Alternatively, slip the buttered or oiled steaks in one layer into a boil-in-bag, seal and slip into a roasting pan of simmering water. Cook in a moderately hot oven (375°F/190°C/Gas 5) for about 8–10 minutes.

Suggested Wine. Best white.

Fresh Salmon Leaves with Vegetables

This is one of my favourite ways of cooking a light and delicate salmon dish for just a few people (without vast grills it is not practical for large numbers, but it is an ideal restaurant dish). The salmon must be filleted then cut into little slices or leaves (a good fishmonger will do this for you) that take but a moment to grill. If Simon comes home with a nice fish I sometimes prepare a whole side, cut into leaves, package and freeze it ready to remove some slices to cook; it works well but don't keep it frozen for too long. Wild salmon has much more texture for this dish than farmed salmon, which varies a lot from producer to producer.

Ingredients
Serves 4–6

¾ lb–1 lb (350–450 g) boned, skinned and
  sliced salmon – allow 2–3 oz (50–75 g)
  per person
3 teasp best olive oil or sunflower oil
2 oz (50 g) butter
1 teasp very finely chopped shallot
1 oz (25 g) celery ⎫
3 oz (75 g) prepared carrots ⎪ all cut into 3 inch (7 cm)
3 oz (75 g) long spring onions ⎬ long fine julienne strips
3 oz (75 g) cucumber (discard ⎪
  seeds and soft middle) ⎭
1 teasp fresh chopped or ¼ teasp dried
  tarragon
8 tbs dry white wine
2 tbs dry vermouth
2–3 tbs very reduced fish fumet or a
  little corner of fish stock cube
  (optional)
⅓ pt (200 ml) double cream
salt and pepper

a little chopped tarragon and chives
4–6 cubes or shapes of cooked puff pastry
  (optional)
sprigs chervil for garnish

Fillet the salmon, remove any bones and cut like smoked salmon into slices, allowing 2–3 per person. Set aside. Heat the oil and butter in a wide sauté pan or sauce pan then add the shallots, celery, and carrot julienne strips; cook without browning for 3 minutes then add the spring onion and cook for a further 2 minutes before adding the cucumber and tarragon for a final 2 minutes. Now add the wine, vermouth, and fish fumet or stock cube if used, boil up and add the cream and seasoning. Simmer half-covered for 5 minutes then strain the vegetables from the sauce.

Make little piles of vegetables on individual warm wide plates, or on one serving dish that will fit under the grill; then lay 2–3 slices of salmon on each pile so they do not overlap. Pop the plates or dish under a very hot pre-heated grill for about 2 minutes to cook the salmon which should be only *very* lightly cooked and 'tacky'. Boil up and reduce the sauce until lightly coating. Correct seasoning. Add chives and tarragon and spoon over the salmon; top with a cube of warm puff pastry, garnish with a chervil sprig and serve at once.

Suggested Wine. Best white (ideally fine dry Loire like Savennières, or a white Burgundy).

Tronçons of Salmon with a Classic Sauce

You know those wonderful classic sauces you taste in the restaurants of Cherbourg and all over Normandy? Well, they are not at all difficult to make if you have some good fish fumet, preferably with a hint of prawn in it (this lasts well in the freezer so keep a supply); it goes wonderfully well with salmon or even trout. Actually, I like to use an Alsace wine, preferably a Pinot Gris or Riesling, which consorts well with fish and you can drink the rest of the bottle as an apéritif or with the meal (the better the wine, the better the sauce).

I rather like to fillet and skin the salmon then cut it into generous lengthways tronçons like a large fish finger; I drop these into a hot, buttered grill pan and grill briefly; I like the browned outside to contrast with a tender, lightly cooked centre (it is also a good way of cooking farmed salmon which does not have that wonderful firm chewy texture of fresh wild fish). Salmon, brushed with dill and lime butter or beurre maître d'hôtel and plain grilled, is also excellent but add no extra flavours if you use this classic sauce. I can find nothing that improves its perfect simplicity.

Ingredients
1½–2 lb (675–900 g) centre cut of salmon
1 oz (25 g) butter
salt and pepper
chervil for garnish

Classic Sauce
8–10 fl oz (225–300 ml) good fish fumet
    (p. 23)
4–5 fl oz (100–150 ml) good dry white
    wine (preferably Alsace)
1 tbs shallot, finely chopped
¼ oz (6 g) butter
½ teasp flour
7–8 fl oz (200–225 ml) good double cream
2 oz (500 g) best unsalted butter
salt and pepper

Serves 4 as a main course or 6–8 as a starter

Classic Sauce. Place the fish fumet, which should be virtually unsalted, and the shallot in a small saucepan and reduce by half; then add the wine and reduce again to about 8 fl oz (225 ml). In another pan, melt the ¼ oz (6 g) of butter, add the flour and cook gently; then draw off the stove and add the reduced fish fumet and wine and all but 1–2 tbs of the cream. Simmer and reduce by about half by which time, if it was good fish fumet, it will be tasting pretty good. Now whisk the remaining diced butter into the simmering sauce, one piece at a time, whisking hard. Finish with the last of the cream and correct the seasoning (keep warm in a bain-marie if not using at once but don't let it get too hot or it could separate; alternatively, whisk the butter in only when serving).

To Cook the Salmon. Fillet the salmon and remove the skin; pull out any bones and trim off any brownish fat at the midline. Cut each piece of salmon into 4 even lengthways tronçons rather like a large fish finger; the two from the back will be thick, the two from the belly rather thinner; you will get 8 pieces from the 2 sides of salmon. Divide it into the 4 thicker pieces, which will take a little longer to cook, and the 4 thinner. Season just before cooking.

Heat the grill until very hot and heat a heavy grill pan. Drop diced butter into the grill pan and, once sizzling, lay in the thickest salmon sticks; turn in the butter and put the pan under the grill, about 2–3 inches (5–8 cm) from the heat; after about 2 minutes, add the remaining salmon and grill for about 3–4 minutes until the tronçons have just lost their squidgyness (I don't know how fierce your grill is or how hot you get the grill pan so precise timings are impossible to give, but the salmon should come out whilst still tender and almost soft inside).

Serve at once, a thick and a thin slice, on a little pool of the sauce, garnished with chervil, or hand the sauce separately in a sauceboat. Serve alone, or with some steamed new potatoes and a delicate green vegetable such as mange-tout, beans or courgettes, simply cooked or steamed.

Suggested Wine. Best white (preferably Alsace Pinot Gris or Riesling).

Salmon Caviar

Should you find yourself with a good hen salmon full of roe, you can make some excellent salmon caviar. It's very simple to do but it is a slow and fiddly job to separate the eggs from the fine membrane that holds them together; but it's worth it. I have the method from Barney and Belle Rhodes in California. First wash and separate the roe in a 4% salt solution; that is 4 grams of salt (I use sea salt) to each 100 ml of water and therefore 20 g to each ½ litre. Delicately remove the membrane (the use of a carefully wielded fork can help), slip the tine between the eggs to lift the membrane, but each time a little egg pops one curses. Allow about an hour or so for this task, but think of the caviar! Now strain carefully in a sieve then soak in a 7% salt solution (7 g to each 100 ml therefore 35 g to ½ litre). Soak for 15 minutes only then drain thoroughly and pack into tiny clean jars (I boil them for 10 minutes), right to the top so there is no air space. Cover with a circle of Bakewell or greaseproof paper and screw on the lid. Keep in the fridge and preferably use within a week once opened. Serve the caviar with brown bread and butter or toast, lemon, black pepper and, if you like, finely chopped shallot. Or serve with blinis and melted butter and sour cream and onion which is a most wonderful luscious experience and merits a special party for good friends.

Suggested Wine. Crisp white or iced vodka. Try adding 2 strips of lime or lemon zest and 4 peppercorns to a bottle of vodka. Keep in the freezer all day, then serve in tiny glasses.

Salmon and Spinach Pie

As a lot of my salmon recipes seem to be rather last-minute and to need careful cooking, I wanted to include a nice pie that can be prepared well ahead and which will keep warm and wait for your guests. I also wanted a dish that uses less than prime fish or leftover cooked salmon. Include the pine nuts and raisins for a slightly unusual note; sweet stuffings were used with salmon in mediaeval times, but if it does not appeal you can happily leave it out without spoiling the dish. You can make it without the spinach if you wish and put it in a smaller dish or you can add hard-boiled eggs to make it go further. You could also sandwich two fillets of salmon with the spinach stuffing, wrap in pastry and bake. I do like to use home-made puff pastry for this, but you could get away with the best bought brand, or use Fast Puff (p. 182), Flaky (p. 191) or even Shortcrust Pastry (p. 186). I also intend to try a filo pastry pie; I used to make one in Cyprus with spinach and cream cheese so why not salmon. You would have to cut out the sauce or the pastry would never be crisp.

Ingredients

Serves 4–6

1–1½ lb (450–675 g) cooked filleted, boneless, skinless salmon
12 oz–1 lb (350–450 g) cooked spinach
1½ oz (35 g) butter
2 tbs pine nuts
2 tbs raisins
nutmeg
salt and pepper

8 oz (225 g) puff pastry
egg wash

Sauce

1½ oz (35 g) butter
1½ oz (35 g) flour
½ pt (300 ml) fish fumet (p. 23) or salmon head stock (p. 38) court-bouillon or mixed wine, water and herbs used to cook the fish
5–8 fl oz (150–225 ml) milk
2–3 tbs cream
2–3 good tbs chopped chives, parsley, fennel or dill
a tiny bit grated lemon rind
pinch ground mace
salt and pepper

Heat the butter until just browning, add the pine nuts and raisins and fry until the pine nuts brown and the raisins swell. Toss with the well drained and squeezed spinach, season, add nutmeg and mix well. Place in the bottom of a 2½ pt (1.5 l) greased pie dish.

To Make the Sauce. Melt the butter in a saucepan, add the flour and cook, stirring, over moderate heat for several minutes. Draw off the stove and add the fumet and milk; bring to the boil, whisking, and simmer for several minutes; add the cream, herbs, lemon rind, mace and seasoning, fold in the salmon in generous flakes and pour over the spinach. Leave until cold.

Pastry. Roll the puff pastry thinly; cut a ½ inch (1 cm) strip and attach with cold water to the rim. Moisten this with cold water, cover the pie with pastry and seal down. Trim and decorate and preferably rest in the fridge for ½ hour or so before cooking. Brush with egg wash and bake in a hot oven (400°F/200°C/Gas 6) for 20–30 minutes until well risen and brown; turn down to moderately hot (375°F/190°C/Gas 5) and continue to cook for a further 20–30 minutes to cook the pastry right through. Serve hot, warm or cold. It is complete but new potatoes and a salad go well with it.

Suggested Wine. Modest white.

Salt-Baked Sea Trout or Salmon

This is a wonderful natural way to cook a fish; the flesh stays moist and the true flavour is very apparent without it becoming too salty. If you use a tail end, tie a piece of Bakewell paper over the cut surface to protect it from becoming too salty. Timings are tricky for different-sized fish; allow 12–15 minutes to the pound but take into account whether the fish is deep and solid or long and thin. The salt can be used several times but, if kept for long periods, tends to have a less clean and attractive aroma.

Ingredients   *Serves 3–4*
1½ lb (675 g) sea trout or tail end of fresh
   salmon
3 lb (1.35 kg) sea salt (approx.)

Gut but do not scale the fresh fish. Make a bed of sea salt on a long ovenproof dish. Lay the fish on it (wrap the cut surface of a fish in Bakewell or greaseproof paper first) and cover completely with salt. Bake the fish in a moderately hot oven (375°F/190°C/Gas 5) for about 20 minutes. Leave to stand for 5 minutes or so then break off the salt crust, remove the skin and serve the fish, either *au naturel* with beautiful baby vegetables and new potatoes or with My Mother's Herb Sauce (p. 58), Green Mousseline Sauce (p. 70), Sauce Louise (p. 75) or Sorrel Sauce (p. 45).

Suggested Wine. Best white (perhaps top class Alsace Riesling).

illustrated opposite: Salt-Baked Sea Trout (see above), Salmon and Spinach Pie (see page 79)

Trout or Salmon Zeviche

Fresh raw trout or salmon can be simply marinated in lime juice for a delicious starter. Half to one hour is long enough to marinate and in fact, eating Nile perch this way with David and Petal Allen at Lake Turkana in Kenya, 10 minutes' marinating was quite enough. Many Scandinavians freeze (for 1–4 days only) all sea fish before serving it raw to eliminate any danger of worms.

Serves 4–6

Ingredients
12 oz–1 lb (350–450 g) cut of salmon or
   2–3 trout
juice of 3–4 limes (or lemon)
1–2 shallots, finely chopped
1 tbs olive oil
fresh chopped parsley or coriander
a little chilli (optional)
salt and pepper

Skin and bone the fish and cut into strips ¾ × ½ × ½ inches (2 × 1 × 1 cm); place in a dish and scatter with shallot; pour over the lime which should generously coat, if not cover, the fish; toss and leave for ½–5 hours. Add oil, toss again, garnish with herbs and serve with bread and butter. A little chopped fresh chilli can be added to the marinade if you wish.

Japanese Raw Fish

Absolutely raw slices of perfect fresh fish can be served in small quantities, tastefully arranged on a plate in the Japanese style with a sprig of herb. Hand a little bowl of dipping sauce made up of 1 tbs lemon juice, 1 tbs rice vinegar (or 2 teasp wine vinegar, pinch sugar and 1 teasp water), 2 tbs light soy sauce and 1 tbs Chinese wine or sherry with a little grated ginger. It's fresh, slimming, nutritious and delicious.

Suggested Wine. Crisp White.

FEATHERED GAME

Pheasant

The brilliantly hued, gaudy pheasant should look out of place in Britain's gentle countryside, but since the pheasant (*Phasianus colchicus*) was introduced from China, he has made himself so at home that we are no more surprised, when he flusteringly breaks with rainbow flashes from our October hedgerows, than we are of a bolting rabbit. Pheasant is now the most prolifically bred and shot bird in the country and those who are lucky enough to get plenty of shooting sometimes tire of eating them, though never of the chance to shoot a high bird. There are wives who seem to have a slightly hunted look as another triumphant bag is displayed; often the only escape is the freezer which gradually gathers booty all season, whence it must be cleared in summer for the next shooting season's glorious harvest! This *embarras de richesse* is almost as inexplicable to those who have to buy all their game as is the idea of tiring of caviar, but I know it happens. Therefore I have included some great classic pheasant dishes for those who are cooking game for the first time as well as evolving many good ways of profiting from any surfeit you may have. I also include a summer dish or two that won't seem out of place and which will help to thin out the freezers of those fortunate enough to have them full. Some of my recipes also cater for badly shot, dog-chewed or ancient carcasses. I have tried to give useful dishes to turn these into something delicious and have gone rather long in this chapter where I think people are most in search of ideas.

---

illustrated overleaf: Stuffed Spatchcock Pheasant (see page 95), Pheasant with Armagnac, Prunes and Walnuts (see page 92), Summer Pheasant in a Green Sauce (see page 101)

Pheasant varies from the corn-fed, yellow-fatted fellows, tender and mild-flavoured, barely able to elevate themselves for the gun's benefit, to the horny hill birds, lean and sinewy who scream over the tops from the high hills, whistling down the wind and looking like jet-propelled sparrows to the guns in the valley far below. The best sporting bird does not always make the best eating bird, though a bird killed 'in a gentlemanly way' will keep and cook better than one 'much mangled by shot'. Nevertheless, don't pay too much lip-service to tender succulence because flavour, used correctly, is just as important and the Oh-so-slow casseroles, in which a young bird would disintegrate, will produce a magnificently flavoured dish with an old bird. So choose your recipe to suit your bird and you will find there is a recipe to make the most of every bird and a dish to suit most occasions.

The first pheasant I cooked as a very young bride was in Hong Kong for a rather self-conscious little food and wine group. It came from China, the flavour was magnificent and it was well hung. Some hanging is agreed by all to be necessary for the fine flavour of pheasant; I like properly hung birds but will concede it is a matter of upbringing and taste, though I rather deplore the present restaurant trend of serving them almost fresh and like chicken. I definitely do not think they should be allowed to reach the stage where the flesh has so tenderised that it becomes almost a paste, because at this stage the fine flavour of the bird is masked. Over the years I have tried all sorts of ways of cooking these, not always easy birds to keep succulent, and many of the recipes illustrate a particularly successful method, such as the 'sealed pot', the 'not quite cooked' and the 'Oh-So-slow' which you can adapt to all sorts of recipes of your own.

Choosing Pheasant. Young birds can be still quite immature in October and November but fully grown after Christmas. They will not be tough until their second season by which time their short round spurs will have become pointed and their feet and beaks will look as if they have used them. A young bird's lower beak should bend or break if you pick it up by it, holding the beak horizontal and letting the weight hang down; and a very young bird will have a pointed first wing feather which soon becomes rounded. The only infallible test is one I was shown years ago by a member of the Game Conservancy; you insert a tapered matchstick into a hole to be found between the vent and tail (on both male and female); this blind-passage or bursa closes up with age. The match will go almost half an inch into a young bird but there is no real entry to an old one. Hen birds, though considerably smaller and less handsome than cocks, are nevertheless more succulent, tender and delicately flavoured so choose them when you may.

A well-grown hen will feed 2–3 people whilst a fat cock should do 3–4 though up and down the country birds vary considerably in size. Some of the largest, plumpest and tastiest I have seen came from Kent. Their situation and feeding, be it a wild Welsh hillside or cosseted lowland wood where they may be hand-fed for almost their whole life, will play a vast part on their size, tastiness, fattiness, and tenderness.

Pheasant comes into season on 1 October but can still be very young and immature then. I think they are at their best in November and December and, in a mild winter, when they have not lost condition, can still be good till the season closes on 1 February.

Sealed Pheasants with Chestnuts

I have various ways of ensuring pheasant is moist and tender when cooked. One of them is the sealed pot method where old-fashioned huff paste is used to seal the casserole hermetically which then goes into a hot oven; steam, unable to escape, is driven into the bird to make it succulent. All sorts of recipes can be adapted to this method. You will notice the bird is *not* stewed; only a very little liquid is added to the pot, so any sauce may need to be added at the end. Chestnuts are beastly to prepare, but I do have the best method (p. 207). Do them in the autumn while they are plump, fresh and easy to peel then freeze for later; or cheat with tins of whole, prepared chestnuts!

Ingredients   *Serves 3–4*

1 young pheasant
1–1½ oz (25–35 g) butter, oil or chicken
  fat
4 tbs port
potato flour or arrowroot (optional)
salt and pepper

Chestnuts
24 or so large peeled fresh chestnuts
¾ pt (450 ml) good stock
1 teasp sugar
1 oz (25 g) fat or butter
salt and pepper

Huff Paste
½ lb (225 g) plain flour
½ teasp salt
¼ pt (150 ml) cold water

Melt the butter, oil or any tasty fat in an ovenproof casserole (preferably earthenware or cast iron). Wrap the pheasant in a sheet of Bakewell paper and tie it in place. Place the pheasant, breast down, in the casserole, season lightly, add the port and seal the lid on with the huff paste. When ready to cook, place the casserole in a hot oven (425°F/220°C/Gas 7) for 45 minutes (or 50–60 minutes for a large bird). Leave to rest out of the oven for about 30 minutes before opening, if possible. Break off and discard the huff paste. Set the pheasant on a serving dish, jointed if you wish, and surround it with the prepared chestnuts. Degrease and reduce the pan juices before pouring over the pheasant. You can thicken the pan juices with a little slaked potato flour or arrowroot if you wish.

Huff Paste. Combine the flour, salt and water in the food processor to make a pliable dough. Roll into a long rope and use to seal the casserole lid in place.

Chestnuts. Place the peeled chestnuts in a small pan and just cover with good stock; add sugar, fat and a light seasoning. Cover and simmer gently for about 1 hour by which time the chestnut should be tender but still whole and all the stock should have been absorbed.

Suggested Wine. French provincial red.

Pheasant with Cider and Orange

A useful casserole with a tasty, copious sauce that is good served with white or brown rice or really soft, creamy mashed potato. It is a good dish to freeze because there is enough sauce to cover the pieces satisfactorily.

Ingredients
Serves 3–4

1 plump pheasant	1 orange
1½ oz (37 g) butter	bouquet garni
1 tbs oil	thin slices of orange
1 sliced onion	a few browned almonds
½ oz (12 g) flour	salt and pepper
½ pt (300 ml) good tasty cider	

Joint the pheasant into 4 pieces, dry well and sauté in the hot butter and oil until a light brown on both sides; remove to a casserole. Cook the sliced onion in the butter until golden, sprinkle on the flour and cook for 1 minute; draw the pan off the stove, wait for the sizzling to cease and add the cider. Bring to the boil, whisking, add some julienne strips of orange rind and the juice of one orange; season and pour over the pheasant. Add a bouquet garni and cook, well covered, in a slow oven (300°F/150°C/Gas 2), or simmer very gently on the stove, until just tender. Correct the seasoning. (Remove the pheasant joints and boil the sauce hard, uncovered, to reduce if the sauce is too copious.)

Serve surrounded by thin slices of orange and scatter over a few browned almonds.

Suggested Wine. French provincial or light red.

Pheasant à la Crème

This is a very simple but wonderful way to cook pheasant. The initial cooking, which is in effect pot-roasting on top of the stove in a little butter and with an onion, ensures the pheasant cooks legs first and the breast is not overdone, and that there are good tasty browned pan juices to dissolve into the cream when it is added. Make sure you boil the cream down to a proper coating sauce at the end. There is no flour in it so it will not curdle. If you must joint the pheasant to re-warm later, beware your pheasant juices do not thin down the sauce – overthicken a little to start with or re-boil at the end if necessary.

Ingredients
Serves 4

1 plump pheasant	juice ½ good lemon
2 oz (50 g) butter	1 tbs paprika
1 medium onion, quartered	salt and pepper
½ pt (300 ml) double cream	

Heat the butter in a heavy casserole which will just hold the bird comfortably. Turn the trussed bird in the hot butter until it is filmed all over with butter; add the onion, cover closely and cook over moderate heat for 35–45 minutes or until the bird is nearly done. Now add three-quarters of the cream, the lemon juice and paprika to the buttery juices, season with salt and pepper and continue to cook over very low heat for 15 minutes or until the bird is just done. Remove the bird, carve into quarters with a sharp knife and keep warm. Boil down the sauce fast until it coats a spoon, whisking well and adding in remaining cream to smooth it out. Correct the seasoning and strain over the bird. Serve at once. It can be jointed once cool then re-heated later in its sauce in the casserole. To serve, remove the joints to a serving dish, boil the sauce fast, whisking to re-amalgamate, pour over and serve.

Suggested Wine. Best red.

Pheasant with Grapes and Walnuts in the Georgian Style

Here is an early Georgian recipe from Russia, a way of cooking pheasant that I found in *Larousse Gastronomique* and which is unusual in the use of tea to add an astringent undertone to the sweet grape juice and orange sauce. It was Jane Grigson who really brought this recipe to general attention in a newspaper article and her lovely book *Good Things* some years ago. One should, but I don't, pour boiling water over the walnuts and skin them which would improve the dish a little; but I do strive to get good fresh walnuts (I keep good French shelled walnuts or ones we have brought back from the Dordogne in the freezer), but so many ready shelled walnuts are sold stale and rancid. During the pheasant season fresh walnuts and late season grapes are in the shops and marry admirably so get out your nut crackers.

Ingredients   *Serves 4*

1 plump pheasant	5 fl oz (150 ml) sweet white dessert wine or
4 oz (100 g) shelled walnuts	Malmsey Madeira
1 lb (450 g) white grapes	juice of 1–2 oranges
1 teasp green or china tea leaves	½–1 teasp potato flour
2 oz (50 g) butter	salt and pepper

Pour 4 fl oz (100 ml) of boiling water over the tea in a cup and leave to steep. Fit the pheasant, with 1 oz (25 g) butter inside it, into a comfortable sort of casserole without much spare room. Process the grapes briefly and sieve over the bird, add the wine, orange juice, strained tea and walnuts to the casserole and season. Cover very closely with butter paper or tinfoil and lid. Cook in a moderate oven (350°F/180°C/Gas 4) for about 45–50 minutes until the bird is tender, or simmer very gently on top of the stove.

Remove the pheasant and keep warm, or pop into a fierce oven to brown for a few moments if you wish. Joint while the juice reduces by about a third to a richly flavoured sauce. Thicken the sauce lightly with a little potato flour, slaked in cold water, added off the stove. Bring through the boil, whisking. Correct the seasoning and, if you wish, finish with the remaining butter whisked in to give the sauce a shiny gloss. Serve in a sauceboat with the pheasant or pour over the carved pieces and serve or keep warm.

Suggested Wine. Best red.

Whiskied Pheasant

This is a simple and delicious way with pheasant (or chicken for that matter for I evolved this dish years ago in Germany where I could only get good chickens) and has been a great favourite of ours over the years. The mustard should always be added once the sauce has finished cooking for its flavour is spoilt if it boils. Two pheasants will need barely more of the sauce ingredients than one.

Ingredients   *Serves 3–4*

1 plump pheasant	⅓–½ pt (200–300 ml) double cream
2 oz (50 g) butter	1 tbs Dijon mustard
1 onion, finely chopped	1 lemon
2 fl oz (50 ml) whisky	salt and pepper

Melt the butter in a casserole and gently fry the onion until golden; add the pheasant and brown on all sides, taking 10–15 minutes. Pour over the whisky, heat and flame (beware you don't burn your eyebrows!). Season then cover the casserole closely and finish cooking over very low heat for 25 minutes (the bottom heat helps the legs to cook before the breast is overdone) or cook in a moderate over (375°F/190°C/Gas 5) for 40–50 minutes until the pheasant is tender.

Remove and joint the bird; keep warm. Place the pan over high heat and boil up the juices until only 2–3 tbs remain, stirring all the time; then add double cream gradually, boiling down until you have a nice coating sauce. Draw off the stove, add mustard and correct seasoning; sharpen with lemon juice, pour over joints and serve. It can be kept warm in a low oven for a short time.

Suggested Wine. Best red.

Pheasant Sauté à la Clamart

Pheasant cooked with petits pois, bacon and little onions makes a most succulent and tasty casserole, good for a shooting lunch or an easy supper; you could just use the legs if you have taken the breasts off for another dish. It is nicest done before Christmas when the little pickling onions are still around.

Ingredients   *Serves 4*

1 large cock or 2 small hen pheasants or just use legs and keep the breasts for another dish	1 lb (450 g) petits pois, thawed from frozen
	1 head lettuce
	2–3 teasp sugar
2 oz (50 g) smoked bacon, thick-cut	a few tbs stock (if necessary)
2½ oz (65 g) butter	1 teasp potato flour, slaked with water or cream
24 little pickling onions or spring onions	
a little fresh chopped tarragon or summer savory (optional)	salt and pepper

Joint the pheasant into four or eight portions and dice the bacon small. Melt the butter in an ovenproof casserole (not iron or aluminium), place the pheasant joints in it in one layer and fry them very gently until sealed but not brown. Turn and seal the other sides. Add onions and bacon and fry for a little, season with salt and pepper (a little tarragon or summer savory is good too), cover with the pheasant carcass if there is room and close tightly. Place in a slow oven (300°F/150°C/Gas 2) for ½ hour. Shred the lettuce and drain the peas if they were frozen. Remove the carcass from the casserole, add the peas, shredded lettuce, sugar and, should it be necessary, a little stock. Stir well together, cover closely and continue to cook at 300°F/150°C/Gas 2 for another ½ hour. Then turn up to moderate (350°F/180°C/Gas 4) for 30–60 minutes more until the pheasant is done and the peas soft and tender. Remove the pheasant joints to a serving dish and keep warm.

Thicken the peas with a little potato flour mixed with water or cream, boiling it down if there is too much; you could use egg yolks and cream for a richer dish if you wish. Pour the peas over the pheasant joints and shake the dish to settle them. Heart-shaped croûtons of fried bread are attractive served round this dish.

Suggested Wine. French provincial red.

Pheasant Breasts in Rich Garlic Sauce

Getting the breast and leg of pheasant perfectly cooked at the same moment is notoriously difficult; by the time the legs are done, so often the breast is dry. One way to avoid this is to remove the breasts and cook them separately for a special dinner, using the legs up in a casserole, or Confit (p. 100) or Devilled Game (p. 198). This rich garlic sauce, using two heads (yes, two *heads*) of garlic is delicate (once we have blanched the garlic) and very good. You can omit the butter if you want to keep the calories down; of course garlic is very healthy anyway, since it breaks down cholesterol.

Ingredients
Serves 4

2 plump pheasants (or 4 pheasant breasts)
2 tbs olive oil
1 onion, finely diced
1 carrot, finely diced
1 stick celery, finely diced
4 oz mushrooms
1 teasp flour
1½ pts (900 ml) game or chicken stock, not salty

3–4 young parsley stalks, a good sprig of thyme, a bay leaf and 4 juniper berries
1–2 heads garlic
½ pt (300 ml) good red wine
1 tbs olive oil
4 oz (100 g) unsalted butter (optional)
potato flour, slaked with water (optional)
salt and pepper

Carefully remove the pheasant's legs and set aside to use for something else. Take the breasts from the carcass with a sharp knife and remove the skin and the tendon in the fillet. Set the breasts aside while you prepare the sauce.

Chop up the carcass, and roast in a hot oven (400°F/200°C/Gas 6) for 20–30 minutes until browned. Drain off the fat and deglaze the pan with a little of the stock.

In a heavy casserole, soften the onion, carrot and celery and mushroom stalks in the olive oil until soft and golden; sprinkle over the flour, fry for a few moments then add the stock.

Bring to the boil, stirring, then add the browned pheasant bones, the deglazing stock and all the herbs. Simmer quite vigorously, uncovered, and skimming from time to time until reduced by half. Strain.

Break up the garlic and throw it un-peeled into a pan of cold water; bring to the boil and boil for 3 minutes. Drain, peel and poach the garlic in the wine in a semi-covered pan for 30–40 minutes until absolutely tender and the wine has reduced. Purée the garlic, which looks a most horrid purple colour at this stage, with a little of the wine and set aside. Add the remaining wine to the reduced stock, reduce until only 10–12 fl oz (300–350 ml) remain and then taste to see that it is becoming well flavoured. Add the garlic purée to the sauce and season. Slice and sauté the mushrooms caps in a tablespoonful of olive oil and set aside.

Oil a shallow dish to hold the pheasant breasts in one layer but not too tightly packed. Pour over the sauce, cover with a piece of oiled Bakewell paper and, when ready to cook, poach them in a hot oven (400°F/200°C/Gas 6) for about 6–8 minutes only, until the thickest part of the breast just stops feeling squidgy. Pour off the sauce, boil up and reduce until only 6–8 fl oz (175–225 ml) of nicely flavoured sauce remains, and whisk in the butter in small pieces. Finally add the mushrooms, drained of any juice, and pour the sauce over the pheasant breasts. Serve at once, either handing the dish so everyone takes a steak-like pheasant breast or slicing each breast and setting it on individual plates with the sauce spooned around.

Either way, serve at once for the breasts can exude their juices and lose succulence if kept too long and the sauce, once buttered, will not hold. If not using the butter, you may wish to thicken the sauce very lightly with a tiny bit of potato flour.

Suggested Wine. Best red.

Pheasant with Armagnac, Prunes and Walnuts

Don't be daunted and do try this stuffing because it's quite delicious and makes this a good dish for a party. The pheasant can be all jointed up and will keep warm or re-heat well. The interesting stuffing mixture with prunes and walnuts, based on an old French recipe, helps make a small pheasant go further and can be used in several ways: to stuff the bird, though I don't favour this as you tend to have to overcook the bird slightly to get the stuffing cooked; or it can be formed into a roll, the prunes hidden down the centre, and roasted in a roaster bag then served sliced around the bird. Another way is to make it into patties, a prune in each, and fried. Finally, it is also a delicious mix to use to stuff a hare or rabbit for roasting or to make forcemeat balls to accompany any game. The remaining prunes are cooked in with the pheasant, though you can take some (choose very large ones), stuff them with stuffing mix, wrap them in thinly cut streaky bacon, cook them on a rack in a hot oven (or fry them) and serve around the bird as a contrasting garnish.

Serves 4–6

Ingredients

1 plump pheasant	1½ oz (35 g) butter
16 good-sized prunes	4 fl oz (100 ml) port
6 tbs Armagnac	3 oz (75 g) shelled walnuts
1 tbs oil	salt and pepper

Stuffing (optional)

12 oz (350 g) belly of pork	2 tbs Armagnac from soaking prunes
2–4 oz (50–100 g) sliced smoked ham	1 egg yolk
liver, heart and gizzard of pheasant (if available)	¼ teasp quatre-épices, mace or ground allspice
3 slices bread	3 oz (75 g) shelled walnuts
milk or water for soaking	8 of the soaked prunes
handful parsley heads	flour (optional)
2 tbs cream cheese, yoghurt or cream	salt and pepper

Sauce

1½ oz (35 g) butter or oil	½ stick celery, diced
1 slice bacon, diced	bouquet garni (parsley stalks, thyme, bay leaf)
1 onion, finely chopped	1 tbs flour
1 carrot, finely diced	½ pt (300 ml) good stock

Soak the prunes in the Armagnac for 2 hours or so.

Stuffing. Cut the skinned belly of pork into pieces, removing the gristly bits, and process (or mince) with the ham, pheasant liver, heart, gizzard and parsley heads until finely chopped. Soak the bread in a little milk or water, squeeze out and add with the cream cheese, 2 tbs of Armagnac from soaking the prunes, the egg yolk, quatre-épices and seasoning. Process until fairly smooth. (Fry a little to test the seasoning.) Finally add in the walnuts and process briefly to mix in. Either form the mixture into 8 patties with a prune in the middle of each, flour and fry to accompany the bird; or flour a roaster bag, place half the mixture down the centre, place prunes in a row and the remaining mixture on top. Fashion into a roll, seal the bag, snip the corner and roast in a hot oven (400°F/200°C/Gas 6) at the appropriate moment for 35–40 minutes before slicing and serving around the bird.

Pheasant. Heat the oil and butter in a heavy casserole and gently brown the bird well all over, taking 15–20 minutes to do so. Pour over 2–3 tbs Armagnac from soaking prunes and flambé the bird. Add the port, prunes and seasoning, cover closely and leave the pheasant to finish cooking on a very low heat for 25–35 minutes (the bottom heat helps the legs cook before the breast is overdone). Prepare the sauce while the pheasant cooks.

Try to catch the pheasant when the inside legs are still a little pink but they can always be returned to cook for a moment or two longer. Joint up the pheasant, discarding the backbone, or leave whole and carve at the table. Remove excess fat from the pan juices (a fat and lean gravyboat is quickest for this). Pour in the prepared sauce and remaining walnuts, reduce to a good consistency, adjust the seasoning and return the pheasant joints, or serve in a sauceboat. Keep warm or re-heat very gently when required.

Sauce. Heat the oil in a heavy saucepan, fry the bacon, onion, carrot and celery to a good golden brown; sprinkle the flour over and fry gently to a good colour. Draw off the stove, wait for the sizzling to cease then add stock and bouquet garni. Bring to the boil, whisking, and simmer for 15–20 minutes until reduced a little and thickened; skim if necessary. Strain into the pheasant casserole and finish as above.

To Serve. Set the pheasant joints on a meat plate, spoon over the prunes and a little sauce and surround with the stuffing slices or patties. Serve remaining sauce in a sauceboat.

Suggested Wine. Big red.

Speedy Spatchcock Pheasant

When you don't feel like plucking, have a go at skinning a pheasant instead. I did this at the 1981 Game Fair at Stowe and, with a little practice, it will only take you three minutes! Many people tell me they rarely pluck now. To keep the bird moist (because, of course, if it is skinless, it will dry out very easily), spatchcock it so it is almost flat and the heat penetrates the legs before the breast so they are cooked by the time the breast is done; also cover it with muslin and baste it to keep the moisture in. You might also experiment using a roast-in bag.

Ingredients   *Serves 3–4*

1 plump pheasant, unplucked
3 oz (75 g) butter
1 small onion
1 bay leaf
salt and pepper

a piece of muslin or even a J-cloth
2 cocktail sticks or skewers

Sauce
2 fl oz (50 ml) dry white wine
1 tbs brandy
1 tbs Redcurrant and Green Peppercorn
   Jelly (p. 199)
4 fl oz (100 ml) whipping or double cream

To Skin Pheasant. Cut off the head and the end joints of each wing. Cut carefully round the skin at the bottom of each drumstick. Cut the skin carefully down the back of the bird and cut off the parson's nose and tail. Now roll back the skin, working from the back towards the breast, pulling the skin and feathers off the wing and the leg as you go. Remove the crop and discard. It is easier to spatchcock the bird and then draw it, so take the scissors and carefully cut through the backbone from neck to tail. Snip round the vent then spread open the bird and remove the innards, reserving only the liver and heart. Snip through the wishbone, press the bird out flat, bending up the legs and skewering them in place.

Melt the butter gently in a small saucepan. Slice the onion thinly and place in the middle of a small roasting pan with the bay leaf; on this, lay the pheasant, breast uppermost, and season with salt and pepper. Take a double layer of muslin that will just cover the bird and dip in the melted butter; lay this over the pheasant and pour over any remaining butter. Roast the pheasant in a hot oven (400°F/200°C/Gas 6) for 30–40 minutes, depending on size, basting the muslin every 10–15 minutes and covering lightly with tinfoil if it gets too brown. Add a few drops of wine, stock or water to the pan if the juices are threatening to burn. Remove the pheasant to a serving dish and set to rest.

The Sauce. Wring the butter out of the muslin into the roasting tin and then replace the muslin over the pheasant. Add the diced liver and heart to the roasting pan and cook for a few moments; then add the wine and brandy and boil up fast to reduce and amalgamate with the buttery juices. Now add the Redcurrant and Green Peppercorn Jelly and stir to melt. When the pan juices are well reduced, add the cream and boil fast until it thickens to a sauce of coating consistency. Correct seasoning and pour over the pheasant which can be carved or served jointed into four.

Suggested Wine. Big red.

Stuffed Spatchcock Pheasant

This is a really tasty, flavoursome dish with no pretensions to elegance but one much loved by family and friends. Vignotte, a tall cylinder of firm creamy cheese, is very reliable and a great standby for cheese board or cooking though you can use other cheeses, even a blue cheese like Cambozola or Dolce Latte if it is to your taste. This dish is perhaps best done with a small hen pheasant, split between two as the carving is not very easy!

Ingredients *Serves 2–3*
1 good young (preferably hen) pheasant
½ lb (225 g) button mushrooms
a little oil, olive for preference
1 clove garlic
6 oz (175 g) Vignotte or other French
   cheese
1–2 tbs finely chopped parsley
3–4 tbs white wine or stock
salt and pepper

Slice the mushrooms and fry briskly and lightly in a little oil, adding the finely chopped garlic for the last few moments. Cool a little and mix with the cheese, parsley and seasoning.

Cut the pheasant straight down the backbone, snip the wishbone then press out flat with the heel of your hand. Carefully slip your finger between skin and breast flesh and loosen the skin all over the breast and over the legs if you can reach them. Pack the mushroom and cheese mixture under the skin, spreading it evenly. Rub the skin carefully and thoroughly with a little oil and roast the bird in a hot oven (400°F/200°C/Gas 6) for 30–40 minutes until well browned and just cooked. Stir the wine or stock into the pan juices, deglazing well.

Split in two or carve and serve, perhaps with a gratin of spinach and baked potatoes.

Suggested Wine. Big or French provincial red.

Oh-So-Slow Game Casserole

The idea is to cook the dish at such a slow temperature that the protein in the meat never has a chance to toughen and coagulate. You know how scrambled eggs, if you over-cook them, suddenly go firm and wet? The protein has coagulated and, rather like from a sponge, the juices come out of it; over-cooked fish and chicken are the same. If you keep the cooking very slow and gentle with the temperature of the food never rising above 180–190°F/80–85°C, even for many hours in the case of tough meat, the meat will remain moist and tender when cooked. The connective tissue, collagen, that surrounds threads of muscle or meat gradually changes to gelatine which dissolves during cooking and finally allows the fibres to fall apart, as in the case of over-cooked meat. Acid helps this break-down, hence marinades, added wine, vinegar or lemon juice in long slow-cooked dishes.

The problem is to find an oven which keeps to such a low temperature. Take an oven thermometer and try your oven at its lowest setting. I have finally found that my Belling hot cupboard is the place, but of course it means leaving the casserole cooking for 6–8 hours (even longer for really tough old birds). The taste and texture of the casserole dishes is certainly a revelation. I have also made a haybox to cook in this way when I had not got an oven that would cook as slowly as this.

To Make a Haybox. Take a large cardboard box at least 5 inches (12 cm) bigger all round than your casserole. Place a thick layer of screwed-up balls of paper (much more available and less messy than hay) in the bottom, set in your casserole and pack balls of newspaper tightly round it. Ease it from the nest and prepare your casserole in it; make sure it is actually simmering for 15–30 minutes then, without lifting the lid, transfer quickly to the haybox and cover quickly with a thick layer of newspaper balls. Close the box, cover with a rug or duvet and leave for hours. This wonderfully economical method of cooking is sadly overlooked in these days of electrical appliances but is still valid, not only for its fuel saving but for the flavour and tenderness it gives the dish; large casseroles are advisable as tiny ones would cool down too quickly. It's wonderfully useful for shooting lunches and large gatherings, and in many ways much easier than trying to regulate a recalcitrant oven.

Many recipes can of course be adapted to this way of cooking but I have included two especially, this Oh-So-Slow Game Casserole and Duck with Zampona and Lentils; both can be cooked a little faster if you wish but do try the Oh-So-Slow Method – it is so good.

Ingredients _Serves 6–8_

2 pheasant or 8–10 legs, or use grouse, partridge, duck or hare
1 pig's trotter, split
6 oz (175 g) thick-cut smoked streaky bacon, Zampona, or saucisson de Toulouse, or other smoked sausage
2 tbs oil
2 onions
2 carrots
1 stick celery

1–2 cabbage hearts
3 cloves garlic
bouquet garni of parsley stalks, thyme and bay leaf, and including 4 juniper berries and 1 clove
1–2 tbs tomato purée
½–¾ pt (300–450 ml) good stock
1 tbs spiced or wine vinegar
potato flour (optional)
salt only if necessary, pepper

Place the pig's trotter in plenty of cold water; bring to the boil, skim and simmer for 20–30 minutes; rinse, split and set aside. Dice and fry the bacon in the oil; remove and set aside.

Joint the game and brown it well in the fat; set aside. Dice and fry the vegetables until golden and slice the cabbage thickly. Pack everything into a heavy casserole, tucking in flattened garlic cloves, bouquet garni, and grind of pepper. Mix the tomato purée with some stock and the vinegar and moisten the casserole. Cover tightly and bring to the simmer; then cook in a very, very slow oven (170–180°F/75°C/Gas ¼ or less) for 6–8 hours until absolutely tender. De-grease the sauce, remove loose bones from the pig's trotter, reduce the strained-off sauce by fast boiling if necessary and thicken lightly with potato flour if you wish. Season if necessary. You can flour the joints before frying and sprinkle with flour for a thicker gravy if you wish.

Suggested Wine. Big or French provincial red.

Pheasant Braised with Pineapple and Lime

Later on, after Christmas, you may be looking for something a bit different to do with pheasant. Try using those small and relatively inexpensive pineapples, which are available then, for I think their flavour and sweetness admirably complement pheasant and an older bird can be braised gently into submission.

Ingredients   *Serves 3–4*

1 good pheasant	1 small ripe pineapple
1–2 limes, depending on size	3 tbs sultanas
a little seasoned flour	1 tbs soft dark brown sugar
1½ oz (35 g) butter	2 teasp tomato purée
1 onion, finely chopped	a few drops Tabasco or chilli sherry
3 tbs rum	salt and pepper

Joint the pheasant into 4 or 8 pieces; squeeze the juice of half a lime over it, season with salt and pepper and roll in flour. Heat the butter in a heavy frying pan and gently brown the pieces of pheasant on all sides before adding the onion to soften gently. Spoon the rum over the joints, heat and set light but watch out for the flames! Shake the pan until the flames subside; remove the joints from the frying pan to a casserole.

Cut the skin off the pineapple, quarter and core. Chop briefly in the food processor until fairly finely chopped then add to the frying pan with the sultanas, brown sugar and tomato purée; boil up, adding a few drops of Tabasco or hot sauce and seasoning. Pour over the joints in the casserole and cover closely. Cook in a slow oven (225°F/110°C/Gas ¼) for 1½–2 hours or until tender. Check the seasoning, remove the joints and reduce the sauce by fast boiling if necessary. Serve with Burghal Pilau (p. 212) or saffron rice.

Tender birds can be cooked as a sauté dish by following the recipe until flamed; then cover the pan and continue to cook, gently, until just done; the sauce should be made once the pieces are removed from the pan and then poured over them.

Tough old birds can be cooked by the Oh-So-Slow method (p. 96) for many hours. All three methods of cooking this dish will give very satisfactory results so choose the best for your pheasant.

Suggested Wine. Big or French provincial red.

Pheasant in the Alsace Style

This is a very authentic and most delicious Alsatian way of cooking pheasant though I must say I do cut the quantity of fat a bit, and with an old bird I set it to cook gently in the sauerkraut for a long time in a slow oven. Of course partridge can also be cooked in this way and the sauerkraut alone makes an excellent vegetable with game. I find people love it rinsed and prepared like this and all sorts of odds and ends and legs of game can be cooked in it with smoked sausage to make a most appetising dish.

Ingredients
Serves 3–4

1 pheasant
a thin sheet of pork back-fat or 6–8 rashers
  thin-cut streaky bacon
2 lb (900 g) sauerkraut (tinned or bottled)
6 oz (175 g) goose, duck or pork dripping
  (lard at a pinch or oil)
1 onion stuck with 2 cloves
½ teasp juniper berries
¼ teasp black peppercorns
1 clove garlic
12 fl oz (350 ml) Alsace or other dry white
  wine (preferably Riesling)
4 fl oz (100 ml) water
8 oz (225 g) thick-cut, smoked, streaky
  bacon
salt and pepper

Empty the sauerkraut from its jar and rinse it in cold water, plucking the strands apart. Squeeze well then rinse in warm water and squeeze again to get it as dry as possible. Place all but about 2 tbs of the goose fat in the bottom of a casserole, lay on it the sauerkraut and slip the onion, stuck with cloves, into the middle. Add the juniper berries, peppercorns, crushed clove of garlic and pour over 8 fl oz (225 ml) of the wine and 4 fl oz (100 ml) of water; salt lightly, cover the casserole and cook for 1 hour over medium heat or in a moderate oven (350°F/180°C/Gas 4). Reduce the heat, or turn the oven down to 325°F/170°C/Gas 3 and continue to cook for a second hour, but watch that the sauerkraut does not catch on the pan.

Season the pheasant and slip 2 crushed juniper berries inside, bard with a thin sheet of pork back-fat or thin rashers of streaky bacon. Cut the smoked bacon into lardons or cubes. Heat the remaining goose fat in a frying or sauté pan and sauté the pheasant and bacon cubes gently for about 30 minutes to a good golden colour on all sides.

Remove the pheasant and smoked bacon cubes from the fat and bury it, breast down, in the sauerkraut which has already cooked for 2 hours. Drain the fat from the frying pan and deglaze with the remaining 4 fl oz (100 ml) of wine. Pour this over the pheasant and sauerkraut, cover closely and cook for 1 further hour in a hot oven (400°F/200°C/Gas 6). Serve the jointed pheasant on a bed of sauerkraut.

Suggested Wine. Alsace Riesling.

Pheasant Braised with Pig's Trotters and Red Wine

The gelatine and lip-sticking richness of pig's trotters nourish the dry pheasant meat and contribute to a fine shiny sauce. This is a true, rich gamy dish, especially when finished with the purée of livers and heart. It's a good recipe in which to use up the pheasant legs when you have removed the breast for another dish, and you can make good stock with the carcasses. A garnish of separately cooked mushrooms, little onions or other vegetables can be added.

Ingredients
Serves 3–4

1 fine pheasant
1 pig's trotter, salted or plain
2–3 tbs dripping or oil
about 3 tbs flour
2 onions
2 carrots
1 stick celery
1 pt (600 ml) good full-bodied red wine
½ pt (300 ml) good stock

bouquet garni of parsley stalks, thyme, bay
    leaf, basil and 1 teasp of juniper berries
1 clove garlic
1–2 teasp liqueur de cassis
potato flour
liver and heart of the bird ⎫
1 tbs brandy or sherry   ⎬ (optional)
salt and pepper   ⎭

Simmer the pig's trotter in plenty of water for 30 minutes, then discard the water and split the trotter. Joint the pheasant into 4 or 8 pieces, roll in flour and brown in hot dripping or oil, adding the onion, cut up roughly, and the carrot and celery in generous pieces. Remove the joints to a casserole as they brown and continue to fry the vegetable and the neck and back bone if you include them for flavour (the browner they are the better) until at least some of the onion is a good brown. Sprinkle 2 tablespoons of flour over the pan, stir in and cook for a few moments; then, off the stove, add the wine; stir until smooth and bring to the boil. Bubble fast for 5 minutes to reduce then add the stock and pour over the pheasant in the casserole; tuck in the pig's trotters, the bouquet and a half-flattened clove of garlic. Season, cover closely and cook gently on the stove or in a slow oven (200°F/100°C/Gas ¼) for 1½–2 hours or until tender (you can of course cook this by the Oh-So-Slow method (p. 96)).

Pour off the sauce, leave to settle, then de-grease. Boil it hard in a wide pan to reduce until rich and syrupy, skimming as necessary; add a little cassis to enhance the flavour and thicken if necessary with ½ teasp or so of potato flour and water. Remove any unwanted bits of neck or backbone from the casserole, de-bone the pig's trotters and chop up and return the meat if you wish; return the sauce to the casserole and keep warm. (This sauce would be superb with separately sautéed breast of pheasant in haute cuisine style, using the legs for a pâté.)

To add additional rich gamey flavour to the dish, process the raw liver and heart until smooth; add the brandy or sherry and keep aside until ready to serve. Stir this into the casserole and just simmer for a moment or two before serving, long cooking or simmering will cause the sauce to go gritty and grainy and spoil the flavour and texture. Serve this with Burghal Pilau (p. 212).

Suggested Wine. Big red.

Confit of Pheasant

This is a wonderful dish for those with endless pheasants. The idea came to me in California where I was demonstrating and was given incredibly fatty, reared birds; why not make a confit as goose and duck is preserved in France? Well, of course, you will have to gather up some good fat for pheasants are leaner in this country, but goose fat can be brought back from France in tins; duck, chicken or pork fat can be begged from the butcher or gathered and frozen until you wish to make the dish; or you can use lard though the flavour is not so good. The salting and slow cooking gives a very interesting flavour (most useful when you have a lot of pheasants and are always looking for ways to vary the flavour) and of course the cooked birds can be kept in the fridge for several weeks or longer, ready to use whenever it suits you. The confit is also extremely versatile; joints can be served hot, added to soups, stews or bean dishes like cassoulet, made into salads or processed into pâtés or stuffings.

Traditional English potted pheasant was prepared in much the same way though clarified butter was used in its preparation. For long preservation, be sure no meat juices get into the pot with the meat and fat for it is they that can go off. Saltpetre, available from chemists, keeps the meat pinky (as in bacon) and is a great preservative but should only be used in the smallest quantities as it may not be good for us. Game bird hearts and gizzards also make an excellent confit. They are included in many tasty and rustic salads in France where they are much enjoyed at the best restaurants, so do a jar if you ever get enough! You can always save them up in the freezer until you do.

Ingredients *Serves 4–6*

1 good pheasant (or other game)
some coarse sea salt
good pinch saltpetre (optional)
1–2 sprigs thyme

2 bay leaves
2 lb (900 g) pork fat (flead or back-fat) or
    duck or goose fat or lard

Joint the pheasant or other game. Weigh and sprinkle with coarse sea salt at the rate of ½ oz (12 g) to 1 lb (450 g), adding a pinch of saltpetre if you wish. Add the thyme and bay leaves and leave in a cool place for 24 hours, turning occasionally. Render the pork fat in a slow oven and pour off. Remove the joints from the salt, brush off any excess salt, pack into a deep casserole and tuck in the bay leaves and thyme. Cover with pork fat and cook, covered, in a slow oven (300–325°F/150–170°C/Gas 2–3) for 2–6 hours until the meat is completely tender. Remove the joints to a sieve and carefully separate the liquid fat from the juices. Pack the joints into a very clean crock, jar or casserole and pour over fat until they are completely covered; once cool, cover and keep in the fridge for 2–3 weeks or more.

Remove joints, fry lightly to heat through and serve with potatoes, fried in the fat, and a salad dressed with a mustardy vinaigrette. Or make the confit, scraped of all fat and cut up, into interesting salads with salad leaves, croûtons and a garlic dressing.

You probably won't need much extra pork fat if doing more than one pheasant – just enough to cover generously.

Suggested Wine. Big or French provincial red.

Summer Pheasant in a Green Sauce

I'm not really a believer in game out of season, but still frequently find myself with pheasants lurking in the freezer in summertime. So I thought I should evolve a nice cold summer pheasant dish that can be used for summer lunches or buffets. Do remember a long slow thaw in the fridge for 2–3 days is preferable to a quick thaw. If you don't like the flavour of coriander (it took me twenty years to get to like it – but now I love it!), you could use a mixture of fresh summer herbs like basil and chervil with a little tarragon and lemon thyme or sweet marjoram; anything you fancy as long as it ends up bright green, fresh flavoured and balanced. Cook the pheasant how you like. I favour this Chinese style for really succulent meat, but of course it only works for a tender bird.

Ingredients
Serves 3–4 depending on pheasant size

1 good young pheasant
salt and pepper

To Cook the Pheasant

4–5 pt (2.25–2.8 l) good stock
2–3 spring onions
2–3 slices ginger
2 cloves garlic
1–2 carrots

1 stick celery
4 tbs sherry
bay leaf and bundle of mixed herbs
½ teasp sugar

Sauce

2 oz (50 g) blanched almonds
1 spring onion or slice sweet onion
good handful fresh coriander
good handful fresh parsley
1 small fresh chilli, de-seeded, or cayenne
grated rind and juice of about 1 lemon

4–6 tbs good olive oil, or use light
    sunflower oil and 1–2 tbs of almond,
    walnut or hazelnut oil
4–6 tbs reduced stock
5 fl oz (150 ml) whipping cream
salt to taste

To Cook the Pheasant. Bring the pheasant to room temperature (important for the cooking time). Season inside and out with salt and pepper and preferably leave for 20 minutes or so. Heat the stock with all the ingredients in a heavy casserole. Boil for 3–4 minutes then add the pheasant; cover and simmer for a further 15 minutes then remove from the heat and leave, without opening the casserole, for 4–6 hours or until cold. Cooking like this on descending heat ensures lovely moist and tender flesh. Once almost cold, remove the pheasant, drain, pat dry. Joint or bone and cut flesh into generous bite-sized pieces.

Take some of the stock and reduce until very strongly flavoured for the sauce; cool.

Sauce. Place the almonds, onions and herbs in a liquidiser or food processer; add the chilli, salt and lemon rind and process until smooth, gradually dripping in the oil, stock and lemon juice until you have a smooth green mixture. Press this through a sieve if you wish. Whip the cream, fold the sieved green sauce into the cream and adjust the seasoning.

Fold the pheasant meat into the green sauce and serve on a bed of lettuce or with fine pasta, just cold and dressed with fresh tomato pulp, oil, herbs and seasoning. The flavour of the pheasant will be best when it has just cooled to room temperature.

Suggested Wine. Big white or light red.

Grouse

The red grouse (*Lagopus lagopus scoticus*) is indigenous only to the British Isles and, sad to say, is now rather rare in most of Wales, on the West Country moors and in Ireland. Not only is it arguably the most exciting game bird to shoot and the finest to eat but it is all our own, though its cousin the willow grouse (*Lagopus lagopus*) is common in north America, northern Europe and Russia. We have been lucky enough to have the chance to walk it up in Scotland and drive it at Blubberhouses in North Yorkshire and there is simply nothing like it. I think one of its attractions is that it is such a sporting contest with the odds usually heavily on the grouse as they scream over at head height with zero notice. Sad to say, the five million acres of heatherclad grouse moorland is rapidly diminishing and disease is always a problem.

The great chefs have devised few complex recipes for it thinking, generally quite rightly in my opinion, that simplicity is the way to handle this treat, though the following recipes are all great favourites of ours. Young birds are always at a premium, available in smart restaurants in London on The Twelfth and as far afield as Hong Kong by the next day (but beware; last year's birds may be frozen in the feather to be brought forth on 12 August, a lot less trouble for the restaurateur and distinctly offside).

If you don't often have a chance to cook grouse, a fine roast young bird is unbeatable but if you are fortunate and have a few more, spread your wings a little further.

Magret of Grouse

All dark game meat such as venison, wild duck or grouse is superb when served very rare, *so long as it is young*. Some years ago, eating a *magret d'oie* down in the Armagnac, I thought how superb grouse would be cooked like that – and it is. A magret is the breast removed in one piece, often cooked briskly like a steak and served rare as a steak or nowadays frequently sliced in wafer slices by the chef and arranged beautifully in tiny quantities in the centre of a huge plate! Keep this for your nearest and dearest, cook with great care and don't try to do too many.

Ingredients   *Serves 4*

2 or 4 plump young grouse (allow ½ or 1 grouse per head, depending on their size and your menu)	4 or 8 slanting slices stale French bread (to make croûtes)
4 tbs oil	½ lemon
1½ oz (35 g) butter	1 bunch watercress
	salt and pepper

Remove each side of the grouse breasts in one piece with a very sharp knife (keep the legs for another dish such as Devilled Game (p. 198), soup or a Game Pie (p. 185). Trim the breasts, brush with oil and season with pepper; they are like plump little fillet steaks.

Heat 2 tbs oil and the butter in a frying pan and sauté the croûtes of bread to a golden brown on both sides; keep warm. Wipe the pan, turn up the heat, add a little more oil and, when very hot, cook the grouse breasts for 2 minutes on each side for rare when they will have a feeling of pliant resistance when pressed with a finger and have a beading of rosy blood on the top surface. Cook them 3 minutes each side for medium, a firmer resistance to your finger and beads of clear blood on the top crust. Season and sprinkle with a few drops of lemon juice.

Place each magret on a croûte of fried bread and rest in a warm place for a few minutes before serving, garnished with watercress.

Suggested Wine. Best red, probably finest claret or Rhône.

Drambuie Grouse

Two years of sponsorship by Drambuie at the Game Fair gave me the chance to discover how this luscious spicy herby liqueur can be used to enhance game. Grouse, with its own powerful flavour, makes a great marriage with Drambuie in this recipe. Pot-roasting in a covered casserole in a hot oven is the perfect way for grouse to imbibe the sealed-in Drambuie vapours and keep moist and succulent. You can also use this method with other birds and other flavours such as wine, sherry, port or Madeira, Grand Marnier or one of the eaux-de-vie. But Drambuie does have that special something with grouse.

Ingredients
Serves 2 (or 4 if birds are halved)

2 young grouse
½–1 lemon
2–3 vine leaves or a slice of apple or potato per bird
2½ oz (60 g) butter
1 small chopped onion

5 tbs Drambuie
6–8 fl oz (175–225 ml) strong well-reduced game or chicken stock
about ¼ teasp potato flour
salt, pepper and cayenne

Prepare the grouse, season inside by rubbing in salt, cayenne and a few drops of lemon juice. Then tuck in a few vine leaves, apple or potato slices to keep it moist. Melt the butter in a heavy casserole and carefully and gently brown the grouse on all sides, taking about 10–20 minutes, adding the chopped onion to brown half way through. Once browned, season lightly and add about 3–4 tbs of the Drambuie. Cover closely with tin foil and a tight fitting lid and place the casserole in a hot oven (400°F/200°C/Gas 6) for 15–20 minutes until the grouse are just done (do not overcook). Remove the birds and rest where they cannot go on cooking.

Deglaze the pan (which should now have some very brown onions) with the remaining Drambuie and the stock, added in small quantities, stirring in all brown flavouring bits and boiling fast to amalgamate. Remove from the stove, add a tiny bit of potato flour, slaked with cold water; boil up and reduce until a nice sauce consistency with a good flavour. Add a good squeeze of lemon juice and adjust the seasoning. Strain the sauce to remove the over-browned onions, which have coloured and flavoured the sauce but are now unnecessary, and serve in a sauceboat or poured around each grouse, set on a plate.

Serve perhaps with Burghal Pilau (p. 212) and Sweet Red Cabbage (p. 207) or a creamy garlic mashed potato and broccoli or spinach.

Suggested Wine. Big red (not Drambuie!).

Braised Grouse in Mexican *Mole* Sauce

Old grouse (well, any old birds really) are always a little difficult to use but I find this adaptation of a Mexican *mole* sauce rather successful (I've cut 2 tbs chilli down to ⅛–¼ teasp!). The birds can be very gently cooked until you know they have capitulated, then be sauced and finished cooking or be reheated later or what you will and the flavour will just get better. The pig's trotter is not essential but I always keep several in the freezer and they do add gelatine to the stock.

Ingredients   *Serves 4–6*

2–3 old grouse or any other mature birds
1 pig's trotter, split (optional)
4–6 oz (100–175 g) thick-cut smoked
   streaky bacon
2 tbs oil

1 onion, roughly cut up
1 carrot, roughly cut up
bouquet garni of parsley, thyme and bay leaf
1½ pts (900 ml) stock
salt and pepper

Mole *Sauce*

2 tbs oil
1 teasp chopped rosemary
1 large onion, finely chopped
1 stick celery, finely chopped
2 tomatoes, diced
2 red peppers, seeded and diced
2–3 cloves garlic, finely chopped
1–2 de-seeded and chopped red or green
   chillies or ⅛–¼ teasp chilli powder,
   more if you want

1½ pts (900 ml) stock from the grouse
½ oz (12 g) dark chocolate
2 good pinches ground cloves
good grate nutmeg
grated rind of most of 1 small orange
squeeze of lime or lemon juice
salt and pepper

Place the split pig's trotter in plenty of cold water and boil for 20–30 minutes; drain, rinse and dry and place in a casserole; blanch the bacon for 1 minute too if you think it needs it; put the bacon skin in one piece in the casserole.

Take a sharp pair of kitchen scissors and cut the backbones out of the grouse and discard (I find them very bitter). Remove the legs and split the breasts. Season the joints. Joint other birds into appropriate pieces. Cut the bacon into lardons, brown gently in the oil and remove to the casserole with the pig's trotter. Brown the grouse joints gently and pack into the casserole with the onion and carrot, tuck in the bouquet garni and pour the stock over. Cover and cook in a very slow oven, preferably by the Oh-So-Slow method (p. 96) at 170°F/75°C for 6–8 hours until tender but otherwise at 225°F/110°C/Gas ½ for 3–6 hours. Strain off stock for sauce and discard the pig's trotter and bacon skin.

Mole Sauce. Heat the oil in a heavy, wide frying pan or casserole with lid; add rosemary, onion and celery and soften gently; cook until golden then add the tomatoes, the red peppers, garlic cloves and the chilli. Cover and cook gently until the pepper has completely softened. Turn up the heat and start to add some of the grouse cooking stock; let it boil rapidly and reduce. Add in the chocolate, cloves, nutmeg, orange rind and seasoning. Keep adding more stock but keep some back. When rich and tasty, process and sieve the mixture to make a smooth sauce. Either reduce again or add reserved stock then correct the seasoning, add a squeeze of lime or lemon and pour over the grouse; it should nearly cover the pieces and be thick and rich. Return the casserole to a slow oven to complete the cooking or leave aside for the flavours to blend; reheat and finish cooking the next day.

Serve with a crispy noodle cake, Pilau Rice (p. 192), Burghal Pilau (p. 212) or pasta.

Suggested Wine. Big red.

Grouse in a Butt

Named after the circular stone butts we use at Blubberhouses in Yorkshire, this dish of lightly cooked dice of incredibly tender grouse breast in a simple rich sauce is served in a circular vol-au-vent like a puff pastry butt. Bordering on haute cuisine, I know, it can nevertheless be prepared ahead with very little last-minute work (you could, I suppose, serve the breast this way without any pastry). It's also useful if your numbers don't quite fit for two good grouse will feed three people. The legs can be removed and kept to make Devilled Game (p. 198) or the flesh from them can be made into a purée with egg white, sieved and cooked as tiny quenelles to include in the butt, adding a touch of elegance and a nice change of texture. I would like to beg you to use home-made puff or Fast Puff pastry (p. 182) for the butts; it is *so* much better than the bought stuff, which may rise but has no true butter flavour. It keeps in the freezer so you can make it any time.

Ingredients   *Serves 4–6*
4 young grouse
1½ oz (35 g) butter
salt and pepper

Sauce   *Grouse Leg Quenelles (optional)*
grouse bones and skin   boned leg meat of grouse
2 tbs oil   1 egg white
1 onion, finely chopped   3–4 tbs double cream or more
1 carrot, finely chopped   salt, pepper and nutmeg
1 stick celery, finely chopped
1 tbs flour   *Puff Pastry Butts*
3–4 tbs port (optional)   ½ batch Fast Puff Pastry (p. 182)
½ pt (300 ml) good red wine
1 pt (600 ml) good game or chicken stock
1–2 tbs redcurrant jelly
¼–½ teasp potato flour, if necessary
1–2 oz (25–50 g) unsalted butter
salt and pepper

Carefully skin and remove the breasts of the grouse and set aside. Remove the legs and, if making the quenelles, remove the skin and scrape all flesh from the legs. Set aside.

Sauce. Break up all the grouse bones, removing and discarding the bitter backbone. Heat the oil in a heavy sauté pan, add the grouse bones and skin and the diced vegetables and fry for 20 minutes or so until a good brown. Sprinkle the flour over the contents of the pan and stir in and cook for several minutes. Now, off the fire, add port, wine and stock; bring to the boil, stirring, then simmer half-covered for about 1 hour or more, skimming as necessary. Once well reduced to about 8 fl oz (225 ml), season and add the redcurrant jelly to taste; stir until dissolved then strain, preferably through muslin and a fine sieve, pressing the debris well. Set aside in a small pan, reduce further or thicken with a tiny bit of potato flour if necessary to make a light coating sauce.

Grouse Leg Quenelles. Process the grouse leg meat in a food processor until smooth; add egg white and process again. Scrape the mixture through a sieve to separate the sinew and threads. Chill the smooth paste, then work in seasoning (salt will tighten the mixture so don't add it until after you have sieved it) and beat in the cream, but keep the mixture still holding its shape. Bring a shallow pan of salted water to the boil and poach small teaspoonfuls of the mixture, formed with a wet spoon and tapped on the bottom of the pan to dislodge. Poach for 2–3 minutes until they firm up and rise then remove and drain; set aside.

Puff Pastry Butts. Roll the pastry to ¼ inch (¾ cm) thickness and, with a very sharp knife, cut 5½ inch (14 cm) circles (using a saucer as a guide). Turn these circles (which can be cut and kept carefully in the freezer until ready to use) over on to a greased and dampened baking sheet. Brush carefully with egg wash, not letting any drip down the sides of the pastry. Score lightly in a circle 1 inch (2.5 cm) in from the outside, like a vol-au-vent. Score the 1 inch (2.5 cm) border lightly in a stone-wall pattern then bake the butts in a hot oven (400°F/ 200°C/Gas 6) for 10–15 minutes until well risen and browned; then turn down to moderately hot (375°F/190°C/Gas 5) for a further 15–20 minutes until cooked right through; cover if getting too brown. Remove from the oven, lift off the top and scrape out any centre pastry to make a nest for the grouse filling; keep the butts warm or re-heat when required.

Grouse Breast. Cut the grouse breast into thumbnail-sized cubes and season with salt and pepper. Melt the butter in a sauté or frying pan and, when foaming, add the cubes; shake and sauté until just firmed and no longer feeling squidgy. Add in the quenelles to heat through. Reheat the prepared sauce until boiling, correct seasoning then whisk in the butter in small pieces to thicken the sauce lightly and to enrich and polish it. Pour this sauce over the cubes of grouse, shaking the pan to amalgamate and at once spoon into the warm butts and serve. Once the butter is added, the sauce must be used at once because it will not hold.

Everything can be prepared and left ready for the final frying of the grouse and reheating and buttering of the sauce. You could fry the grouse breast briefly ahead of time but it tends to ooze juice which can change the consistency of the sauce which should be just coating but not heavy and binding.

Suggested Wine. Best red, probably fine claret or Rhône.

illustrated opposite: Grouse in a Butt (see page 105)

Dalmigavie Grouse Casserole

First cooked with the spoil from a wonderful holiday at Dalmigavie on the Findhorn, all the family having walked up grouse all day on the glorious late summer Invernesshire hillside.

Roasting young grouse is the superlative way to have them but sometimes it is not convenient to give the last-minute attention so necessary for perfect roasting. So then you need a recipe for a really good casserole to prepare ahead that only needs keeping warm or re-heating. This is also useful if you can only offer half a bird a head, for the casserole can be bulked out a little and will be perfectly generous.

You don't want to detract from the wonderful grouse flavour so the treatment needs to remain relatively simple with no competing flavours, but the presentation should make rather more of it than any old casserole. I favour a *salmi* in which the birds are part roasted then jointed and just heated through to finish cooking in a carefully prepared sauce. They are garnished with mushrooms and croûtons and some English or Scots fruit in season like blackberry, cloudberry, redcurrants or apple, pear or quince.

Ingredients

Serves 4 or more

4 young grouse
a bundle of bacon rinds (optional)
8 fl oz (225 ml) good red wine
½ lemon
3 oz (75 g) butter
1 large onion, sliced
1 carrot, diced
1 stick celery, diced
2 rashers streaky bacon, diced
the mushroom stalks from the garnish
2–3 tbs brandy
1–1½ oz (25–35 g) flour
2 pts (1.2 l) good game or chicken stock
3–4 parsley stalks
1 bay leaf
sprig lemon thyme or thyme
4–6 juniper berries (optional)
2–3 tbs Rowan Jelly (p. 200) or redcurrant
  jelly
salt, pepper and cayenne

Garnish

8 oz (225 g) little pickling onions
8 oz (225 g) button mushrooms
½ oz (12 g) butter
pinch sugar
sprig lemon thyme or thyme
croûtes of fried bread
halves of cooked pear, apple or quince
a few blueberries, cloudberries, redcurrants
  or cranberries
a few sprigs watercress
salt and pepper

If using bacon rinds, blanch for 10 minutes in plenty of boiling water. Boil down the wine by half if you wish to save time.

Wipe out the grouse, making sure they are well drawn and season inside and out with salt, cayenne and a few drops of lemon juice. Melt the butter in a large, heavy casserole, add the grouse, onion, carrot, celery, diced bacon, mushroom stalks and any neck, gizzards or hearts and gently brown the grouse on all sides, taking about 10–15 minutes. Add the brandy, cover closely and set the casserole in a hot oven (450°F/230°C/Gas 8) for 10–15 minutes. Remove grouse to cool.

Continue frying the vegetables and bits until all the juices have evaporated and the vegetables are a good brown and are really frying again. Sprinkle over the flour, fry gently until brown then draw off the stove and add the reduced wine and stock. Bring to the boil, whisking. Add in the blanched and rinsed bacon rinds, parsley stalks, bay leaf, sprig thyme and juniper berries if used.

Halve the grouse, snipping out the back bones with a sharp pair of scissors, and set aside. Add the back bones to the sauce and simmer gently for ½–1 hour or longer, skimming if necessary, until well reduced, adding more stock or water if it reduces too fast or gets too thick.

While the sauce simmers, prepare the onions and mushrooms. Place the onions in one layer in a saucepan; just cover with water, add ¼ oz (6 g) butter, a pinch of sugar, seasoning and a sprig of thyme; boil fast until the water has gone and shake well at the end to glaze evenly; set aside.

Heat the remaining ¼ oz (6 g) butter in a sauté pan, add the mushrooms and seasoning, cover and heat for 3–4 minutes; remove the lid and toss and fry until all the liquid has gone and the mushrooms are cooked; set aside.

Add the rowan jelly, a little lemon juice and seasoning to the reduced sauce then strain through muslin and a fine sieve. Lay the half grouse, which should be pink, quite tightly in one layer, in a dish. Tuck in the prepared mushrooms and onions, if used, then pour over the sauce which should almost cover them. Cover and reheat later but the reheating dish should never quite boil.

On Serving. This can be served straight from the re-heating dish but it will have more impact if the grouse are removed to a large serving dish, set around with croûtes of bread, fried in butter and olive oil (heart shapes, diamonds, circles or crescents), and halves of cooked pear, apple or quince, set with several poached blueberries, cloudberries, redcurrants or cranberries and little sprigs of watercress. Or you can make nice arrangements on individual plates if that suits you better.

Suggested Wine. Finest claret or red Rhône.

Partridge

Gone are the days, at least for the time being, when covey after covey swept over the guns, crouching behind the hedgerow with their loaders; really expert guns were unhappy to take less than four birds from the covey. The numbers of the English or Grey Partridge (*Perdix perdix*), once our most prolific indigenous game bird, have been declining since the last century due to more intense agriculture, the use of pesticides, lack of hedgerow cover and a shortage of autumn stubble. Some people have even stopped shooting partridge and, other than on the relatively few estates that can afford some of the ½–1 million birds now released each year, the best places to shoot partridge are in naturally farmed or unusual places like the Army training areas on Salisbury Plain where the tank has a less adverse effect than the spray. The Game Conservancy has launched a scheme, aimed at aiding farmers in the controlled use of herbicides and insecticides and the provision of suitable habitat which it is hoped will reverse the trend.

The French or Red-legged Partridge (*Alectoris rufa*) was originally introduced in 1673 and has since spread over much of England. It is larger than the grey and seems to be better able to adapt to modern farming, but is not so highly esteemed for the table, the flesh being rather darker and of less fine flavour. Young birds are best in September and October; both breeds have yellowish legs, dark beaks and softer bones than their parents. The two outer primaries are also pointed in the young and coloured cream in the red-legged. Roast when young and serve simply. Old birds need long casseroling and they have a great affinity with cabbage and cream.

Partridge with Little Plums

Partridge come into season in September and the early birds should just catch the yellow mirabelle plum season. I use the last of the honey-sweet gages from a western wall with a splash of eau-de-vie and the result is fabulous. If I don't get partridge until later I use damsons but, being sharp, they give an altogether different dimension to the dish. The large French partridge is halved for this dish but the smaller and more delicate English bird can be cooked whole, allowing a little longer.

Ingredients
Serves 4

- 2–4 young partridge, depending on size
- 2 oz (50 g) butter, preferably clarified
- a few drops oil
- a little sprinkling flour
- 1–2 tbs eau-de-vie de mirabelle, prune, kirsch, quetch or gin!
- ¼ pt (150 ml) dry white wine
- 8 oz (225 g) mirabelle plums, gages or damsons
- 8 fl oz (225 ml) double cream
- salt and pepper

illustrated opposite: Partridge with Little Plums (see above), Barbecued Quail with Herbs and Polenta (see page 118)

Halve the partridge lengthways, wipe dry with kitchen paper and season lightly. Heat the butter and oil in a wide sauté pan that will hold all the birds in one layer. Sauté gently until golden on both sides then sprinkle a little flour over them; season and shake the pan. Add the eau-de-vie and flame the dish. Now add the wine, cover and simmer gently for about 15–20 minutes until the birds are done, adding the plums for the last 5 minutes or so. Dish up the birds and plums on to a warm dish. Boil up the sauce, adding the double cream. Reduce until it is a good consistency, correct the seasoning and pour over the birds.

Serve at once. Crispy green vegetables and a bland accompaniment like Burghal Pilau (p. 212) are all that are needed.

Suggested Wine. Best red.

Partridge in an Overcoat

A very old way of keeping birds moist and succulent and cooking them without any fat is to wrap them in a huff paste for roasting. The salty flour paste, which nourishes the bird and keeps all its flavour in, is discarded after cooking; this is also a very healthy way of cooking and the birds truly just taste of themselves. It's very easy for the cook-hostess though your timing must be quite snappy. If you are clever (like Raymond Blanc) you can fashion a head and wings from extra paste to make your parcel look truly bird-like and gild it with egg wash; but don't let the paste get much thicker or you may upset the cooking times.

Ingredients   *Serves 4–6*
4–6 young partridge (or try grouse, teal or
    quail)
8 black peppercorns
12–16 blackcurrant or vine leaves
    (optional)

Salt Huff Paste
1½ lb (675 g) plain flour
6 oz (175 g) salt
1 egg white
12–15 fl oz (350–450 ml) cold water

Salt Huff Paste. Mix the flour, salt, egg white and water to a pliable dough and rest for 2 hours in the fridge.

To Cook the birds. Wipe the birds, slip two peppercorns into each and wrap them in blackcurrant or vine leaves, if available.

Divide the paste into 4 and roll out thinly into ovals. Lay the birds breast down on the paste, gather it up and seal the paste. Turn the birds breast up and roast, set well apart, in a very hot oven indeed (500°F/250°C/Gas 10) for 30–32 minutes. Rest for only 5 minutes before serving or the birds may lose juice into the crust. Let everyone remove and discard their bird's overcoat, which is definitely not for eating!

Allow only 20–22 minutes for quail, 25–30 for teal and 30–35 for young grouse and adjust the timing for other varieties of game. Remember that if you pack more than just a few birds into the oven they will take longer.

Serve with delicate crisp vegetables such as courgette, mange-tout or carrot and perhaps a celeriac and parsley purée or creamy gratin dauphinois or Chou Bonne Maman (p. 206).

Suggested Wine. Best red, probably fine Burgundy.

Partridge in Noisette Sauce

The delicate flavour of roast hazelnuts is added to a light Hollandaise style of sauce, made with the cooking juices of partridge, a fine sauce that could be equally well served with pheasant or quail. You can serve it with a handful of crisp fried shreds of cabbage leaf, rather like Chinese fried seaweed; the colour, textures and flavours combine well. These shreds go with many game dishes.

Ingredients
Serves 2–4

2 plump partridge
4–6 oz (100–175 g) unsalted butter
2 sheets pork back-fat (or Bakewell paper)
2–3 tbs dry white wine

1–2 tbs lemon juice
1½ oz (35 g) whole hazelnuts
1 egg yolk
salt and pepper

Fried Cabbage Shreds (optional)
2–4 outer green cabbage or kale leaves
oil for frying
dusting of icing sugar

Wipe the partridge inside and out, season with salt and pepper and tuck in a nut of butter. Bard with a sheet of pork back-fat or well buttered Bakewell paper. Melt 3–4 oz (75–100 g) butter in a cocotte that will just hold the birds and fry gently until browned on all sides, taking 15–20 minutes, but do not let the butter burn. Add wine and lemon juice, cover and continue to cook very gently for about 10–15 minutes until the partridge is just done.

Meanwhile roast the hazelnuts until a good golden brown and rub off skins in a kitchen cloth. Place the nuts in the food processor with metal blade and process until very finely chopped; add in the yolk and process again until as smooth as possible. Pour the hot buttery juices from the partridge down the tube with the machine running, and add the remaining butter either just melted or in soft nuts. Pass the sauce through a sieve (not essential but the sauce is nicer smooth), season, add more lemon if necessary and keep warm in a bain-marie; the sauce must *not* boil.

Fried Cabbage Shreds. Take 2–3 large green cabbage leaves, perfectly dry and a little wilted if possible. Roll up tightly together lengthways and cut with a sharp knife across and across into the thinnest shreds. Heat about ½ inch (1 cm) oil in a pan and, when smoking hot, add a handful of cabbage shreds. They will be crisp in a moment so lift out with a slotted spoon on to kitchen paper and once the oil is hot again, do another handful. Sprinkle with a dusting of icing sugar.

Serve the partridge, whole or halved, coated with the sauce and accompanied by a little pile of fried cabbage shreds.

Suggested Wine. Best red.

Braised Partridge with Cabbage

A classic dish where all the components contribute to make a wonderful whole. You can use mature but not *very* old partridge or you can use an old bird and then serve a young roasted half-partridge on top to have the best of both worlds. Also excellent with pheasant and most elderly game birds. Try to get a decent poaching sausage.

Ingredients   *Serves 2–4*

1–2 old partridge	1 onion, diced
1½ lb (675 g) cabbage	8 fl oz (225 ml) good jellied stock (or add a
2 tbs fat or oil	piece of blanched pork skin)
6 oz (175 g) thick-cut streaky bacon	¼ pt (150 ml) cream
8 oz (225 g) spicy poaching sausage,	salt and pepper
smoked boiling ring, or Zampona	

Brown the partridge gently all over in fat then set aside. Cut the bacon into chunks, blanch and drain. Pour boiling water over the sausage and leave for 10 minutes. Slice the cabbage, remove tough core and blanch for 1 minute in boiling salted water; drain and press well to expel water.

Fry the bacon gently in the fat from the partridge and remove it as it begins to colour. Add the onion and soften gently. Slice up the sausage into big chunks. Halve the partridge.

Pack the cabbage, bacon, onion, sausage and halves of partridge into a heavy casserole, preferably earthenware, burying the partridge in the middle. Pour the stock over, simmer gently or put into a very slow oven (250°F/120°C/Gas ½) for 1½–2 hours. Add the cream to the casserole and continue cooking for a further 1 hour. Once the partridge is well cooked, pour off the juices and boil down, removing any scum that may form. Pour back over the dish when there is just enough to moisten it nicely. By leaving the lid ajar, you may be able to get it to reduce enough as it cooks, but I usually find I have to pour it off and reduce.

Pile the cabbage, bacon and sausage into a serving dish and top with the braised partridge (or separately roasted birds) or serve from the pot. Not elegant but oh-so-good.

Suggested Wine. French provincial red.

Quail

Quail (*Coturnix coturnix*) are now protected in Britain though they breed and are shot in much of Europe and Asia, migrating south in winter. There are tales of so many quail settling on a galleon in the Mediterranean that it capsized and certainly many quail were caught in nets on the north coast of Africa as they arrived exhausted. Now the Japanese quail (*coturnix japonica*) is bred and farmed in this country and is available all the year round; it is a little bigger than the wild quail so you will find the cooking times in old books a bit short.

Quail eggs are also available all year; the birds start laying at six weeks and obligingly keep it up daily for a year or so. Quail adapts to many recipes and is very versatile, has a great affinity with vine leaves and grapes and is perhaps at its best fast cooked on a rôtisserie or spatchcocked under the grill for a crispy brown skin and juicy tender flesh. It needs to be fully cooked but over-cooking will dry it out. The perennial problem is how many to offer. I cook them frequently and tend to offer an average 1½–2 per person. With two, people are inclined to just eat the breast, leaving most of the leg and tasty bits which is a pity. Fingers are by far the best way to finish your quail or any other small game bird.

Quail in My Way

Endlessly looking for recipes for dinner parties where all, or nearly all, the work can be done ahead, I have come up with this fine quail dish. The quail are marinated in a Chinese-style seasoning then stuffed and quickly browned. They are then left ready to cook on a prepared mirepoix base and covered in vine leaves. Once cooked, the sauce takes but a moment to finish with grapes and cream. It is my frequent choice for dinner parties for 10–12 people.

Ingredients   *Serves 2–6*
4–6 quails
2 oz (50 g) cream cheese
6 oz (175 g) large grapes
1½ oz (37 g) butter
2–3 tbs olive oil or a bit more
10–12 vine leaves
1–2 tbs double cream
salt and pepper

Seasoning

1 teasp sugar	1 tbs vermouth or dry white wine
½ teasp salt	½ teasp grated fresh root ginger
1 tbs soy sauce	1 teasp finely chopped shallot

Sauce

1 oz (25 g) butter	a bouquet garni of parsley stalks, thyme or
1 slice bacon	lemon thyme and ½ bay leaf
1 onion, finely diced	8 fl oz (225 ml) dry white wine
1 carrot, finely diced	1 teasp brandy
1 stick celery, finely diced	salt and pepper

Mix up all the seasoning ingredients. Pat the quail dry on kitchen paper and rub with the seasoning mix inside and out; leave to marinate for 1–2 hours or overnight, even better.

Sauce. Melt the butter in a heavy frying pan or casserole, dice the bacon and add with the diced onion, carrot and celery. Cook gently without browning until tender then add the bouquet garni, wine, brandy and light seasoning to this mirepoix. Boil fast until reduced by half. Spread this mixture in the base of a roasting tin to hold the quail, not too tightly packed.

Stuff the quail with a halved grape and a spoonful of seasoned cream cheese (this keeps all game birds very succulent). Heat the olive oil and brown the quail briskly on all sides (a wok is good because its shape fits the quail). Set the quail on the vegetables, spread the breasts with butter and cover with a mat of vine leaves (or Bakewell paper) but leaving gaps round the edge for moisture to evaporate.

Skin, halve and de-seed the remaining grapes and sauté for a moment in a scrap of butter. Place the roasting tin of quail in a very hot oven (450°F/230°C/Gas 8) for 20 minutes when they should be perfectly cooked and succulent. They can then rest in a very slow oven or food-warmer at under 170°F/75°C for 20 minutes or so.

To Serve. Remove the quail to a serving dish, remove the bouquet garni from the sauce (of which there should now be only a small quantity left). If too much has evaporated, add a splash of white wine or water or if it is not rich and well reduced, boil fast for a moment. Boil up, add the grapes and 1–2 tbs cream to smooth out the sauce. Correct the seasoning and spoon rich, smooth sauce, diced vegetables and grapes over the quail and serve at once.

Suggested Wine. Best red, probably fine Burgundy.

Quail with Pears and Blackcurrant Leaves

I have adapted this from an old French recipe for cooking thrushes. Quail are suitably delicate in flavour and it is an interesting dish with its use of blackcurrant leaves which have a lovely flavour (redcurrant leaves have none so watch out!). Again I use Bakewell paper as a substitute for elusive thin bards of pork back-fat; use these if you have them but make sure they are very thin or the extra fat from them will unbalance the dish. This is a dish to cook and enjoy with good friends; true French cooking is not really suitable to pre-cook for a dinner party.

Ingredients   *Serves 4–6*

8 oven-ready quail	4 oz (100 g) butter
24 blackcurrant leaves or vine leaves (if from a packet, thoroughly rinsed)	2 large or 4 small firm but ripe pears, peeled, cored and halved
8 juniper berries, slightly crushed	a little grated nutmeg
16 black peppercorns	3 tbs eau-de-vie de poire
pork back-fat (or Bakewell paper)	salt and pepper

Roll and crush 8 blackcurrant or vine leaves between your fingers; then pop one inside each bird with a slightly crushed juniper berry, 2 peppercorns and a little salt. Cut 8 strips of Bakewell paper about 2 inches (5 cm) wide and 6 inches (15 cm) long. Season the birds lightly and place a blackcurrant or vine leaf on the breast and back of each; wrap in pork back-fat and tie with string. Heat half the butter in a sauté or deep frying pan that will take the birds in one layer. Add the quail and cook for about 15 minutes, turning from time to time, until browned and done, without letting the butter burn. Remove the quail, take off the paper and blackcurrant leaves and keep warm; add the pears to the butter in the pan, season lightly with salt, pepper and nutmeg and cook for 7–8 minutes, turning once, until tender. Return the quail to the pan and reheat; add the eau-de-vie de poire to the pan, flame and shake the pan until the flames extinguish.

Remove the quail and pears to a serving dish. Add a little water and deglaze the pan if there is no juice; then add the remaining butter, cut into small cubes; heat and whisk until amalgamated, pour over the quail and pears and serve at once. Spinach, which has a great affinity with pears and cuts a rich dish, would go well.

Suggested Wine. Light red.

Barbecued Quail with Herbs and Polenta

Quail are easy to come by and make a lovely winter or summer dish. In summer I cook them on skewers on the barbecue, sometimes spatchcocking them or, at other times, following a tip of Alice Waters of Chez Panisse (in San Francisco) by putting some butter, creamed with soaked, chopped dried *cèpe* mushrooms inside them and a cube of stale bread wedged in the back end to keep the butter in and absorb the juices; absolutely delicious and she also puts little spicy sausages and bay leaves between each quail and that's nice too. In winter I cook them, still on skewers for easy turning, on a rack in a fierce oven over a dish of polenta to catch their drippings. This is a classic Italian way for little birds.

Polenta is the Italian name for maize meal and it is cooked into a porridge that is then either turned out on to a board, baked under a dish, like this, or stamped out and fried. It makes a good, non-assertive accompaniment to many game dishes; one that tends to grow on people.

Ingredients   *Serves 4–6*
8 quail

Marinade
2 tbs olive oil
2 tbs tasty duck or chicken fat
½ lemon, rind and juice
3–4 sprigs lemon thyme or thyme
5–6 leaves of fresh or a little frozen or dried
    basil
4–5 sprigs parsley
good pinch sugar
4 tbs white wine or sherry
½ teasp salt
peppermill mixture or pepper
a thumbnail of lovage leaf
12 fresh or dried bay leaves

Polenta
1½ pt (900 ml) stock or milk or water
½ lb (225 g) coarse polenta (maize meal)
½ teasp salt or to taste
1 large onion, diced
2 tbs duck or chicken fat or oil
2–3 cloves garlic (optional)
pepper

For the Marinade. Bruise the herbs and heat gently in the oil and fat with a little grated lemon rind, or use Spiced Oil for Game (see p. 25); then combine with the remaining marinade ingredients. Wipe the quail dry, season inside with salt and pepper and brush all over, inside and out with the marinade; leave at kitchen temperature for an hour or so, turning from time to time. Take long flat skewers, pass one neatly through the wings and body and another through the legs and body to hold the legs tight to the body; place a bay leaf on each skewer, then another bird. Fit 3–4 birds on each pair of skewers and season generously. Soak dried bay leaves to soften in hot water before using.

Polenta. Prepare the polenta before cooking the quail. Bring the stock to the boil in a large, heavy pan; whilst boiling, stir and gradually add the polenta in a fine stream, like making porridge and it will thicken to a similar consistency; simmer gently for about 15 minutes, stirring frequently as it can easily stick. Meanwhile, sauté the onion gently in the fat until a good golden brown; then add the finely chopped garlic, if used, and soften that without browning. Stir onion and garlic into the polenta with seasoning to taste, then turn out into a greased baking tray that will fit under the quail in the oven and spread to a ½ inch (1 cm) layer all over.

To Cook the Quail. Place the skewers of quail on a rack in a very hot oven (450°F/230°C/ Gas 8) and set the polenta a shelf below them. Roast the quail for about 18–20 minutes, brushing with the marinade frequently and turning the skewers over once. Remove from the oven. Cut the polenta into squares and serve a quail on each square, perhaps with a dish of tomatoes baked with basil or a well-dressed chicory salad on the side.

Quail are best eaten with fingers so have napkins or finger bowls ready.

Suggested Wine. Lots of choice; probably something Italian like Chianti Classico.

Quail with Grapes and Brandy

A classic but simple way to do quail for small numbers though I would hesitate to try to finish the sauce for large numbers in this way (the reducing takes too long for a hostess to be out of the dining room). But it is quick and so delicious for just a few and also perfect for partridge.

Ingredients *Serves 2–4*

4 quail
2 oz (50 g) cream cheese
2 oz (50 g) soft butter
4 vine leaves (optional)
4 thin sheets of pork back-fat or blanched
   streaky bacon
4 croûtes of fried bread (use butter and
   olive oil)
3 oz (75 g) white grapes, skinned, seeded
   and, if large, halved
2 tbs brandy
4 tbs white wine
6 fl oz (175 ml) double cream
salt and pepper

Season the cream cheese and put one quarter inside each quail; rub the birds with softened butter and cover with a vine leaf (if available) and a layer of pork back-fat, Bakewell paper or bacon, tied on with thread or string. Set in a roasting pan and roast for 18–20 minutes in a hot oven (425°F/220°C/Gas 7), basting twice. Remove the back-fat, string and vine leaf, set each quail on a croûte and keep warm. Set the roasting pan on the stove to boil up, add the brandy and flame; then add the white wine and grapes, and boil hard to reduce to a few syrupy spoonfuls before adding the cream. Reduce to a beautiful rich sauce, season and spoon over the quail. Serve at once.

Suggested Wine. Best red.

Roast Quail in Buckwheat Noodle Nests with Pine Nuts

Allow 1–2 birds per person, depending on appetites and the rest of the menu. Roast the quails, basting well, and then leave in a switched-off or very low oven (under 200°F/90°C so the birds do not go on cooking or dry out) for up to 30 minutes. The noodles ought to be boiled at the last minute but if they must be kept, leave them in the saucepan with a little oil and just enough of their cooking water not to dry out. Dish up when ready to serve.

Ingredients   *Serves 2–6*
4–6 quail (or young partridge)
sprigs of celery or bunch watercress

Marinade

1 teasp sugar
½ teasp salt
1 tbs soy sauce
1 tbs vermouth or sherry
½ teasp grated fresh root ginger
1 teasp finely chopped shallot
2 teasp oil

Buckwheat Noodles

2 oz (50 g) buckwheat flour
8 oz (225 g) strong white flour
2 eggs
2 yolks
1 teasp pine nut, hazelnut or olive oil
1 teasp salt
1–2 tbs cold water if necessary

To Finish

2 tbs pine nuts
a little pine nut, hazelnut or olive oil

Wipe the birds dry. Mix up the marinade, rub the birds with it and leave to marinate, turning from time to time, for 1–2 hours or overnight.

Buckwheat Noodles. Process the flours, eggs and yolks, oil and salt in a food processor until crumbly then gradually drip in water as the mixture processes until it forms polystyrene-like granules which can be pressed together to form cohesive lumps. Press into 4–5 lumps and keep in a polythene bag.

Roll each piece through the pasta-roller, set at its widest, until smooth: then progressively through thinner rollers to the thinnest but 2 setting. Hang on a cloth whilst you repeat with remaining pieces. Leave to dry for 30 minutes before cutting if you wish, or cook at once. Then pass through the fine noodle cutter and toss in piles on a tray. Alternatively make up the pasta by hand; knead for 5–10 minutes then roll out very thinly, flour well, roll up and cut into fine noodles. Shake out on to a tray.

To Cook the Quail. Roast for 18–20 minutes until done in a hot oven (425°F/220°C/Gas 7), brushing with the marinade frequently. Fry the pine nuts in a little oil until golden.

Toss the noodles into plenty of boiling salted water to which a teaspoon or so of vegetable oil has been added. Boil for 3–5 minutes until *al dente* then drain, not too thoroughly. Toss the noodles, seasoning and pine nuts with their oil in the roasting-pan juices.

Form mounds of noodles using a fork to twist the noodles round, into nests, on a serving dish and top each nest with a roast bird. Tuck in sprigs of celery leaf or watercress and serve at once. Serve with a juicy vegetable such as Chou Bonne Maman (p. 206).

Suggested Wine. Light red.

Spatchcock Quail Salad

A modern hot salad like this makes a lovely summer or autumn lunch or supper dish for a few people. As well as quail, which are now commercially available anytime, you can use really young pigeon, adjusting the grilling time to keep them pink and tender. Grouse, teal or partridge are also excellent spatchcocked and grilled with a salad or vegetable.

Ingredients *Serves 2–4*

4–6 quail	4 tbs walnut oil
1½ oz (35 g) soft butter	2 tbs sunflower or other light oil
a few drops oil	2 tbs tarragon wine vinegar
3–4 oz (75–100 g) smoked, streaky bacon, cut in a thick slice and cut into lardons	mixed salad leaves of chicory, lettuce, watercress, radicchio, rocket or endive
½–1 oz (12–25 g) pine nuts	salt and pepper

Cut the quail down the backbone and spread flat to spatchcock. Push the legs up tight and slip the drumsticks through a slit in the skin; fix in place with a skewer or cocktail stick. Place a quarter of the softened and seasoned butter under the breast skin of each bird. Rub the skin with a drop of oil and season heavily on both sides with salt and pepper. Pre-heat the grill and when ready to serve, with the salad and dressing ingredients prepared, grill the quail, breasts down, for 5 minutes; turn over and grill for 5 minutes breast up. Give them a further 5 minutes breast up, moving slightly further from the heat if they get too brown. Meanwhile, fry the bacon gently until golden brown; add the pine nuts and fry a little until just colouring, then add the walnut and other oil to the pan with the vinegar and heat through gently, mixing well. Drain most of the dressing over the prepared salad, season and toss.

Arrange the salad on individual plates and place grilled quail on each bed of salad; add any grilling juices to the bacon, pine nuts and remaining dressing and spoon over each bird. Serve at once. You could add croûtons of fried bread, perhaps fried in walnut oil, to this salad.

Suggested Wine. Light red.

Quail with Broccoli and Light Sabayon Sauce

I adapted this from a recipe of Michel Guérard that I found in an American magazine. The very light sabayon sauce is a lovely idea that can be used for many things. I adapt and also use it for fish, or shellfish, perhaps in a puff pastry *feuilleté* or with asparagus and other vegetables and of course it would suit partridge, guineafowl or pheasant breast as well as quail. Allow 1, 1½ or 2 birds per head, depending on appetites and the menu.

Ingredients   *Serves 2–6*
4–6 quail
1–1½ oz (25–35 g) butter
salt and pepper

4 croûtes of bread, fried in butter and olive
    oil
1 lb (450 g) perfectly cooked broccoli
    spears

Light Sabayon Sauce
1 fl oz (25 ml) lemon juice
2 fl oz (50 ml) water
8 oz (225 g) best unsalted butter
2 egg yolks
2 tbs water

You can smoke the quail for 10–15 minutes in a home-smoker if you wish to give them a delicate smoked flavour (pp. 19 and 53). In this case, cut the cooking time by about 5 minutes.

Season the quail, coat with softened butter and place in a covered meat roaster or casserole. Roast in a hot oven (450°F/230°C/Gas 8) for 20–25 minutes (timing can depend on the thickness of the casserole) until just cooked.

Cook the broccoli spears in plenty of boiling salted water until just tender, or steam them if you prefer; drain and serve with the quail. Dress the quail on croûtes, coat with sauce and garnish with broccoli. Serve at once.

Light Sabayon Sauce. Meanwhile, boil the lemon juice and water in a heavy pan, add the diced butter and keep whisking and boiling the mixture. The butter will melt and foam, thickening the mixture into a light sauce. Set aside.

Place the egg yolks and water in a bain-marie, or bowl, over a pan of hot water over gentle heat and whisk until the sabayon thickens, leaves a trail and greatly increases in volume. Immediately whisk the sabayon into the foamy butter sauce and serve at once. Each half of the sauce can be made ahead and reheated by bringing the butter sauce back to the boil and re-whisking the sabayon and combining.

Suggested Wine. Best red, probably fine Burgundy.

Pigeon and Dove

The pigeon has lots of qualities; it makes good eating, it is plentiful, it has no close season and it's cheap. The feral pigeon (*Columba oenas*) and collared dove (*Streptopelia decaocto*) make rather better eating than the wood pigeon (*Columba palumbus*). Young birds are a great delicacy from May to September and wood pigeons younger than two months can be distinguished by the lack of the adult's white collar. They are generous breasted with thinnish thighs; the legs of the young birds are orangy-pink and scaleless, maturing to reddish-purple, while the claws change from pink to brown; the young skin is also paler and the still flexible beak looks especially large.

I like to use young birds in many different ways – roasted, grilled, spatchcocked or in my favourite way with the breasts just briefly cooked like steaks. Mature birds make tasty casseroles, often using just the breast which can easily be taken by slitting the skin and removing *without* plucking. As well as the recipes in this chapter, you could adapt the Moroccan Hare with Honey and Prunes (p. 177) or the Italian hare or wild boar recipes. Pigeon breast makes good pies and pâtés and is useful as a part of mixed game dishes.

Hot Squab, Pigeon or Quail Salad

This idea of serving a hot honey roast spatchcock bird on mixed salad leaves, with pan-tossed slices of peach (or pear) and a hot peach vinegar dressing with cream *is* really rather delicious and can be adapted to use with partridge, woodcock or young teal or even the breasts only of young mallard or pheasant. It can be a starter or main course, depending on the size or number of birds you offer.

Ingredients
Serves 4 as a main course or 8 as a starter

4 tender young squab, collared dove, wood pigeon, or 8 quail
a little grated lemon rind
4–6 tbs pear or peach vinegar
4–6 tbs olive oil
2 tbs honey
mixed salad leaves of lettuce, spinach, rocket, sorrel, chicory or radicchio with a very little, finely shredded lovage if possible

2–4 pears or peaches, depending on size
a little wine (optional)
6–8 tbs double cream
salt and pepper

Split the birds down the back, snipping out the backbone and through the wishbone with a pair of scissors; press out flat to spatchcock, season generously inside and out with salt, pepper and a little grated lemon rind and sprinkle with 1 tbs vinegar mixed with 2 tbs oil. Toss, rub in and leave to marinate for an hour or so then skewer into shape with one skewer (I use wooden *sate* skewers) through wings and breast and one through thigh and drumstick to keep the shape. You can get 1–2 pigeon or 3 quail on each pair of *sate* skewers which makes it easier to turn them in the oven. Before cooking, brush the birds all over with the honey, warmed and mixed with 1 tbs vinegar.

Wash, dry, pick over and mix a large bowl of salad leaves (leave in a sealed bag in the fridge to crisp until ready to serve). Peel, core and halve the pears or skin, stone and halve the peaches; sprinkle with a little vinegar and have ready for when the quail are cooked.

Cook the spatchcocked birds in a very hot oven (475°F/240°C/Gas 9) for about 20–25 minutes until a good brown, turning and brushing with honey twice (watch the roasting pan juices do not burn, if necessary adding 1 tbs wine or water if they get very brown). Remove the birds and keep warm for a moment. Add the remaining oil and vinegar and the cream to the pan and boil up, stirring in all the brown roasting juices. Heat the pear or peach halves through in the dressing then remove and slice thinly; keep together ready to fan out on the plate or, heat in a microwave or alternatively slice and toss the fruit in hot oil separately. Boil the dressing down to a good coating consistency and correct the seasoning.

Place generous salad leaves on each plate, top with a bird (or two), arrange sliced pear or peach halves, fanned out on each plate; then spoon over some hot cream dressing. Serve at once and napkins or fingerbowls are essential!

Alternatively, if you are using the breast only of a larger bird such as mallard or pheasant, just cook briefly on each side in hot oil with a sprinkle of vinegar until done (keep mallard very rare, cook pheasant a little more); then slice thinly and arrange on the salad leaves. With any of the breast only presentations, you won't, of course, have the intensified flavours of the roasting pan juices in the dressing which is very much part of this recipe. A delicious cold salad dressing can be made with oil, cream, lemon and fruit vinegar.

Suggested Wine. French provincial red (for the breast only version, you may like something a little finer, probably a medium quality red Bordeaux or Rhône).

Pigeon with Prunes

The dark meat of pigeon responds well to a touch of sweetness and the prunes are especially successful. If in doubt about the age of the birds, cook them even slower by the Oh-So-Slow method (p. 96) until they are tender when the flesh won't be so dry and dense. They could also be excellent cooked in the Chocolate and Wild Cherry Sauce for Wild Boar (p. 178).

Ingredients   *Serves 4–6*
1 pigeon per head (depending on size)
½ lb (225 g) prunes
1½ lb (675 g) onions
2 oz (50 g) butter or dripping
4 rashers thin-cut streaky bacon per bird
a little dripping, fat or oil
1 bay leaf
sprig thyme
¼ pt (150 ml) red wine, cider or good stock
salt and pepper

Soak the prunes in tea or water for 5–6 hours or overnight (if you use those succulent Agen or Californian prunes they can go straight in). Slice the onion finely and fry gently in a casserole in the butter or dripping until soft and golden; allow 20–30 minutes for this. Cut the breast, with leg and wing attached in one piece from each side of the pigeon. Sprinkle the pieces with pepper and bind up each piece in two rashers of bacon, impaling with a cocktail stick to secure them.

Heat a little fat in a frying pan and brown the pigeon on both sides. Then bury them in the golden onion, slipping in a bay leaf and sprig of thyme; season with salt and pepper and add the wine, cider or stock. Cover with tinfoil and a lid and place in a slow oven (300°F/150°C/Gas 2) for about 2 hours. Add the drained prunes and cook a further ½–1 hour till tender. Serve with mashed potatoes or buttered noodles seasoned with nutmeg.

Suggested Wine. Big Red (or try something with some sweetness like a Vouvray Demi Sec or a Rhine Spätlese from the Palatinate).

Spatchcock Grilled Pigeon with Stuffed Mushrooms

Pigeon, being a dark meat, is delicious served rare like a steak if it's young; nothing can be tougher than an old bird! Spatchcock them for quick cooking but as most of us don't have the facilities for grilling more than a few spatchcock birds at once, this will probably have to be a dish for family or just a few friends and you may have to do the mushrooms in the oven. Cooked in this way, you can also serve the birds on all sorts of interesting salads.

Ingredients

Serves 4

4 tender young pigeons or squabs, or use grouse, partridge, teal or quail
oil
4 large cap mushrooms
2 large tomatoes (optional)
½ shallot or very small onion
handful parsley and little sprig fresh thyme
2 oz (50 g) wholemeal breadcrumbs
2 oz (50 g) butter
bunch watercress
vinaigrette dressing
salt and pepper

Spatchcock the pigeon by cutting down the back, snipping out the backbone and through the wishbone with a pair of scissors. Bat out flat, tuck the wing bones under the carcass and keep in place with cocktail sticks; tuck the drumstick ends into slits in the skin so they look a bit like frogs! Season with salt and pepper and brush with oil. Grill for 6–8 minutes on the breast side under a very hot grill, adding the mushroom caps (see below) and halved tomatoes when you turn the pigeon to cook for a further 5–7 minutes on the underside. Grouse will take about 15 minutes to grill and should be rare and pink: partridge about 15–20 minutes and should be just cooked: teal about 14–18 minutes and rare: quail about 15 minutes to be fully cooked (see recipe p. 121). All can do with marinating in a little flavoured oil and seasoning for an hour or so before grilling if you wish.

Stuffed Mushrooms. Separate the mushroom caps and stalks. Combine finely chopped shallot, thyme, mushroom stalks and parsley with breadcrumbs and seasoning; add a few drops of melted butter to bind *or* chop in the food processor with a metal blade; first the shallot, adding in the parsley and mushroom stalks until finely chopped; then add the breadcrumbs, seasoning and ½ oz (15 g) butter. Chop finely but do not overprocess. Melt 1½ oz (35 g) butter in a small pan and dip in or brush each mushroom cap with butter; grill the caps for 1–2 minutes then turn and fill with stuffing; trickle over any remaining butter and grill for 5–6 minutes.

Serve the pigeons, which should be still pink inside, surrounded by the stuffed mushrooms, grilled tomato halves and bunches of fresh watercress dipped in vinaigrette dressing with the excess shaken off.

Suggested Wine. French provincial red.

Marinated Pigeon with Mediaeval Flavours

This is a nice warming winter dish. It's quick and easy to prepare but allow plenty of time for the cooking; 4–6 hours at a very low temperature seems to produce the most succulent bird and the most savoury juices. It's also excellent in summer when the fresh herbs abound and could just as easily be turned into cold pigeon *en gelée* by following the Lapin en Gelée recipe (p. 168); any leftover meat can be turned into excellent Potted Pigeon (p. 56). I sometimes lard the pigeon breasts with little matchsticks of pork or bacon fat (see larding (p. 17) to keep the dry breast meat more succulent.

Ingredients   *Serves 4*

4 pigeon
24 small matchsticks of back-fat or bacon
   fat (optional)
6 cloves garlic
good handful parsley
4 sprigs lemon thyme or thyme
4 sprigs sweet marjoram
4 leaves sage

juice ½ lemon
½–1 pt (300–600 ml) stock
¼ teasp ground cinnamon
¼ teasp ground ginger
pinch ground cloves
potato flour (optional)
salt and pepper

Marinade

1 onion, finely chopped
1 carrot, finely chopped
8 fl oz (225 ml) (or more) red wine
2 tbs oil

2 slices orange
½ teasp coriander seed
1 bay leaf

Lard the birds, if you are going to. If you marinate the birds, mix all the marinade ingredients and pour over the wiped and seasoned birds (I do this in a plastic bag so you can draw it up and seal it for maximum contact); leave for 12–48 hours. You can cook without marinating by just tossing all the marinade ingredients into the pot with the pigeon.

Slightly flatten the garlic cloves and remove their paper waistcoats. Tuck one into each bird with a bunch of parsley and a sprig of the other herbs; if using dried herbs, a pinch of each would do. Pack the pigeon tightly into preferably an earthenware casserole. I have a bellied pot with quite a small lid which is ideal for this sort of dish. Tuck in remaining garlic, add marinade ingredients, lemon juice, spices, seasoning. Pour over the stock. Cover with a butter paper or circle of Bakewell paper. Fit the lid on tightly and cook in a very slow oven (225°F/110°C/Gas ½) for 4–8 hours (I usually give it about 20 minutes in a hot oven just to get the dish warmed and the cooking started, for otherwise it takes about 2 hours to heat enough to start cooking); it can also be cooked at 300–325°F/150–170°C/Gas 2–3 for 3–4 hours. Look from time to time and cook until the pigeons are tender and the legs move easily in their sockets with no elastic feeling. Pour off the juices, strain if you wish though this is a simple dish and it's not essential; boil down hard until strongly flavoured then thicken lightly, if you wish, with a little potato flour, mixed with cold water.

Serve with Chestnut Purée (p. 207) or Sweet Potato Purée (p. 208) and braised kale or broccoli and maybe try some Skirlie (p. 212) if you like its nutty oatmeal flavour.

Suggested Wine. Big red.

Woodcock and Snipe

The woodcock is a short-legged, long-beaked, night-feeding woodland bird which breeds here, though large numbers of northern birds visit during bitter weather when shooting may be suspended as a form of protection. Woodcock (*Scolopax rusticola*) make some of the most exciting and testing shooting and although you may no longer join the Bols Woodcock Club on shooting a right and left, you most certainly should apply to the Shooting Times Woodcock Club, with statements from two witnesses. Young birds have ragged and worn tips to their primaries whereas old birds are intact. This clean little bird, living on a diet of earth worms and insects, always defecates as it takes off in flight so is usually cooked without being drawn, the gizzard only being removed. The head is often split after cooking because the brain is a delicacy. Gourmets choose this bird in preference to almost all others, its rich flavour being said to bring out the best in a fine wine. I find variations on a theme of roasting and flaming the most exquisite way to serve it with a sauce or croûte made with the trail.

Snipe (*Gallinago caelestis*) is a tiny, long-legged, long-beaked marsh bird, probably evolving from the same stock as the woodcock. As marshland is drained, so habitat decreases and the majority of birds are now found in the wilder parts of Ireland and Scotland, including the Hebrides where we have had a lot of good sport. They are exciting and testing to shoot and are superb to eat with the same characteristics as woodcock for which the recipes could be adapted; they are also generally cooked undrawn. A voracious eater to keep its tiny body weight up, especially in winter, it mostly eats at dusk and during the night. In spring the male can be heard 'drumming' in a mating display to protect his territory. He dives through the air at 45 degrees and two tail feathers vibrate to make this amazing and evocative noise which he keeps up during the almost continuous hours of daylight of a northern summer.

Classic Roast Woodcock with Brandy *opposite*

You can use VSOP Cognac or Armagnac (not your three star cooking stuff), a good Calvados or really any eau-de-vie for this dish. Woodcock really suits this classic way of cooking and is said to bring out the fine flavour of wine so serve your best with this dish.

Ingredients *Serves 2*

2 woodcock
2 thin sheets of pork back-fat, speck or buttered Bakewell paper
1½ oz (35 g) butter (preferably clarified)
2 tbs fine champagne or VSOP Cognac or Armagnac, Calvados or eau-de-vie
4 × 2 inch diameter croûtes of stale white French bread, fried golden in butter

8 fl oz (225 ml) good game stock, reduced down to 1–2 tbs
a few drops lemon juice
pinch cayenne
1½ oz (35 g) best unsalted butter
salt and pepper

To remove the Gizzard. Make a little slit in the skin of the abdomen on the right side and locate the little hard round sack; hook it out with a skewer and snip it off. (Bought birds

should have had the gizzard already removed.) Leave in all other innards (of course they can be removed if you prefer but the sauce won't have the flavour). The crop must of course be removed but the head is left on; eyes removed. Season the birds and truss with the sharp beak passed through thigh and body; cover the breast with the bards of fat or buttered Bakewell strips and tie in place. Heat the, preferably clarified, butter in a roasting or sauté pan of the right size (birds not touching and room to spare all round but not excessively large – too large and the butter burns, too small and the pan juices won't reduce). Roast in a hot oven (450°F/230°C/Gas 8) for 15–18 minutes, basting every 5 minutes and removing the bards for the last 5 minutes.

Have the Cognac or whatever ready-warmed in a small pan, the croûtes fried and keeping warm and the well-reduced stock or fumet warm. Once done, prepare the *rôti*; that is scrape all the 'trail' or innards from the birds on to a plate, set the birds to rest and keep warm (see resting p. 29). Mash up the innards (a nugget of real foie gras *should*, but probably won't be added!) with a ½ oz (12 g) butter, salt, pepper, a drop of lemon and cayenne; spread half on the 4 croûtes, set the birds on two and keep warm or halve the birds and set on all four.

To make the sauce, pour the roasting butter off the pan (it's delicious for frying potatoes or croûtes) leaving all pan juices and sediment. Set fire to the warmed Cognac and pour into the pan; heat and stir round, adding the stock and deglazing the pan; stir in the remaining crushed innards, stirring and crushing well, season with a few drops of lemon, a pinch of cayenne and beat in the remaining best unsalted butter in little bits; check the seasoning. Set a bird on a croûte on each plate, spoon over the sauce and add the extra crisp croûte to each plate.

Serve at once. Glazed turnips, braised kale and perfectly mashed potatoes go with this dish.

Suggested Wine. Best red.

Woodcock en Cocotte

Young woodcock have tender whitish flesh and mature birds are quite dark-meated and are stronger in flavour. They can be beautifully plump and with delicious fat when in prime condition. Then treat them like this or roast them but, if you only have one or it is dark and in poor condition, make Savoury Woodcock Croûtes (p. 194). Not everyone likes the trail so here I have drawn them and used a simple cream cheese stuffing. You can please yourself.

Ingredients   *Serves 2–4*

2 plump young woodcock
2 slices streaky bacon or pork fat bard
1 oz (25 g) butter
1 tbs onion, finely chopped
1 tbs carrot, finely diced
1 tbs celery, finely chopped
2–3 pieces crumbled dried *cèpe* mushroom (optional)

1 bay leaf
1–2 slices truffle (optional)
2–3 tbs Madeira
2–3 tbs good stock
good squeeze orange juice
a few drops lemon juice
salt and pepper

Stuffing

2 oz (50 g) cream cheese	pinch cayenne
1 tbs shallot, very finely chopped	2 tbs breadcrumbs
chopped liver and heart (optional)	salt and pepper

Remove the crop and draw the woodcock. Mix up the stuffing ingredients, adding chopped liver and heart if you wish. Season the woodcock inside and stuff. Stretch a bacon rasher over each breast and secure with a tooth pick.

Heat the butter in a heavy pan or cocotte that will just hold the birds, add the onion, carrot, celery and the woodcock and fry gently to brown the birds all over, taking about 20 minutes. Add the crumbled mushroom, bay leaf, truffles if available, Madeira and stock. Season lightly, cover and cook either slowly on top of the stove or in a hot oven (400°F/200°C/Gas 6) for 10–12 minutes. Once done, add a good squeeze of orange juice and a few drops of lemon and leave aside until ready to serve.

Serve woodcock whole, or split on fried or toasted croûtes, or on squares of polenta (p. 118) fried crisp. Spoon the sauce over them, sieved or not as you please.

Suggested Wine. Best red.

Snipe à la Minute

Baroness Robin Wedell Wedell-Sborg gave me this recipe which she used to do in Ireland when snipe were plentiful; simplicity is the key.

Ingredients   *Serves 3–4*

6–8 snipe, head, crop, feet and gizzard
   removed (see p. 128)
6 oz (175 g) best butter
2 tbs breadcrumbs
4 tbs good dry sherry (dry oloroso is
   particularly good)
juice 1 small lemon
salt and pepper

Heat the butter in a sauté pan that will hold the snipe in one layer. Season the snipe and sauté gently for about 10 minutes, turning frequently until browned and nearly done. Remove the snipe, add the breadcrumbs, sherry and lemon juice to the pan and stir it all together. Return the snipe to the sauce and serve when done. Burghal Pilau (p. 212) to mop up the rich sauce and a simple vegetable like spinach or broccoli go well with this dish.

Suggested Wine. Best red.

Snipe with a Mushroom and Marrowbone Ragoût

Snipe are usually cooked with their innards (the trail) in. If you don't like this idea, draw them and stuff with the same cream cheese stuffing used for the woodcock. You can then include the trail in the Mushroom Ragoût if you wish for it adds a good depth of flavour. The Mushroom Ragoût can be served with any game bird, with or without its enrichment of bone marrow. Marrowbones are almost given away by butchers, keep in the freezer, have a wonderful flavour and richness and can be poached and the marrow spread on croûtes or diced and included in sauces. They should be used much more widely as they used to be.

Ingredients   *Serves 4*

8 snipe
about 4 oz (100 g) butter (clarified is best)
8 bards pork back-fat or butter and
   Bakewell paper
2 large marrowbones, knobbly ends sawn
   off (optional)

4 thickish oval slices stale bread on which 2
   snipe will fit
2–3 tbs red wine
salt and pepper

Mushroom Ragoût

8–10 oz (225–275 g) mushrooms
½ pt (300 ml) good red wine
1 tbs oil
1 oz (25 g) butter
1 slice bacon, diced
the innards (trail) from the snipe (optional)

1 clove garlic, finely chopped
a little chopped or pinch dried thyme
½–¾ teasp plain flour
prepared and poached marrow from one
   bone (optional)
salt and pepper

Remove the crop and gizzard from snipe (see p. 128). Draw, if not cooking with the trail *in situ*, and set the trail aside to add to the mushrooms. Season and stuff the snipe with cream cheese stuffing (pp. 119 or 133) or a seasoned ¼ oz (6 g) knob of butter and truss with the sharp beak passed through thigh and body. Bard with pork fat or butter and Bakewell paper tied in place.

Mushroom Ragoût. Boil the wine down to half quantity in a small pan. Thickly slice or quarter the mushrooms. Heat the oil and butter in a sauté pan, add the bacon and trail and fry, squashing and pressing for 1 minute. Add the mushrooms, toss and cover and cook over moderately high heat for 2–4 minutes. Uncover and continue to sauté until all juice has gone and the mushrooms are browning. Add the garlic, thyme and seasoning, sprinkle over the flour and cook for a moment before drawing off the stove to add the wine. Bring to the boil, stirring, and reduce until thick and rich. Let the marrowbones come to room temperature then push the marrow out of the bones in one piece and poach in salted water for 8–10 minutes. Keep hot in the water until ready to use. Drain, dice and add half the hot poached bonemarrow to the ragout. Correct the seasoning and make very hot before serving.

To Cook the Snipe. Heat 2 oz (50 g) butter in an appropriate roasting pan and turn the snipe in the hot butter; roast, basting once, in a very hot oven (450°F/230°C/Gas 8) for 10–12 minutes.

Toast the croûtes of bread on both sides (or fry until golden in the roasting drippings if not using the marrow), spread with the poached, drained marrow from one of the bones (leave the other for the sauce) and set 2 snipe on each croûte. Pour off the roasting fat, deglaze the pan with 2–3 tbs wine and pour over the birds. Serve with the mushroom ragoût.

Suggested Wine. Best or big reds.

Guineafowl and Rook

The rook (*Corvus frugilegus*) is a friendly and familiar bird one remembers about the place as a child. Alas, the huge elm tree rookeries are no more and the rook population has declined by 45% from 1945 to 1975. Nevertheless, 'branchers', that is fledglings just ready to take flight, are still sometimes shot (using a .22 rifle) during May. They make an excellent pie so watch out for them.

Though not strictly a game bird, guineafowl (*Numida meleagris*) are sometimes shot, usually unintentionally in the final battue round the home policies, inciting wrath in the heart of one's host and anguish for his wife and children. But farmed guineafowl are now widely available in supermarkets. They are particularly popular in France and make good eating though their tasty but dryish flesh needs nourishing and careful cooking and suits delicate flavours and sauces. Many of the pheasant recipes adapt well to guineafowl and this way, stuffed *en cocotte*, is especially good.

Guineafowl Farci en Cocotte

The guineafowl, stuffed with cream cheese and walnuts, is cooked in a casserole with bacon and mushrooms. You could use the sealed method of cooking (p. 87) but in this recipe I wrap the bird in vine leaves and start it breast down, finishing cooking it breast up, another way of getting a succulent bird. Cream cheese makes an excellent moistening stuffing for game.

Ingredients   *Serves 3–4*

a plump guineafowl (or pheasant)	1 small onion
4 oz (100 g) cream cheese	8 oz (225 g) mushrooms
1 oz (25 g) shelled walnuts	2 fl oz (50 ml) white wine
1 teasp olive oil	1–2 teasp potato flour, arrowroot or cornflour
2 oz (50 g) butter	6–8 vine leaves (optional)
4 oz (100 g) smoked bacon, cut in one piece	salt and pepper

Mix the cream cheese and walnut halves together, season with salt and pepper and stuff the guineafowl with this mixture. Rub the bird's skin all over with a little olive oil then, if you are using them, cover its breast with vine leaves and bind on with thread (you could substitute with a strip of Bakewell paper). Melt the butter in a casserole which will just hold the bird and add the bacon, cut into little fingernail-sized cubes; toss and sauté until lightly brown then remove and add the roughly chopped onion and whole mushrooms. Sauté for 5–10 minutes until just beginning to brown then return the bacon to the pan and lay the bird, breast down, on top; season lightly, add the wine then cover with a butter-paper, a layer of tinfoil and a close fitting lid. If you wish to leave it, prepared ahead and ready for the oven, sauté the bacon etc. first and leave to get absolutely cold while you prepare the bird; then pack it all into the casserole and leave in a cool place until ready to cook; allow a little longer cooking time.

Place the casserole in a hot oven (400°F/200°C/Gas 6) for 30 minutes then turn the bird breast upwards and return to the oven for a further 20–30 minutes until just cooked. Strain off the juices into a little pan, remove the vine leaves and thread but leave the bird and bits in the casserole keeping warm (food hot cupboard, warming drawer, or oven just on). Remove any excess butter from the pan juices then lightly thicken the juices with a little potato flour mixed with cold water, adjust the seasoning and keep warm.

Serve the guineafowl on a meat plate, surrounded by the bacon and mushrooms and hand the sauce separately; don't let the carver forget the walnut and cream cheese stuffing!

Suggested Wine. French provincial or light red.

Rook Pie

Young rook were culled from the great swaying, cawing elm tree rookeries in May or so as they teetered on the edge of the nest. They were considered a great delicacy and were often made into a pie with a little fat bacon, moistened with either stock or milk and topped with puff or flaky pastry. The backbones are bitter so it's easiest to split the skin of the unplucked and undrawn birds down the breast, cut out the breast on the bone and detach the leg. There is not much on each bird so allow 6–8 for a decent pie.

Ingredients
Serves 4–6

5–8 young rooks, breasts and legs only
a little milk to soak the rook
8–10 thin rashers streaky bacon, de-rinded
2 oz (50 g) thick-cut fat bacon, diced
a little seasoned flour
1–2 tbs chopped chives
a few leaves lemon thyme

2 fl oz (50 ml) thick cream }
8 fl oz (225 ml) milk }
  or use light cream or creamy milk
  and a bit of butter or use stock
6–8 oz (175–225 g) fast puff pastry, flaky
  or puff pastry
salt and pepper

Soak the rook in mixed milk and water, with 1 teasp salt added, for 12–24 hours then drain and dry well. Line a 1½ pt (900 ml) pie dish with stretched rashers of streaky bacon. Roll the rook joints in seasoned flour and pack into the pie dish with the diced fat bacon and herbs. Season only lightly if at all and pour over the milk and cream.

Roll the pastry, cut a strip, moisten and fit around the rim of the pie dish; cover with the remaining pastry, seal and decorate the edges; make a hole in the centre and cook in a hot oven (400°F/200°C/Gas 6) for ½ hour until well browned; then turn down to moderate (350°F/180°C/Gas 4) for a further hour before serving.

Suggested Wine. Big or French provincial red.

Duck

Most of us with shooting husbands have been duck flighting from time to time and have either endured the bitter fenland east winds, a scurry of snow blinding one at the critical moment when the teal come drifting in, or crouched around a flight pond, hoping for a bit more wind, the tension mounting as you wonder whether they'll be coming in tonight; it's almost dark, the first owl hoots and, suddenly, the whisper of wings and dark shapes appear against the blue black sky.

Many natural watery places are being drained, diminishing the available habitat, and the shyer breeds are easily disturbed but plump mallard (*Anas platyrhynchos*), easy to breed and encourage, and tiny teal are still common. Teal (*Anas crecca*) are the best and I'd settle for one any day, while mallard are plentiful and bigger, and just about as good. Gadwall (*Anas strepera*), which like a very quiet habitat, are said to be excellent (though I don't think I've ever eaten one); widgeon (*Anas penelope*), pintail (*Anas acuta*), pochard (*Aythya ferina*) and tufted (*Aythya fuligula*), should they come your way, can also be good, depending rather on where they have been feeding; sea shore ones can be very fishy, but shoveller (*Anas clypeata*), as you expect, and golden eye (*Bucephala clangula*) are a bit on the muddy side.

Young birds are tender but oldies, which may have migrated for many of thousands of miles, developing good muscles as they go, need gentle casseroling or the Oh-So-Slow method (p. 96). It is tasty red meat and I like it served rather rare. The breast is relatively generous in size, unlike farmyard duck, and it lends itself to going with many flavours or is excellent on its own. Gourmets like dishes which take only the breast, as a Magret or Breast of Wild Duck (p. 140), though the well-cooked steam and roast Chinese style method in Mallard with Wild Cherries (p. 138) is also a firm favourite. Wild rice, really an aquatic grass, has a great affinity with duck and can be used as stuffing or accompaniment. The recipes are

written for Mallard-size duck, but can be adapted for others, allowing for size and weight; and the goose recipes can also be adapted and used. Duck can develop a rather rancid smell in the freezer after several months so don't hoard; enjoy it in the autumn and winter while in condition and at its best. Do not forget to remove the musky preen glands from either side of the duck's tail before cooking.

Wild Duck with Poached Kumquats and Pepper-Glazed Pecans
illustrated opposite

This is a glorious dish though a little complicated and perhaps more suited to a restaurant than for serving at home. I wrote it for *A la Carte* magazine and it is very handsome with the poached kumquats spread out in fans and the crisp fried pecans coated in sweet syrup and heavily peppered. The tiny dice of lemon flesh is important to offset the richness and sweetness of the sauce. The breast should be served very rare and legs used for another dish such as Devilled Game (p. 198). It is the culmination of many experiences from eating duck with noodles and green peppercorns in Hamburg to an idea from an early mediaeval recipe for fruit stuffing for duck.

I have used the Chinese technique for boiling and frying walnuts for a crunchy texture and mellow flavour and their style of finishing them in sugar to serve with savoury dishes. I also indulged my desire to find something worth while to do with kumquats which I find pretty but difficult to use. I do hope some of you will try it for it is exciting, with each necessary component adding to the whole.

The garnish and stuffing can be prepared ahead and it's not difficult to do but does need watching as it roasts, so that the pan juices do not burn.

Ingredients
Serves 2–3

1 plump young mallard
4 oz (100 g) dried mixed fruit, apricots, peaches, apples, pears or prunes
½ pt (225 ml) dry white wine
1 lemon

1 teasp green peppercorns
1 oz (25 g) fresh pecan or walnut halves, roughly chopped
3 oz (75 g) butter
salt and pepper

Garnish

3 oz (75 g) sugar
4–6 kumquats, or 2–3 clementines quartered

8–12 perfect halves of pecan or walnut
oil for frying
coarsely ground or crushed black pepper

Soak the dried fruit in the wine for a few hours or overnight (fruit varies so much these days; some needs no soaking at all), then simmer gently until tender and drain, setting the juice aside to baste the duck.

Take tiny pine-needle julienne strips of zest from the lemon, place in cold water, then bring to the boil; simmer 4–5 minutes then drain and refresh under the cold tap; set aside.

Cut the pith from the lemon and remove the flesh from the skin in segments; set 2–3 segments aside to add to the sauce at the end; cut the remainder into bits and mix with the fruit, the peppercorns, some of the lemon zest and the pecans.

To remove the Preen Glands. These give the bird a strong musky taste. They are on either side of the duck's tail and can be found by locating the gland that exudes oil for the duck to oil its feathers. Cut out the glands which are like tiny, pale kidneys and have a strong musky smell.

Peel back the skin at the neck end and with a sharp knife, remove the wishbone to facilitate carving. Season inside with salt and pepper and stuff with the fruit stuffing. Spread the breast with 1 oz (25 g) of the butter and tie on a strip of Bakewell paper. Set the duck in a roasting pan and roast in a very hot oven (475°F/240°C/Gas 9) for about 10 minutes, then remove the paper and baste with about 4 tablespoons of the reserved fruit juice. Roast for a further 10–15 minutes, basting with the reducing pan juices and adding more if necessary. Once glazed and brown and cooked to your liking (the breast should still feel fairly squidgy under your fingers), set aside to rest for about 20–40 minutes (see resting roasts p. 29).

Garnish. Meanwhile, melt the sugar in ¼ pt (150 ml) water. Cut the kumquats almost into slices, leaving them attached at the stalk end, and poach gently in the syrup until tender and the syrup is very thick and heavy (don't let it boil down to tooth-sticking toffee). Remove to a rack to drain. Or, if you are using clementines, carefully peel the quarters and coat in the heavy syrup. Boil the perfect pecan halves in water for about 5–6 minutes then drain and dry well; fry in 3–4 tablespoons oil for about 5 minutes until crisp and golden. Drop them into the heavy syrup glaze, sprinkle in plenty of pepper then remove the coated pecan halves to the rack.

Once the duck is cooked, remove any excess fat from the roasting pan, deglaze with the remaining fruit juices, or wine, stock or water if they have all gone, and boil down to a syrupy glaze. Off the stove, briskly whisk in the remaining butter in little bits to finish and thicken the sauce. Adjust the seasoning, add a squeeze of lemon and some of the remaining lemon flesh, cut into tiny dice. Keep warm but don't boil.

Remove the legs and carve the duck breast into thin slices. Spoon a mound of fruit stuffing on to each plate, arrange slices of breast, spoon the sauce around and garnish with the lemon zest, poached kumquats and glazed pecans. Serve at once, perhaps with fine noodle pasta, wild rice or Burghal Pilau (p. 212) and a separate simple vegetable like broccoli, braised kale or glazed baby turnips.

Suggested Wine. Best red.

Mallard with Wild Cherry Sauce

There are almost two recipes here. A Chinese-style duck, steamed then roasted, which could hardly be more different from the rare roasted duck, but is equally good in its way. The duck becomes well cooked, very tender and tasty and can be served as it is, rather like Chinese crispy roast duck, or with a sauce. This sauce made with sloe gin and the wonderful Italian wild cherries (Amarena Fabbri, available from I. Camisa, 61 Old Compton St, London W1, and Valvona & Crolla, Leith Walk, Edinburgh) can be all made ahead and the duck can be left all ready for 30 minutes in a hot oven. The sauce is also superb with duck breasts, fried and served like rare steaks.

Ingredients

Serves 2–4

1 plump mallard

Marinade (optional)

3 tbs spiced or herb vinegar
1 tbs sea salt
½ teasp Chinese five-spice powder
　(optional)
4 × 5p-sized slices fresh root ginger
2–3 spring onions

Wild Cherry Sauce

3–4 tbs wild cherries (drained of syrup)
1 shallot, finely chopped
1 small carrot, finely diced
½ stick celery, finely diced
2 tbs olive oil
bouquet garni of parsley stalks, bay leaf
　and lemon or ordinary thyme
3–4 tbs sloe gin or gin

8 fl oz (225 ml) dry white wine
¾–1 pt (450–600 ml) good duck stock,
　including the de-greased cooking juices
¼–½ teasp arrowroot or potato flour
1–2 oz (25–50 g) good unsalted butter,
　diced (optional)
salt and pepper

Cut out the preen glands from the duck's tail (p. 138).

Mix up the marinade ingredients and rub vigorously over the inside and outside of the duck. Pop the slices of ginger and the spring onions inside the duck. Leave to marinade for 4–6 hours or overnight. Remove the duck from the marinade and set in a dish with at least 1½ inches (3 cm) raised sides. Set this in a steamer. (It could be set on a trivet in a roasting pan of water tented tightly with foil and boiled on the top of the stove; that's what I do if I have more than one duck.) Steam the duck, tightly covered, for 50 mins or longer if you think the duck is very mature. Carefully remove the duck from the steamer, draining all juices from inside it. Pat with kitchen paper to dry and leave it on a rack to dry and cool for ½–1 hour or longer.

Wild Cherry Sauce. Leave the duck juices to stand for a few minutes then separate the fat and de-grease. Soften the shallot, carrot and celery in the oil in a wide sauté pan; once soft, add the herbs and sloe gin, bubble up, then add the white wine and reduce by half. Now add the duck stock and 2 teaspoons of the marinade and reduce again, skimming and tasting until very full flavoured and only about 8 fl oz (225 ml) remains. Add a little arrowroot or potato flour mixed with cold water to thicken, very lightly. Strain through a sieve into a small pan, pressing the debris well. Add the cherries to the sauce. Simmer gently for a few minutes, adjust seasoning then keep warm until ready to serve. Beat in the butter in small dice to soften, thicken and lustre the sauce if you wish.

Set the duck on a rack and roast in a very hot oven (450°F/230°C/Gas 8) for 25–35 minutes until golden brown. Serve at once, carved or quartered, alone or with the sauce.

Suggested Wine. Big red or, as something a little different, a big white.

Breast of Wild Duck with the Marquis' Sauce

This includes an old-fashioned sauce that I have taken almost unchanged from Meg Dod's nineteenth-century cookbook. Thin claret sauces, their flavour heightened with ingredients such as shallots, ketchup, lemon, anchovy and mace, were all the thing and this simple sauce was especially recommended for wild duck. You could thicken it very lightly for modern taste if you wish but the butter should do it. Serve it with a plain roast duck or, as in this recipe, with slices of semi-roasted breast gently heated in the sauce. Don't boil the sauce or the meat will toughen.

Ingredients
Serves 4–6

2 plump young mallard
1 tbs oil
2 oz (50 g) good butter
salt and pepper

The Marquis' Sauce

¼ pt (150 ml) claret or good red wine
1 tbs mushroom ketchup
1 tbs lemon juice
1–2 tbs very finely chopped shallot or onion

a little fine julienne or grated rind of lemon
⅛ teasp ground mace
shake cayenne pepper
1 oz (25 g) diced butter (optional)
salt and pepper

The Sauce. Heat all the sauce ingredients (except for the butter) and simmer and reduce for a few minutes. Set aside until ready to use then re-heat and strain before using. It could be thickened with a tiny bit of potato flour if you did not want a thin sauce.

To Cook the Duck. Remove preen glands from either side of duck's tail (see p. 138) (they give a rather musky smell), fold back the neck skin and carefully remove the wish bone to make carving easier. Season the duck, rub with the oil and spread butter over the breast. Roast in a very hot oven (475°F/240°C/Gas 9) for about 10 minutes, basting once or twice; the breast should still feel quite squishy when pressed. Either rest for 10 minutes then carry straight on with the recipe, having prepared the sauce, or set aside to cool.

With a sharp knife, cut down carefully on either side of the breastbone; then cut horizontal slices of breast, cutting in towards the breast bone and catching all the juices (the breast should still be quite rare). Use the wings and legs for another dish, perhaps devilled or as a pie.

Spread the roasting butter around a wide frying or sauté pan and carefully lay in the breast slices and their juices. Strain some of the hot sauce over them. Heat through gently, but never let it boil or the meat and sauce will spoil, shaking the pan so the natural juices and the sauce mingle. When warmed through but still pink, remove the duck breast to a warmed serving dish or straight on to plates; correct the seasoning of the sauce (add an ounce of diced butter and whisk and shake until dissolved), pour over the duck and serve at once. Burghal Pilau (p. 212) and a separate dish of Chou Bonne Maman (p. 206) or braised fennel is good with this.

Suggested Wine. Best red.

Duck in a Brick with Apple and Calvados

A chicken brick, which is a heavy, porous earthenware container, is also excellent for duck or pheasant. It's a very natural way of cooking because you just pack everything in and bake it which is, of course, also a nice easy way for the cook! I find the bricks work best when new, eventually becoming rather grease-clogged and less porous. You can work out all sorts of your own variations on this recipe, adding the herbs, flavourings and vegetables of your choice.

Ingredients   *Serves 2–3*

1 mallard duck
2 eating apples (Cox's for choice)
2–3 shallots, peeled and quartered
2–3 slices smoked bacon or salami, cut in strips
good pinch mace
good pinch cinnamon
sprig lemon thyme and bay leaf or bouquet garni
bay leaf
4 oz (100 g) mushrooms (optional)

2–3 tbs Calvados, brandy or bourbon
1–2 teasp apple, Rowan (p. 200) or Spiced Grape Jelly (p. 199) or Mulberry Conserve (p. 201), or redcurrant jelly
4–6 tbs port or red wine
½–1 oz (12–25 g) butter (optional) or ¼–½ teasp potato flour (optional)
salt and pepper

Soak the chicken brick for 15 minutes in cold water. Peel and core the apples and cut into thick slices. Make a bed of them with the shallots and bacon or salami in the bottom of the brick and add a good pinch of mace and cinnamon and a sprig of lemon thyme or thyme and a bay leaf.

Wipe the duck well, remove the preen glands from either side of the tail (p. 138), season generously inside with salt and pepper and add some sliced mushrooms and a tablespoon or so of Calvados. Lay on the apple base, add any remaining mushrooms, trickle over the remaining Calvados, season and close the brick. Bake in a hot oven (400°F/200°C/Gas 6) for 1 hour. Pour off the juices into a small pan, remove any fat with kitchen paper then boil fast, adding a spoonful of jelly and the port; boil down until well flavoured then, when ready to serve but off the stove, whisk in a little diced butter or thicken with a tiny bit of potato flour mixed with cold water, added off the stove then simmered until lightly thickened.

Carve the duck and serve with a spoonful of the apple mixture and some sauce. Buttered noodles with nutmeg and fried breadcrumbs, braised fennel or glazed carrots are all good with this dish.

Suggested Wine. French Provincial or light red.

Duck with Onion Confiture

There are really two recipes here. The onion confiture can be cooked on its own to a sweet-sour, brown chutney-like mixture to bottle and serve with cold game and meat or can be used to cook with duck. This is for duck that may be rather mature, for you can go on cooking it gently, and for duck that may be fishy. (If you suspect they will be very fishy, blanch in boiling salted water with a ½ teasp of bi-carb of soda added then skin it as well if you wish, or soak overnight in a strong salt solution with other flavourings. I'm afraid I have not much experience of this and only speak from hearsay). Strong-flavoured duck may need the addition of capers, anchovy, pickled walnuts, cayenne and lemon to the sauce to heighten the '*gout*' as they used to say, and which is the way my family adore it. Let me hasten to add this is a tasty way to cook a plump young mallard and need not be kept for your less choice birds.

Ingredients
Serves 3–4

1 big mallard, 2 smaller duck or 3–4 teal
1 oz (25 g) plain flour
½ teasp herbes de Provence or Italian
    seasoning
1 teasp paprika
2 tbs fat or oil
8 fl oz (225 ml) stock
salt and pepper

Onion Confiture

1½ lb (675 g) onions, sweet red-skinned
    for choice
2 tbs oil
3 oz (75 g) Demerara or golden
    granulated sugar
5 tbs sherry vinegar or spiced, wine or
    cider vinegar
8 allspice berries
1 tbs liqueur de cassis (optional)
a good squeeze lemon juice
1½ teasp salt

Optional Flavour Heighteners

lemon, marjoram
1 pickled walnut, mashed
1 teasp capers, chopped
1–2 anchovy fillets, chopped
a little cayenne pepper

Onion Confiture. Slice the onions and fry gently in the oil in a heavy casserole for 20–30 minutes until translucent and soft. Now add the sugar, vinegar, cassis if used, allspice and salt, and cook gently (at this stage mix with the duck). Once the onion is tender and the mixture well reduced and thick, stir in the lemon juice and pot up as a chutney.

To Cook the Duck. Joint the duck and season the flour, adding the herbs and paprika. Heat the oil, toss the duck in flour and brown on both sides. Sprinkle over the remaining flour, cook for a moment, draw off the stove and wait for the sizzling to cease. Remove the duck to the casserole of prepared and cooking onion. Add the stock to the frying pan, bring to the boil, whisking, and pour over the duck and onion. Stir together, cover and cook gently in a slow oven (250°F/120°C/Gas ½) for 1½–4 hours or until tender (it can also be cooked by the Oh-So-Slow method). Add seasoning, lemon, marjoram and any other flavour heighteners you feel may be necessary.

Serve with rice, a crispy noodle cake, garlic mashed potato or something to mop up the sauce.

Suggested Wine. Big red.

Duck with Zampona and Lentils

Though this is written for the Oh-So-Slow method of cooking as the best way of producing old birds in a tender way (p. 96), it can be cooked in a standard slow oven if you wish. I add Zampona, the stuffed pig's leg from Italy, which has a wonderful spicy taste and adds a rich gelatinous texture to the gravy. You can buy a whole one from an Italian delicatessen and it will keep in the cool for months; once opened, cut into chunks and freeze what you do not use, for it is a flavourful addition to have handy for many casseroles and stuffings. Pulses and dryish game meat especially benefit from the addition of some sort of lubricating and gelatine-giving ingredient like Toulouse sausage, smoked sausage, spicy Cumberland sausage or smoked bacon, pig's trotter and pork skin.

Ingredients   *Serves 3–4*

1 large mallard	1 stick celery
8 oz (225 g) brown lentils	3 cloves garlic
6–8 oz (175–225 g) Zampona, smoked	bouquet garni
sausage or smoked bacon	1–2 tbs tomato purée
3–4 tbs oil	¾–1 pt (450–600 ml) stock or to cover
2 onions	salt and pepper
2 carrots	

Soak the lentils in cold water for 6–8 hours.

Remove the preen glands from either side of the duck's tail (see p. 138). Joint the duck and brown well in the oil; set aside. Dice and fry the vegetables until golden. Pack the duck joints, sliced Zampona, vegetables and their oil and soaked drained lentils into a heavy casserole. Add the slightly flattened garlic cloves and bouquet garni. Mix the tomato purée with the stock and add enough to cover the lentils. Season, cover tightly and bring to the simmer; then cook in a very, very slow oven at about (170°F/75°C/Gas ¼ or less) for 6–8 hours or until absolutely tender. Correct the seasoning and serve from the casserole.

To get this very low temperature (which must *not* be above 200°F), you may need to use a food warmer or hay box (p. 96) rather than an oven because ovens cannot always be adjusted low enough. Check with an oven or sugar thermometer.

Suggested Wine. Big red.

Goose

I have no great experience of geese though I know I don't like plucking them, too many tough feathers and masses of down. We have occasionally been flighting and there is certainly something most exciting about that, wondering whether the heavy bomber on the horizon is coming your way as you crouch behind the dyke; in a way, I always rather hope they don't because they are so majestic it seems almost a pity to shoot them. But when thousands halt their migration to settle on growing corn the damage is considerable and the sportsman is more than welcome to help scare off the pest. Not that they are at all easy to shoot being wily and wary and travel a lot faster than their slow wingbeat suggests.

But I do like cooking them, especially in fine condition off stubble and not from the seashore – though they are wonderfully constructed to travel many thousands of miles, muscling up nicely on the way, so young birds are definitely advised. Choosing them is not easy, and you may never have any choice as it is illegal to offer wild geese for sale so you will either have to be given one or shoot it yourself; until mid-November, young birds should have a V notch in their tail feathers. If many geese come your way, acquire the Game Conservancy (Fordingbridge, Hampshire) notes on Aging Geese and become your own expert.

The best eating are the feral Canada Goose, the male averaging 10½ lb (4.75 kg) in feather or about 6 lb (2.7 kg) dressed and feeding about 6 people. The rather smaller Greylag (*Anser cinereas*) (male 8½ lb (3.8 kg) in feather) also eats well and so does the still smaller Pinkfoot (*Anser brachyrhynchus*) which weighs in at about 6 lb (2.7 kg) in feather. The Whitefront (*Anser albifrons*), smallest of all, averaging just over 5½ lb (2.5 kg), is also a fine bird for the table but, as the entire Greenland and Iceland population winter in the British Isles, it needs careful protection; it, like all geese except Brent and Barnacle which are not worth eating, tastes better after feeding on grass or stubble, rather than on marshlands. The females weigh lighter.

For roasting, choose a young, plump and well-conditioned goose with a flexible bill, a V notched tail feather, bright legs and rather under the average weight for the breed. Cook goose fast and serve it rare, or long and slow to become tender; anything in between seems to be a mistake. Most, other than Canada, have little fat on them after all their mileage so they need careful basting and cooking or they will be dry. Goose freezes well but, like duck, I find it goes rancid if kept too long.

If many come your way, slit the breast skin, unplucked, peel back and remove the breast only. It can be used in numerous recipes; young birds fried as a magret, stir-fried as in Sauté of Venison (p. 159) or quick fried like the Venison Steaks and Farthinghoe Sauce (p. 158). Old birds will make a good pie or Bobotie (p. 161), can be adapted to Indian Style Venison (p. 163) or turned into potted goose pâté or terrine.

Pot-Roast Wild Goose with Gin and Juniper and Wild Goose Sauce

illustrated overleaf

Young wild goose, like so much dark game meat, is delicious served rare. As it loses its pinkness, so it becomes tougher and then only a long slow braise can make it palatable again. So keep it fairly lightly cooked and rest it for 30 minutes at least for the pink juices to re-enter all the tissue and for the meat to relax before carving. I have adapted this recipe from one given to me by William Chatham Jr, a celebrated hunter and cook from California. I particularly like the Chatham method of moisturising goose or pheasant by stuffing it with stale bread very generously soaked in Bourbon (I use whisky) and sewing it up again; the aroma really does stay inside and moisturises it during cooking. Do this for a mature bird weighing up to or more than the average for its breed.

Ingredients *Serves 6–8*

1 plump breasted wild goose (up to 7 lb
  (3.25 kg))
3 tbs dripping or oil
2 onions, roughly diced
12 juniper berries
3 fl oz (75 ml) gin
4 oz (100 g) thin-cut streaky bacon
2 bay leaves
1 pt (600 ml) good stock
1 tbs flour
salt and pepper

Optional for older, larger birds
3 thick slices stale bread
3–4 fl oz (75–100 ml) whisky, brandy or
  bourbon

Herb and Onion Stuffing or Dressing
2 onions, finely diced
1 stick celery, diced
3 cloves garlic, sliced
3 oz (75 g) butter
4 oz (100 g) stale bread, diced
herbs (I use sage, thyme and mugwort
  which is good with rich goose)
1 egg, beaten
8–10 tinned water chestnuts, sliced
  (optional but nice and crunchy)
¾–1 teasp salt
plenty of pepper or peppermill mixture

Wild Goose Sauce

4 fl oz (100 ml) port
1 teasp Dijon mustard
1 tbs Spiced Grape (p. 199), Rowan
   (p. 200) or redcurrant jelly
½ teasp ground ginger
a little grated orange rind and juice ½–1
   orange

a little grated lemon rind and juice ½–1
   lemon
¼–½ teasp potato flour (optional)
2–3 oz (50–75 g) best unsalted butter

Wipe the bird inside and out and season inside with salt and pepper. Stuff with Herb and Onion Stuffing if used and sew up or, if using whisky-bread moisturiser, soak the bread in whisky for 20 minutes or so. Tie up the neck end of the bird, pack in the bread and any spare whisky, tuck a piece of Bakewell paper, butter paper or tinfoil inside the cavity so no whisky steam can escape, then sew up the back end so all is sealed inside. Heat the fat or oil in a large oval casserole or pot-roaster and brown the bird on both sides, adding onion to brown as well. Crush the juniper berries slightly. Warm the gin, pour over the juniper berries, set alight and pour, flaming, over the goose breast. Cover the breast with bacon rashers, tuck in two bay leaves, season lightly, add about ¼ pt (150 ml) stock and cover the roaster or casserole. Cook in a moderately hot oven (375°F/190°C/Gas 5) for 1 hour, basting once or twice and adding a little more of the stock if necessary. (Definitely young birds under 4½ lb (2 kg) can be open roasted but baste often and check 4 lb (1.8 kg) birds after 45 minutes). Approximate times are 4 lb (1.8 kg) birds about 1 hour while 7 lb (3.2 kg) birds can take about 1½ hours. The breast still ought to feel slightly squidgy when you press it. Remove from the pan, wrap in tinfoil and rest where it cannot go on cooking (under 170°F/75°C – see Resting Roasts, p. 29) for 30–40 minutes before carving.

De-grease the pan, stir in the flour and remaining stock and simmer and reduce until rich and tasty. Alternatively for a grander sauce, de-grease and strain the pan juices and add to the goose sauce below.

Herb and Onion Stuffing or Dressing. This can be put inside the bird to cook or open baked in a pie dish which I think gives a more interesting flavour and which I do if I've used bread soaked in whisky inside the bird.

Soften the onion and celery in the butter, add the garlic and soften; then pour over the bread, diced in little fingernail-sized cubes; add seasoning; mix in the herbs (preferably fresh but frozen or dried will do) and water chestnuts if you are using them. Bind with the egg and a little more stock to moisten; alternatively, you could use orange juice, flesh and grated rind to moisten the bread. Use to stuff the goose or pack lightly into a greased pie dish and bake uncovered at 375°F/190°C/Gas 5 for 45 minutes until brown.

Wild Goose Sauce. Mix the port with the mustard, jelly, ginger and orange and lemon in a small saucepan. Bring to the simmer for a few minutes, thicken very lightly if you wish with potato flour, mixed with cold water. When ready to serve, whisk in diced butter to thicken and finish the sauce. Do not boil once the butter has been whisked in. The strained roasting pan juices can be added to the sauce.

Suggested Wine. Big or French provincial red.

Slow Cooked Goose

Another example of the Oh-So-Slow method that I found in an old book in America. The goose slow roasts for 12 hours with the oven temperature never above 185°F/82°C so you will need to check that your oven will cook as low as this. The fat renders from the goose and though a large fellow may be quite firm and chewy, it will be tasty, succulent and much enjoyed. The goose will be well cooked of course and quite different from the rare pot-roast goose. Make a separate sauce as there will be no gravy; Seville Orange Sauce for Duck (p. 202) or Wild Goose Sauce (p. 145), The Marquis' Sauce (p. 140) or just equal quantities of Spiced Grape Jelly (p. 199) and good wine, reduced and simmered, thickened and finished with a generous nut of butter. The legs can be made into Baked Brown and Wild Rice with Game (p. 195), or Devilled Game (p. 198), or you can follow the recipe for Pigeon and Cream Cheese Pâté (p. 56).

Ingredients

Serves 4–6 or more

a fine wild goose between 4 and 7 lb
   (1.8–3.2 kg)
1 orange, cut in eighths with the skin on
1 onion, sliced
1–2 sticks celery, sliced
4–6 juniper berries
2 bay leaves
salt and pepper

Combine the orange, onion, celery, juniper and bay with plenty of salt and pepper. Pack into the goose cavity, tuck in a strip of Bakewell paper, sew up the back end and season with salt and pepper. Set on a rack over a roasting tin and place in a very gentle oven at about 165–175°F/72–77°C. Do not allow the temperature to rise above 185°F/82°C. Leave to cook for 12 hours without basting; I did try basting with honey and sprinkling with more salt and coarse pepper; it was nice but the fat did not seem to render out quite so well.

Carve the breast and serve with a sauce and Green Herb Pudding (p. 210) or Wild Rice Risotto (p. 209) or Lentils with Butter and Coconut (p. 206) (if the goose fat is tasty, use it in place of the butter in the lentils). Sweet Potato Purée (p. 208), French Canadian Roast Apple Sauce (p. 204) or Burghal Pilau (p. 212) could also be served with this dish.

Suggested Wine. Big red.

GROUND GAME

Venison

The word venison used to cover most kinds of furred game, and *basse venaison* meant hare or wild rabbit. Now we use it just for deer.

Our native red deer, the largest available here, originally lived in forests but were gradually driven mainly to the hills of northern Scotland, still known as deer forests though they may have hardly a tree. These large animals, especially when culled as mature beasts, need to be carefully hung, take quite some cooking but can be excellent. The Sika is a large Japanese deer which makes even better eating. Originally in captivity in this country, I believe some are now interbreeding with red deer in Scotland. Nowadays red deer is being quite extensively farmed and, depending on its feeding, provides a pleasant, quite juicy, tender meat but without quite the full flavour and texture of the wild beast. A booklet of some of the best red deer farmed venison suppliers can be obtained by sending a SAE to the British Deer Farmers Association, Fairfields House, 5 Roughknowles Rd, West Wood Heath, Coventry CV4 8GX, Tel. (0203) 465957. Farmed venison is also available in many branches of Waitrose and occasionally in Sainsbury's.

Fallow deer, although a woodland dweller like roe, was the deer of deer parks, kept at my lord's pleasure and very handsome in the herd with their distinctive dappled coats. The young animals, fawn in their first year then, if male, prickets with a single straight horn in their second year, were culled in winter to keep numbers stable. They make fine eating; I used to get four or five beasts a year from Buckland near Faringdon; we hung, and butchered them for our freezer dishes, boning out the loin and best end as fillet for our dinner parties.

---

illustrated overleaf: Roast Venison with Baked Pears and Linganberries and False Grand Veneur Sauce (see page 154), Drambuie-Flamed Venison Kebabs (see page 157), Venison with Vermouth and Cream (see page 156)

Roe deer are the smallest of the three, have the finest flavoured meat, which it is a pity to marinate when young, and tend to be the gourmet's choice. The muntjac, commonly known as pig deer, is smaller again, has become feral in this country and can do a lot of damage to crops. It can, as vermin, be shot at any time (but *not* with a shotgun). It also makes very good eating when young though, of course, with all these very differently sized beasts, you will have to adapt the recipes, varying timings and amounts.

But with all deer it is the feeding, tasty heather, beechmast and acorns etc. and the beast's condition that count and any fine fat deer with a bit of suet around the kidneys will eat well.

Venison is a dark, close-textured meat without much fat, and what there is should be firm and white; if in prime condition and a prime cut, such as haunch, loin and best end, it is best served rare when it will be juicy and tender. The less prime cuts of neck, shoulder and shin need long and very gentle cooking and are often marinated. I do not believe marinating has any great tenderising as opposed to flavouring effect under about 4 days, so give it time if you expect to change the texture.

The meat and liver of rutting beasts is not to be recommended.

Hanging allows the meat tissues to change and tenderise; allow about 5–6 days for a small beast in warm weather but up to 3 weeks for a large beast in cold weather; see hanging game for further details (p. 15). Larding, by sewing in strips of pork fat with a larding needle or by my simple method (p. 17) is necessary for red and fallow roasting joints though roe in summer and autumn does not need it. It's not difficult to do and is a rather satisfying technique.

Venison liver is excellent so slice and fry it lightly and serve when only just pink. Kidneys can be used on mushroom caps, added to civets or as part of a tasty fry up when the beast is cut up. Venison Stroganoff with all the best scraps is also excellent. Venison should always be served on very hot plates, for the fat congeals at a high temperature. It used to be usual to have fresh, hot plates for second helpings.

Fillet of Venison with Sweet Red Pepper Sauce

I'm always trying to evolve recipes where all the work and sauce making can be done ahead so the home entertainer has no last-minute time-consuming work to adjust flavours and finish the dish. This rich, full-flavoured sauce, thickened with a purée of red peppers, can be served with roast venison, steaks, medallions, kebabs or a saddle as well as with this fillet of boned-out loin, roasted whole.

Ingredients   *Serves 4–6*
1½–2 lb (675–900 g) trimmed fillet of
   venison
8–10 thin rashers streaky bacon
2 tbs olive oil
1½ oz (35 g) butter (preferably clarified)
salt and pepper

Marinade

1 small onion, chopped
1 shallot, chopped
1 bay leaf
1 sprig thyme
1 clove
2 parsley stalks
½ stick cinnamon
4 fl oz (100 ml) red wine vinegar
2 tbs olive oil

Red Pepper Purée

2 sweet red peppers
1 oz (25 g) butter
2 tbs marinade liquid from above
salt and pepper

Sauce

1 oz (25 g) butter
1 tbs olive oil
all lean scraps and trimming of venison
1 small onion, chopped
1 small carrot, chopped
1 shallot, chopped
1 teasp sugar
¼ pt (150 ml) red wine
¾ pt (450 ml) venison or game stock
vegetables and bits from marinade above
salt and pepper

Marinade. Combine all the marinade ingredients, bring to the boil and cook for 5 minutes. Strain through a sieve (keep the bits for the sauce), let it get cold then pour over the trimmed and tied fillet and marinate for 2–4 hours, turning frequently.

Sauce. Heat the butter and oil in a saucepan and add the venison scraps, onion, carrot, shallot and sugar; fry gently to a good brown, then add the wine and boil away completely until the mixture is frying again. Add the stock, all the bits from the marinade (setting aside the liquid) and a light seasoning of salt and pepper. Bring to the boil and simmer gently, uncovered, for about 2 hours until reduced to under ½ pt (300 ml), skimming from time to time. Strain carefully, pressing all the bits in the sieve to expel the juices. It can be made ahead and reheated or kept warm until required.

Red Pepper Purée. Melt the butter in a heavy pan and add the deseeded, quartered red peppers; season lightly, cover and cook gently for 25–30 minutes until tender; then remove the lid, add 2 tablespoonfuls of the marinade liquid and cook until reduced and thick. Purée and sieve the mixture. Add enough of this purée to the prepared sauce to thicken it lightly and flavour it sufficiently. Keep warm.

The Fillet. Remove the fillet from the marinade, pat dry and season lightly with pepper only. Heat the (preferably clarified) butter and oil in a roasting tin and brown the fillet on all sides; cover with thin slices of streaky bacon and roast in a hot oven (450°F/230°C/Gas 8) for 12–20 minutes, depending on the thickness of the fillet.

Remove the fillet to rest and keep warm in a food warmer or oven set below 170°F/ 75°C. Pour off the fat, add a little of the remaining marinade to the pan juices and boil up, stirring in all brown crusting bits. Strain enough of this into the prepared sauce to sharpen it; check the seasoning and serve in a sauceboat with the carved fillet.

Suggested Wine. Big red.

Roast Venison with Baked Pears and Linganberries and False Grand Veneur Sauce

This is suitable for a saddle of roe or young fallow or for a piece of farmed venison. The latter, though it does not really taste quite like venison to those who know, is nevertheless delicious with a tender, fine texture and for venison, a delicate but attractive taste.

I don't always marinate but if you wish to, use the first or second of the basic marinades (p. 24).

In preparing this with various differently sized pieces, I have discovered what nonsense the 'So many minutes to the pound' way of judging the timing is. Instead, look at the size, shape and density of the joint, a solid round or triangular pelvic joint taking proportionally longer than a long loin or saddle. If there is a bone running though it, it will conduct the heat to the centre quicker.

Judge the thickness and test it as it cooks. A spongy touch under your finger means it's still underdone; once it feels more resistant, insert a skewer to the centre and then test it against the delicate skin of your wrist; if it's cold, it's still not cooked; if just warm, it's rare; if hot, it's well done. Chefs test the skewer on their chin but you could brand yourself for life if the meat were over-cooked!

Red and fallow can be very rare like roast beef if you like that, but I think roe, being paler meat, should be cooked a bit more, perhaps like pink lamb though, like lamb, it's good pink or well done. Allow the meat to rest for 30 minutes or so before carving to relax the tissues and allow the juices to spread back through the joint. Set where the temperature cannot rise above 170°F/75°C so the meat cannot go on cooking; but realise the meat will continue to cook with its own heat while it rests so take it out still squidgy if you want it pink.

A Timing Guide

30 minutes for a 4 lb (1.8 kg) saddle of roe e.g. 6–8 minutes to the pound

35–40 minutes for a 4 lb (1.8 kg) saddle of fallow e.g. 9–10 minutes to the pound

45–50 minutes for a 2 lb (900 g) piece of solid pelvic joint e.g. 22–25 minutes to the pound

1¼–1½ hours for a 5 lb (2.25 kg) haunch of roe or fallow e.g. 15–18 minutes to the pound

In my experience, therefore, somewhere between 6–25 minutes to the pound, depending on the joint, cut and poundage.

This sauce, which gets away without all the complicated reductions and preparations of a classic espagnole, poivrade or grand veneur, still has nice complex flavours and you can easily change it to the sauce of your choice by one of these methods: finish with more spices, gingernuts and cream for a German-style sauce; with eau-de-vie de poire and cinnamon for an Alsace style, or cream, paprika and maraschino cherries for an Italian style; see also the sauce for wild boar (p. 180).

The pears are a classic accompaniment for venison on the continent, especially with a little spoonful of linganberry preserve in the centre of each. Failing linganberry, use cranberry preserve or fresh cooked cranberries.

These cuts of venison are expensive and to get the best from them, it's worth taking the trouble to lard the joint with little strips of fat (p. 17).

Ingredients

3–6 lb (1.35–2.7 kg) saddle of roe or
fallow
2–4 oz (50–100 g) pork back-fat or
smoked spek or bacon fat for larding the
joint (not absolutely necessary but it
keeps it lubricated if dry)
sheet pork back-fat to cover joint (optional)
2–3 tbs oil
2 oz (50 g) butter
6–8 tbs port or red wine
strip lemon rind
1–2 teasp plain flour
¼–½ pt (150–300 ml) good stock
1 teasp Spiced Grape (p. 199) or redcurrant
jelly
a little spiced or fruit vinegar
6–8 peppercorns, crushed
salt

Mirepoix

1 stick celery, diced
1 onion, diced
1 carrot, diced
1 tbs oil
2 juniper berries
½ bay leaf
sprig thyme
a few mushroom stalks or dried
mushrooms

Baked Pears

4–6 pears
3–4 tbs Demerara sugar
2–3 tbs brandy
¼–½ jar linganberry conserve, cranberries
or Spiced Grape or redcurrant jelly

Trim all skin, sinew and bluish membrane from the saddle so only the exposed meat is left. Marinate for 1–2 days if you wish. Lard the joint using a larding needle or the frozen strip method (p. 17) and strips of pork fat. Rub with oil and tie a piece of pork back-fat or buttered Bakewell paper over the top of the joint. Bring the meat to room temperature before roasting.

Mirepoix. Soften the celery, onion and carrot in the oil, adding in the remaining ingredients. Turn into a roasting pan and set the venison on the bed of vegetables. Boil together the butter, wine and lemon zest for about 5 minutes and have ready to baste the joint as required (you could use spoonfuls of marinade). Roast the joint in a very hot oven (475°F/240°C/Gas 9) for 15–20 minutes, basting once; then lower the temperature to moderately hot (375°F/190°C/Gas 5) and continue cooking, basting frequently with the butter and port or wine mixture and adding a little more wine, stock or water if the pan juices caramelise too much; remove Bakewell paper for last 20 minutes.

Once done, remove and rest the joint for 20–50 minutes in a food warmer or oven set below 170°F/75°C. Add the flour to the pan (having poured off excess fat), stir in to take up the fat then, off the stove, add the stock and bring to the boil, stirring in all the brown flavoursome caramelised bits. Add the jelly and a few drops of vinegar, reduce well and add the crushed peppercorns for the last few minutes. Strain, pressing the debris well and serve in a gravy boat.

Baked Pears and Linganberries. Peel, halve and core the pears, set in a baking dish and scatter with sugar. Pour brandy into the hollow centre of each and bake in a moderately hot oven (375°F/190°C/Gas 5) for 30–45 minutes; this can also be cooked under the grill.

Serve with a teaspoonful of linganberry conserve or Cranberry Sauce (p. 204) or Spiced Grape (p. 199) or redcurrant jelly in the centre of each.

Suggested Wine. Big red or big white.

Venison with Vermouth and Cream

You can make this with the whole tender haunch or just use the sauce for a couple of steaks cut from the saddle or haunch, or for strips of tender meat cooked like a stroganoff. Good venison should be served rare but rest the joint (see p. 29) for 30–45 minutes to distribute the pink and relax the meat before carving; do not forget it continues to cook a little as it rests. The lovage in this is good so use it in preference to celery if you can.

Ingredients

Steaks serve 2
Haunch serves 8–10

2 × 4–6 oz (100–175 g) haunch steaks
  of red or fallow deer, cut ¾–1 inch
  (2–2.5 cm) thick
or
5–6 lb (2.25–2.7 kg) haunch of roe or
  piece of fallow deer
butter and/or oil for cooking

Sauce for 2 steaks
1 shallot, very finely chopped
½ small carrot, very finely chopped
1 lovage leaf or ¼ stick celery, very finely
  chopped
3 fl oz (75 ml) white wine
3 tbs dry vermouth (Noilly Prat for choice)
4 fl oz (100 ml) double cream or crème
  fraîche
a little fresh or pinch dried tarragon
salt and pepper or peppermill mixture

Sauce for the Haunch
2–3 shallots, finely chopped
2 carrots, finely chopped
10 fl oz (300 ml) white wine
4 fl oz (100 ml) dry vermouth (Noilly Prat
  for choice)
2–3 lovage leaves or celery leaves, finely
  chopped
2 teasp chopped fresh or ¼ teasp dried
  tarragon
10 fl oz (300 ml) double cream or crème
  fraîche
potato flour or arrowroot for thickening
  (optional)
salt and pepper or peppermill mixture

You can marinate the haunch in the wine and finely chopped vegetables from the sauce if you wish but I prefer not to if it's young and tender.

To Cook the Venison Steaks. Heat the butter and oil in a sauté pan. Season the steaks and sauté on both sides; add the shallots, carrot and shredded lovage or finely chopped celery and cook gently until softened; add the wine and vermouth, season lightly, cover and simmer for 4–5 minutes, depending on the thickness, until the steaks are done but still slightly squishy. Remove them and keep warm. Boil down the pan juices until almost reduced away before adding the cream and tarragon. Reduce again until of a nice coating consistency. Slice the steaks into even slices. Spoon some sauce on to each plate and dress the venison on top of the sauce. Garnish with tarragon and serve at once.

To Cook the Haunch of Venison. Take the joint of venison, pat it dry if you have marinated it, then brown it all over in the hot butter or oil. Set it, uncovered, in a generous-sized roasting pan, then soften the vegetables gently in the fat in the pan; pour over the meat, add the wine and vermouth, the herbs and a very little light seasoning. Set a meat roasting thermometer into the thickest part of the meat, not touching a bone, if you wish. Cook in a hot oven (400°F/200°C/Gas 6), allowing 15–20 minutes per pound and basting every 20 minutes or so. Lower the temperature to moderately hot (375°F/190°C/Gas 5) after 30 minutes. Twenty minutes or so before it's done, add the cream to the pan. By the time it has finished cooking, you should have a good tasty sauce. Remove the meat (thermometer reading 150°F/65°C) and rest at under 170°F/75°C for 30–45 minutes. If the sauce is too thin, boil it down or you can thicken it with a little potato flour or arrowroot.

Always serve venison on very hot plates for the fat congeals at a high temperature.

Suggested Wine. Best red.

Drambuie-Flamed Venison Kebabs

Chefs like the prime cuts for their *à la carte* restaurant work so the price is forced up and a cut like saddle is pretty pricey. Looking for an alternative, I have turned to trimmings of tender haunch steak, cut into cubes and kebabbed. When tender, venison can be served very rare. Because it can be dry, I use a Chinese method of marinating with soy and cornflour which puts a protective velvet coating on the meat. Because household grills don't really get very hot and most of us don't cook much over charcoal, I have turned to cooking the kebabs (speared on wooden *saté* sticks) in a heavy, very hot frying pan. The result is absolutely excellent, crispy brown on the outside and tender, rosy and juicy in the centre. The Drambuie, if you use it, is an excellent flavour with venison and helps to brown the meat.

Ingredients   *Serves 4–6*

allow 4–6 oz (100–175 g) lean, trimmed haunch of young venison per person (1–2½ lbs)
4–5 tbs Drambuie
1 shallot, finely chopped
6 tbs olive oil

1 teasp cornflour
1 teasp dark soy sauce
½ lemon
salt and plenty of pepper or peppermill mixture
watercress to garnish

Cut the meat into generous cubes and marinate for 2–3 hours with 2–3 tbs of the Drambuie, the shallot, 2 tbs oil and plenty of seasoning. Add the cornflour and soy sauce and stir round in one direction until it feels sticky; thread the meat on to 4–6 wooden skewers and fry in a heavy frying pan in about 4 tbs of very hot oil. Cook very quickly (about 1 minute each side), turning once. Pour off the fat, add 1–2 tbs Drambuie and flame, shaking the pan; extinguish the flames with a squeeze of lemon.

You might serve on a bed of pilau rice, garnished with watercress, and accompanied by salad leaves or perhaps with a creamy purée of celeriac and watercress or sweet potato. Alternatively, serve on a salad, but you must serve very quickly as venison needs to be eaten good and hot.

The meat should be crispy brown on the outside but still pink in the middle. Alternatively, you can grill them under a very hot pre-heated grill for about 2–3 minutes on each side, or of course over charcoal (most household grills will not heat sufficiently for really quick, short cooking). To flame, lay the kebabs in a hot pan, pour over the Drambuie, heat and ignite.

Suggested Wine. It rather depends on the occasion. Finest claret would be wasted on a barbecue, but the quality of the dish merits a good red wine of character.

Venison Steaks with Farthinghoe Sauce

The boned-out saddle is the prime cut of venison. Once trimmed of skin, sinew and bone it can be cut into fine medallions or steaks and be shown a hot pan for the merest moment to be pink and rare as the best dark game meat should be. You can also roast it fiercely and briefly to pink perfection like a fillet. Most chefs' sauces are intense reductions and can be lipstickingly good but for those with less time to spend in the kitchen, this simple sweet sauce flavoured with port and cinnamon and sharpened with lemon and based on one by Francatelli, chef to Queen Victoria, has the sweet touch that enhances this sort of game so admirably. I don't often marinate young roe, or fallow or, if I do, it's only briefly and lightly for I feel it's a pity to tamper unnecessarily with the flavour; but you may well wish to marinate red deer venison for some time before cooking, depending on whether it comes from farm or hill. Remember to remove and dry most carefully before cooking.

Ingredients   *Serves 4–6*

a complete best end and/or loin of venison,
    cut in one piece (we use young fallow or
    roe)
2 tbs olive oil
2–3 tbs port, wine or stock

Sauce
1 lemon
5 good tbs redcurrant jelly
2 tbs port
½ stick cinnamon
2 oz (50 g) butter

Bone out the meat carefully as for noisette so it is in one piece lengthways. Now remove every vestige of skin and fat so you are only left the 'noix' of meat. Cut this fillet into steaks ½–¾ inch (1.5–2 cm) thick and season with pepper. Bat out gently.

Prepare the Sauce. Take julienne strips from half the lemon, place in plenty of cold water in a saucepan, bring to the boil and blanch for 5–10 minutes until no longer bitter; drain and refresh under the cold tap. Gently melt and heat the jelly, port, cinnamon and thinly pared lemon rind from the remaining half lemon. Simmer for 5–10 minutes then add the juice of half a lemon and whisk in the butter. When the butter has melted, strain the sauce into a sauceboat and add the julienne strips of lemon rind. Keep warm.

To Cook the Steaks. Heat a little oil in a frying pan until very hot and then cook the venison steaks very fast for about 1½–2 minutes on each side. Dish up on a heated dish, add port, wine or stock to the pan and swirl round to remove the tasty juices and pour over steaks. Serve the sauce separately.

Try serving with a chestnut or celeriac and potato purée, or Sweet Red Cabbage (p. 207); or with a crunchy salad dressed with walnut oil to follow it.

Suggested Wine. Big red, though I might be tempted occasionally to try a big white with lots of flavour and power, like a Rhône or Rioja, or even a rich Gewürztraminer from Alsace or a Spätlese from the Palatinate.

Sauté of Venison with Mushroom and Wild Cherry

This is really a Chinese style stir-fry. It is good done with farmed venison which, though very tender, is sometimes a bit flabby in texture and lacking in flavour. It remains meltingly tender and the sauce has good complex sweet-sour flavours. The wild cherries, available from Italian delicatessen, are a quite wonderful flavouring and an opened tin will keep in the fridge indefinitely. All may be left prepared, then the dish only takes moments to cook in the wok though it can be done in a heavy frying pan if necessary.

Ingredients

Serves 4–6

1½–2 lb (675–900 g) tender venison, cut from the haunch or loin
3–4 tbs oil
2–3 spring onions or 1 onion
2–3 small dried chillies (optional)
1 clove garlic, finely chopped (optional)
2 slices ginger, finely chopped (optional)
8 oz (225 g) button mushrooms, quartered
2–3 tbs wild cherries in syrup (Amarena Fabbri) or Spiced Cherries (p. 201) or 1 tbs Spiced Grape Jelly (p. 199)
salt and pepper

Sauce

1 tbs Demerara sugar
1 tbs herb vinegar
1 pt (600 ml) good stock
1 clove garlic
sprig thyme
2–3 stalks parsley
a few mushroom stalks
any venison scraps
1–2 teasp Spiced Grape Jelly (p. 199) or redcurrant jelly

To Thicken

1 tbs potato flour
1 tbs dark soy sauce
1 teasp tomato purée

Marinade

1 teasp salt
½ teasp sugar
1 teasp sherry
2 teasp dark soy sauce
a very little grated lemon or orange rind
plenty of pepper or peppermill mixture
1 teasp cornflour

The Sauce. Start with this. Sprinkle the sugar over the base of a heavy frying pan and heat until the sugar melts and turns to brown caramel; at once add the vinegar and some of the stock. Boil up, add the remaining ingredients and simmer down gently, tossing in the venison scraps as you trim the meat and skimming if necessary. Reduce to about 6–8 fl oz (175–225 ml) of good, strong flavoured sauce and strain, pressing the debris well.

To Cook the Venison. Meanwhile trim the meat of every vestige of skin, gristle and connective tissue and cut, across the grain, into little oblongs, roughly 1 × ½ × ½ inches (2 ×

1×1 cm). Mix these with all the marinade ingredients, stirring round well and leave for 15 minutes or more until ready to cook.

Cut the spring onions into thin slanting slices or the onion in half, then into lengthways slices. Prepare and have ready all other ingredients. Mix the potato flour with the soy, tomato purée and a tablespoon or so of cold water.

Heat the wok or heavy frying pan, add 2–3 tbs oil and, once smoking hot, add half the meat; stir-fry, tossing around in the pan continuously for 2–3 minutes until just browning and the meat no longer feels springy but is still just pink inside. Remove, reheat the wok or pan, add more oil if necessary and cook the remaining meat; remove, add the remaining oil and heat; add spring onions, chilli if used, garlic and ginger if used; stir round and quickly add the mushrooms; stir-fry them for about 1 minute then add the sauce; stir and add the thickening ingredients and the wild cherries. Bring to the boil, stirring (fish out the chillies if you wish); return the meat and its juices and simmer for a few moments until the sauce thickens. Correct the seasoning.

Serve with noodles, rice, Burghal Pilau (p. 212) or Buckwheat Noodles (p. 120). It can also be kept warm or reheated but the venison should not go on cooking.

Suggested Wine. Big or French provincial red.

Venison Casserole with Spiced Vinegar and Jelly

A rich dark stew made of the marinated lesser cuts, such as shoulder, is a popular and delicious dish, good for buffets and large parties. Of course it's extra good if you use meat from the haunch. I adjust the length of time the meat is marinated in the tenderising vinegar and wine mixture, depending on its age and quality and like to balance the flavour by the addition of some jelly; I favour spiced grape or quince but redcurrant, blackcurrant or even marmalade will do well. This is a dish which benefits by being cooked one day and re-heated and eaten the next.

Ingredients

Serves 4–6

2½–3 lb (1.15–1.35 kg) boned venison
  shoulder
2–4 oz (50–100 g) thick-cut smoked
  streaky bacon
2–4 tbs dripping, olive or sunflower oil
2 onions, sliced
2 carrots, sliced
1 stick celery
1 oz (25 g) seasoned flour
½–¾ pt (300–450 ml) game stock
a generous bouquet garni of parsley stalks,
  bay leaf, thyme, mint and basil

bunch of bacon rinds or piece of pork skin
  (optional)
8 oz (225 g) mushrooms
extra spiced vinegar, if necessary
extra jelly, if necessary
½–2 teasp potato flour, if necessary
Hazelnut Forcemeat Balls (p. 191)
  (optional)
salt and pepper

Marinade

1 tbs olive oil	1 small onion, chopped
2 tbs jelly or jam	1 small carrot, diced
3 fl oz (75 ml) spiced vinegar or shallot, garlic or cider vinegar	1 stick celery, diced
	4–6 bruised juniper or allspice berries
8 fl oz (225 ml) goodish red wine	a little fresh or dried thyme and marjoram
2 fl oz (50 ml) mushroom ketchup	salt and pepper

Cube up the meat into generous 1–1½ inch (2–4 cm) cubes, removing gristle and sinew. Place the meat in a glass or earthenware bowl, add seasoning and the olive oil for the marinade and mix well. Melt the jelly in a little of the vinegar, mix with all the remaining marinade ingredients and pour over the meat. Marinate young roe and fallow for 1–2 days, young red deer for 2–4 days and old venison for 4–5 days in a cool larder or fridge. Stir once a day. Drain well from the marinade in a colander and squeeze out in your hands.

Cut the bacon into lardons and gently sauté, until lightly browned, in the oil in a wide frying pan and remove to a casserole; then fry the onion to a good brown and remove; fry the carrot and celery briefly and remove. Now fry the meat, in batches, to a good brown, using more fat or oil if necessary. Turn into the casserole, sprinkle the flour over the meat and toss well; de-glaze the frying pan with a little stock, stirring off all brown tasty bits and add to the casserole. Now turn the marinade into the frying pan and bring to the boil; boil fast for several minutes then skim the marinade of all foamy scum before adding it to the casserole. Add stock to come level with the meat, tuck in the bouquet garni and bacon rinds, tied in a bundle, or pork skin if used, (these add gelatine and texture to the sauce and are all the better for being blanched first). Sauté the mushrooms, left whole, halved or quartered depending on size, in a little oil and add to the casserole. Cover closely and cook gently in a slow oven (300°F/150°C/Gas 2) for 2–6 hours or until tender. Pour off and boil down the liquid if too copious. De-grease, thicken with a little potato flour mixed with cold water if necessary, correct the seasoning and add a little vinegar and jelly to rectify the flavour if desired. Or leave until the next day to de-grease, re-heat and finish.

Hazelnut Forcemeat Balls (p. 191) can be added for the last half hour or just served around the dish. Fast Puff Pastry (p. 182) diamonds can accompany the casserole or it can be turned into a wonderful Venison Pie if topped with pastry. You could serve the casserole with Baked Brown and Wild Rice (p. 195), Sweet Red Cabbage (p. 207) or Sweet Potato Purée (p. 208).

Suggested Wine. Big red.

Bobotie of Venison (or other game)

This lightly spiced dish of minced venison or mutton with a sweet and sour element is often used in Africa to finish up roast game. An early recipe I found for it intrigued me by using rolled up lemon leaves as a flavouring, tucked into the mixture like little cigarettes; although the two recipes given me by friends in South Africa and Zimbabwe did not have this little refinement, I longed to try it but never did until one day I discovered fresh lime leaves sold in a

Chinese shop. They can be kept in the freezer and add a wonderful Thai flavour to food and a subtle fragrance to this dish and they appeal to me enormously though the dish is delicious even without them.

Use left-over roast venison or any other game (goose breast that you despair of will sometimes surrender to this recipe!), cooked pheasant, rabbit and pigeon alone or mixed is excellent or use fresh minced venison from farmed venison, though you will need to cook the meat partially before pouring over the custard. It's also a useful dish for lamb or beef.

Ingredients   *Serves 4–6*

- 1 lb (450 g) cooked minced venison
- 1 inch (2.5 cm) thick slice of bread, crusts removed, or about 4 oz (100 g) freshish breadcrumbs
- a little milk
- 2 medium onions, roughly chopped
- 2 tbs oil or fat
- 1–2 cloves garlic, finely chopped
- 1 tbs good curry paste (I use Sharwoods concentrated mild curry paste) or you could use curry powder, as long as it's good and fresh

- 1 teasp ground turmeric
- 1 teasp ground ginger
- 1 teasp cumin seed
- 1 tbs apricot jam (I use one of our spiced jellies)
- 2 tbs vinegar (spiced if available)
- 2 tbs nuts (I use half flaked almonds, half sunflower seeds)
- 2 tbs sultanas, currants, chopped apple or banana
- 1 teasp salt

Topping
- 4–6 lime, lemon or fresh bay leaves (optional)
- 2 eggs, whisked
- ½ pt (300 ml) milk

Moisten the bread in a little milk.

Soften the onion in the oil and fry until browning; add the garlic, curry and spices, fry gently for a few moments then add the meat and fry a little (if you use raw meat, fry it until sealed and browning) then add jam, vinegar, nuts, fruit and salt, balancing the sweet, sour and spicy elements to your satisfaction. Squeeze the breadcrumbs dry if necessary and add in.

Butter a 2 pt (1.2 l) pie dish and turn the mixture into it, pressing down lightly only. Roll the lime, lemon or bay leaves, if used, into slim pencils and stick upright in the mixture. Whisk the egg and milk and pour this custard over the mixture. It should come to about ¾ the depth of the meat. Bake in a moderate oven (350°F/180°C/Gas 4) for 35–45 minutes until lightly browned and the custard has set. It is best covered for the first 10 minutes or so if the oven (such as a convection) tends to dry things out. If cooked for too long, the eggs will of course curdle and the mixture go a bit watery so, with raw mince, cook it well covered before pouring the custard over.

Serve Bobotie with rice if you wish. I also like it cold, cut in slices with salads and pickles so try it with Mulberry Conserve (p. 201) or Redcurrant and Green Peppercorn Jelly (p. 199).

Suggested Wine. Big red, probably a South African Cabernet Sauvignon or Pinotage.

Civet of Venison

A nice simple rich braise where the meat is marinated then just packed into a pot to slow cook so the juice gets masses of flavour from the meat. To make it go further, add more vegetable, flour and stock.

Ingredients

2–3 lb (900 g–1.35 kg) braising venison (shoulder)
3 oz (75 g) fresh pork skin or bacon rinds
4 oz (100 g) thick-cut smoked streaky bacon
1–2 oz (25–50 g) plain flour
up to ½ pt (300 ml) game stock
1–2 anchovy fillets, chopped or anchovy paste
Spiced Grape (p. 199) or redcurrant jelly
salt and pepper

To Finish

2–3 tbs chopped parsley
a little grated lemon rind

Marinade   *Serves 4–6*

2 large onions, sliced
2–3 carrots, sliced
1 stick celery, sliced
2 cloves garlic, finely chopped
1 strip thin orange peel
3 tbs brandy
3 tbs olive oil
2 teasp black treacle
2 tbs spiced or wine vinegar
¼ pt (150 ml) red wine
bouquet garni of thyme, parsley stalks, bay leaf and 3 juniper berries
salt and pepper

Cut the meat into generous cubes and place in a large bowl with all the marinade ingredients; marinate for 5–6 hours, overnight or longer.

Boil the pork skin or bacon rinds in plenty of water for ½ hour or so; drain, rinse and cut into tiny pieces (so no one asks what they are or says they don't like them!). Cut the streaky bacon into lardons and fry gently until brown. Toss the meat in the flour and pack all into a wide casserole, preferably earthenware. Add the marinade and stock not quite to cover, season, add the anchovy and stir well. Cover with tinfoil and lid and cook in a very slow oven (250°F/130°C/Gas 1) for from 2½–5 hours, depending on the meat. Once tender, pour off and reduce the sauce if too copious, correct the seasoning and the flavour with jelly, vinegar and black treacle.

Serve scattered with parsley and lemon accompanied by noodles, rice, or Spätzle (p. 210).

Suggested Wine. Big red.

Indian Style Venison in Yoghurt and Spices

There are some very high-class Indian dishes made with game. In this one, the meat is marinated in yoghurt and spices which act as tenderisers. It's not hot though you can make it so, if you wish, by adding chillies or more cayenne; but it has a lovely aromatic spiciness and a little rosewater is added for a truly oriental fragrance. You can use good braising venison or just stewing meat, especially shin, where the long slow cooking turns the interconnective tissue to rich savour; or try it with other game such as hare, pheasant or rabbit. It's very good for a large party, heats up well and of course it freezes well.

Ingredients
Serves 4–6

2 lb (900 g) braising, casserole or stewing venison
2–3 oz (50–75 g) butter, ghee or oil
8 oz (225 g) onions
1 tbs coriander seeds
½ teasp cumin seeds
½ teasp ground cinnamon
⅛ teasp ground cloves
⅛ teasp ground mace

3–4 cloves garlic
1–2 inch (2.5–5 cm) piece ginger, skinned
6–8 fl oz (150–225 ml) stock or water
1 tbs raisins
6 almonds
2 tbs rosewater
1½ teasp salt
pepper to taste
1 teasp paprika
1 teasp salt

Marinade
½ pt (300 ml) natural yoghurt
¼–½ teasp cayenne pepper
juice 1 lemon
1 tbs grated ginger
1 onion, finely chopped

Garnish (optional)
½ lb (225 g) onions, cut into rings and fried until brown and crisp in oil or fat

Cut the meat into generous cubes, discarding any gristle and tendon. Mix the marinade ingredients and combine with the meat; leave to marinate in the cool overnight or for 1–4 days, depending on the quality of the meat and your mood!

Lift the meat from the marinade and drain on a sieve whilst you prepare everything.

Heat the butter in a large, heavy frying pan. Process the onions until very finely chopped, add to the butter and fry gently for 5–10 minutes until soft. Roast the coriander and cumin seeds in a heavy, dry pan until smelling roasted and just darkening in colour. Turn into a mortar and pound; mix with the cinnamon, cloves and mace. Process the garlic and ginger to a pulp and add the stock. Once the onions are soft, turn up the heat and gradually add the meat, cube by cube, turning them over and over in the onion mixture and letting the yoghurt coating fry away. Scatter over the spices as the meat fries and let them fry too. Now start to add the remaining yoghurt marinade, spoonful by spoonful, stirring and frying. Finally aromatise with the garlic, ginger and stock mixture. Add in the raisins. Pound or process the almonds, gradually adding in the rosewater and also add this mixture to the meat. Season with salt and pepper. Turn into a casserole (you may have had to put some of the meat into the casserole already if it would not all fit in the frying pan), bring to the boil and seal the lid on very tightly (use a sheet of tinfoil under the lid). Cook in a slow oven (300°F/150°C/Gas 2) for 1½–4 hours until tender, depending on the quality of the meat. You can use the Oh-So-Slow technique (p. 96) for a very long, slow gentle cook which will ensure wonderfully tender meat if you are in doubt about the quality of the meat.

If you use the garnishing onions, fry them to a crisp brown. Correct the seasoning, if necessary, and scatter with the onion. Serve with rice, Burghal Pilau (p. 212), noodles or Spätzle (p. 210) and accompanied perhaps by Lentils with Coconut Cream (p. 206), dahl, Caribbean Sweet Potato Purée (p. 208), Sweet Red Cabbage (p. 207) or perhaps with a bright green crisp vegetable like beans or courgettes.

Suggested Wine. Light or French provincial red or big white.

Rabbit

Once to be seen scuttering in all directions from every hedgerow and into every bank and wood, the rabbit has now made something of a return after the devastation of myxomatosis. Rabbit makes a splendid dish and lends itself to many flavours but heed Meg Dod's excellent advice that 'rabbit cannot be too slowly boiled'. Note also the gallant Major Pollard who, in his *Sportsman's Cookery Book* in 1926 states that 'nature built him for a casserole'. Rabbit (*Lepus caniculus*) is a healthy fatless meat, close-textured and dense so either simmer very gently in a rich lubricating sauce or cook very fast and lightly as in the Fillets of Rabbit.

To Age Rabbit. Young rabbit, rarely weighing more than 3 lb (1.35 kg) undressed, is plump, has smooth sharp claws, soft ears that tear and a soft coat. Old rabbits are usually larger with greying coats, long rough claws and tough ears.

Choose those with bright eyes, with no suggestion of swelling around the eyes nor any balding patches which could show a touch of myxomatosis. Rabbit should be paunched in the field as it is shot; this is not essential as the French don't gut until skinning and preparing it, though you may have to discard the thin belly skin which can go greenish. Press out pellets, slit the stomach skin and carefully remove all the innards except for liver (carefully detach the green gall bladder without breaking it) and kidneys. The kidneys should have a little white fat around them.

Rabbit should not be hung long and 2–4 days is enough or the flavour will get rather strong.

To Skin a Rabbit. Cut off all the paws, peel the skin down each back leg, working from the stomach cut. Then hang the rabbit up again and draw off the skin like a child's jumper; either carefully skin the head or, more usually these days, cut it off. Remove heart, liver and kidneys from inside the rabbit (check gall sack was removed) and set aside. The liver is quite delicious and several make a lovely pâté. The heart, liver and kidney make a good breakfast or supper dish served on toast or on a large mushroom cap.

Sometimes rabbit is soaked in salted water for an hour or so but I don't like this as it becomes horrid and slimy when wet and I feel it toughens it; but if you feel it is rather an old strong flavoured buck, do by all means soak then marinate or even simmer for 2–3 minutes and drain.

To Joint a Rabbit. The back fillets can be removed from each side of the backbone and the tiny filet mignon from the under side of the back can be roasted or cooked in one piece; but the more usual division is to remove the front legs and then the back legs, following the curve of the pelvic bone and divide into 2–3 pieces. Then snip off the rib cage and any loose flaps of skin and divide the back into 4–5 pieces. This is best done, so as not to splinter the bone, by inserting the tip of a heavy knife between the backbone joints then tapping it sharply on the back of the blade to separate the bones.

Rabbit can be marinated in a red wine or white wine marinade, depending on the dish, or in a delicate olive oil and lemon juice mixture. Wild thyme, savory, tarragon and marjoram are all good herbs with rabbit, and juniper and mushroom have a good affinity.

Roast Rabbit with Spring Onion and Tarragon Sauce

In the introduction I rather steered you away from roasting rabbit but let me now say that when I get a young rabbit then I will roast it in this excellent way.

Ingredients

Serves 3–4

1 young rabbit, whole
2 oz (50 g) butter
4 rashers green or smoked streaky bacon, blanched if salty
2–3 spring onions

a little fresh or dried tarragon
6–8 tbs dry white wine
½–1 teasp flour
4–6 tbs cream
salt and pepper

Stuffing (optional)

6–8 good tbs dryish breadcrumbs
1 spring onion, finely chopped
2 tbs chopped parsley
a little chopped tarragon (or other herbs)
a little milk

1 egg
liver, heart and kidneys, diced and sautéed in a little butter
salt, pepper and nutmeg

Stuffing. Mix the breadcrumbs, onion and herbs and moisten with a little milk and the egg; stir in the diced and briefly sautéed heart, liver and kidney and a seasoning of salt, pepper and nutmeg.

Wipe out the rabbit, remove its head and season all over. Pack the stomach cavity with the stuffing and sew up or skewer (long *sate* skewers are very good for this), pulling the front legs back along the body. Spread with half the butter, lay in a roasting tin and cover with the bacon or a sheet of Bakewell paper. Slice the spring onion and soften in the rest of the butter in a small pan; add the tarragon and wine and boil together for 3–4 minutes until it forms an emulsified mixture. Roast the rabbit in a hot oven (425°F/220°C/Gas 7) for 20 minutes, basting with a spoonful or so of the mixture every 5–10 minutes. Remove the bacon after 20 minutes but leave it in the pan; baste again and sprinkle the rabbit with a little flour. Return to the oven for a further 20–25 minutes until well browned and cooked. Baste frequently with the pan juices and the last of the onion-wine mixture then with the cream, a couple of tablespoonfuls each time, until you have a thick rich goldenish sauce (add a little more wine or some water if it looks like burning or separating).

Remove the rabbit to a serving dish, stir all crusty bits into the sauce and smooth with the last of the cream; season if necessary and, if you wish, finish with further flavourings such as Norwegian cheese or Dijon mustard. Serve the sauce in a sauceboat. Carve the back of the rabbit lengthways and don't forget the stuffing.

Suggested Wine. French provincial red.

Rabbit with White Wine and Grapes

This is another lovely dish redolent of the French countryside. It contains many of the little tricks of creating and intensifying flavours, the browning, flaming and reducing the sauce before adding more and all these combine to make rabbit into something quite special. Wild rabbit may take an hour to cook but the timings here are for hutch-bred rabbit.

Ingredients *Serves 4–6*

1 rabbit
2 oz (50 g) butter
2 tbs eau-de-vie de marc or brandy
12 fl oz (350 ml) dry white wine
8 oz (225 g) little pickling onions
12 oz (375 g) large white grapes, peeled and de-seeded
6 fl oz (175 ml) crème fraîche or double cream
sprig fresh or good pinch dried thyme
a little freshly grated nutmeg
salt and pepper

Joint the rabbit into 10–12 pieces and season lightly. Peel the little onions, leaving the root base intact. Heat the butter in a sauté pan which will take all the pieces in one layer, add the rabbit and fry until golden on all sides, sprinkling over it the thyme leaves, stripped from their stalk, or dried thyme; add the onions and continue to fry, shaking the pan until the onions are golden. Add the eau-de-vie or brandy and flame, then add half the wine and a light seasoning of salt, pepper and nutmeg; half cover the pan and simmer for 30–40 minutes (remove the onions when they are done) or until the rabbit is tender, all the liquid has gone and the pieces are browning in the pan again. Remove the rabbit and keep warm. Add the remaining wine, de-glaze the pan and add in the peeled and de-seeded grapes; boil up once or twice to heat and cook them then remove to keep warm with the rabbit. Boil the wine down until reduced by about one third, then add in the cream and reduce again, whisking, until of coating consistency. Correct the seasoning and return the rabbit, onions and grapes to the pan. Heat through and dress on a warm serving dish.

Suggested Wine. French provincial red or modest white.

Rabbit in the Most Delicious Sauce

I find that wine, cream and *cèpe* mushrooms with a hint of lemon and mace make a most delicious sauce. Glynn Christian showed me how to boil up the mushrooms and add a little sherry to get the most intense flavour from them. Buy *cèpes* from a good delicatessen or Italian grocer (where they may be called 'porcini') and they keep for ages, adding much flavour to dishes. Ordinary mushrooms could be fried and added instead, but the flavour will be different. I also make this dish with milk instead of cream; but it can curdle so I just sieve it through muslin at the end.

Ingredients   *Serves 4*

1 rabbit
5–6 good bits (1 small packet) dried *cèpe*
  mushrooms
¼ pt (150 ml) water
2 tbs sherry
½ oz (12 g) flour
1 tbs oil

1 oz (25 g) butter
8 fl oz (225 ml) dry white wine
8 fl oz (225 ml) single or whipping cream
2 strips lemon rind (or zest)
good pinch mace
a little nutmeg
salt and pepper

First cover the dried pieces of *cèpe* mushrooms in water in a small saucepan. Leave to soak for a few minutes then simmer quite briskly until the mushrooms are soft and the water is well reduced; add the sherry and simmer again until only a little liquid is left.

Meanwhile, joint the rabbit into 9–10 pieces, trimming carefully and discarding the rib cage; wipe dry, season and toss in the flour. Heat the oil and butter in a heavy sauté or frying pan until the frothing starts to subside then sauté the rabbit pieces until golden on all sides. Sprinkle any remaining flour into the pan, shake well to absorb the butter then add the wine and boil up, shaking the pan vigorously until the sauce is smooth. Boil for a few moments before adding the cream, lemon zest, the pieces of *cèpe* mushroom and their liquid (watch for and exclude any sand at the bottom), mace, nutmeg and a light seasoning. Cover, turning into a casserole, if you are not using a sauté pan with a lid, and cook very gently ('Rabbit cannot boil too slowly') either in a slow oven (300°F/150°C/Gas 2) or on the stove for about 1–2 hours until the meat is tender. Remove the pieces of rabbit and keep warm. Boil the sauce down until rich and tasty, remove the lemon zest and correct the seasoning. Return the rabbit pieces and heat through.

Serve with a creamy Italian risotto, saffron rice, noodles or Spätzle (p. 210) and a green vegetable like broccoli, beans or courgettes.

Suggested Wine. Light red or big white.

Lapin en Gelée

If you use the back fillets of a rabbit with the Lime Butter Sauce (p. 170) or any other way you fancy, use up the legs by making this simple but tasty classic country dish from France. It's wonderfully fresh and healthy with none of the fat that goes into a rillette, another more luscious way of using up the legs. Serve it as a first course or as a light summer luncheon or supper dish with a salad and bread or new potatoes. The legs of 1 rabbit will serve 2 as a main course or 3–4 as a starter. A whole rabbit will do 4–6.

Ingredients   *Serves 4–6*

1 whole rabbit or the legs of two
½ pt (300 ml) dry white wine
a wide strip lemon rind with no white pith
2–3 oz (50–75 g) lean bacon, smoked or
  green
1–2 cloves garlic
2 shallots, finely chopped
8–10 peppercorns

2 sprigs or ½ teasp dried tarragon
2–3 sprigs chervil and parsley
3–4 good sprigs lemon thyme
2 large carrots (optional)
2 teasp gelatine
a little lemon juice, if necessary
salt and pepper

Cut the rabbit into small joints and marinate in the wine with the lemon rind, diced bacon (all fat removed), flattened but whole garlic, the finely chopped shallots, peppercorns, herbs and salt. Leave to marinate for 1–3 days (if you do this in a small earthenware casserole you can cook it in that too). Sprinkle the gelatine on to a little cold water or wine, leave to swell then add to the rabbit (you can, if you prefer, add a little gelatine at the end or cook a blanched pig's trotter with the rabbit). Cut wafer-thin lengthways slices of carrots, or take ribbons with a peeler, and cover the top of the rabbit, which should be just submerged in the marinade with them or press a disc of Bakewell paper on to the rabbit. Cover closely and cook in a very slow oven, preferably under 180°F/80°C/Gas 'S' for 6 hours or so until the rabbit is absolutely tender and comes easily off the bone. Strain off the liquid, through muslin if possible; it should be lovely and clear.

Pick the meat off the bones, leave in middling sized chunks and pack into a clean terrine. Taste the liquid, adjust the seasoning, add lemon juice if necessary and pour over the rabbit; leave until cold. It should only be set in the lightest of jellies and have a piquant herby flavour, the rabbit being as tender as butter.

Serve from the terrine or on a plate with herbs and good bread or with a salad.

Suggested Wine. Light red.

Lapin aux Pruneaux

A classic rich country dish from northern France and what a happy combination rabbit and prune are. Once again, this recipe shows how a touch of sweetness points up the flavour of game. Be sure to reduce the sauce until it is rich and tasty but don't boil the mustard. Marinate with a little oil, herbs and brandy for several hours if you wish.

Ingredients
Serves 4–6

1 young rabbit
4 oz (100 g) prunes
1 oz (25 g) plain flour
4 oz (100 g) thick-cut streaky bacon
2 small onions
2–3 tbs dripping or oil

½ pt (300 ml) beer
bouquet garni
1 clove garlic (lightly flattened)
1 tbs Dijon mustard
salt and pepper

Joint the rabbit. Soak the prunes if they are hard. Heat the dripping and sauté the drained, floured rabbit joints with the bacon cubes; remove to a casserole and add the quartered onions to the pan; fry until brown, sprinkling in the remaining flour and browning lightly. Draw off the stove and, when cooled a little, add the beer; boil up, whisking hard and pour over the rabbit to which you add the bouquet. Add garlic. Season and cook in a moderate oven (350°F/180°C/Gas 4) or simmer very gently on the stove for 1 hour. Add the drained, stoned prunes and cook for a further 30 minutes or until tender.

Remove the joints to a serving dish, boil down the juices if not rich and strong, then stir in the mustard, mixed with a little sauce, and pour over.

Suggested Wine. French provincial red.

Fillets of Rabbit with Lime Butter Sauce and Pink Pepper Berries

illustrated opposite

Chefs have recently raised rabbit from his pie or stew image and now serve him up in tender, lightly cooked morsels. How right they are because rabbit is succulent if lightly cooked when the protein in the meat has had no time to firm; once well cooked, rabbit, like most other game, can become a little too firm and dry. I find it intensely satisfying to remove the back fillets of rabbit; the bones are so fine and delicate and the tip of the filleting knife, wielded with precision, strips off the meat in a most rewarding way – do try it. I would only do it for a few people for it must be carefully cooked and quickly served. The legs can be used to make an excellent and delicious Lapin en Gelée (p. 168) to serve cold as a starter or as a light lunch dish while all the scraps and bones will make some good stock. The sauce is a *beurre blanc* but flavoured with lime and pink pepper berries.

Ingredients *Serves 2–4*

backs of 2 rabbits
1 oz (25 g) butter, preferably clarified
salt and pepper

Lime Butter Sauce with Pink Pepper Berries

3 tbs finely chopped shallot
4 tbs dry white wine
2–3 tbs white wine vinegar
1 lime

4 oz (100 g) unsalted best butter, diced
¼–½ teasp pink pepper berries
salt and pepper

With a sharp knife, remove both the long fillets of meat running along the back of the rabbit. Having discarded the skin and bone, you will still find the fillets covered in a bluish membrane; loosen the membrane at the thickest end then set the fillet, membrane side down, on the table and, like skinning a fish, draw your knife along at a 45 degree angle to separate membrane from fillet. Set the fillets aside at room temperature until ready to cook.

Sauce. Place the finely chopped shallots, wine and vinegar in a small (non-aluminium) pan and cook gently for 20 minutes or so until the shallots are absolutely tender and the liquid all but gone. Add a little grated lime rind and some juice and leave aside until ready to serve.

To Finish. Place the pan over high heat, add 2–3 dice of butter and whisk like mad; as the butter melts and emulsifies into the sauce, add more dice of butter, whisking the while; draw off the stove before the last of the butter has quite melted. If the sauce looks like breaking and becoming oily, add a teaspoon or so of cold water. Finally whisk in the pepper berries and season to taste. Serve at once.

To Cook the Rabbit. Heat the butter in a heavy frying pan, add the fillets and cook over fairly high heat, rolling and turning them for about 3–4 minutes until they no longer feel squishy at the thickest place. Season, remove and slice quickly into diagonal slices and dress on a plate with the sauce. The rabbit fillets could also be briefly roasted in a hot oven. A purée of turnip tops would go well with this.

Suggested Wine. Best red.

Hare

Once hares covered the country in vast numbers as Cobbett saw on his rural rides near Salisbury. Can you imagine an acre packed solid with a flock of hares? Now it's sad to note that hares are much scarcer, due to modern farming, removal of hedges, pesticides and such like. Some people ban all shooting of hares in an effort to increase numbers though in other areas they are still abundant and need to be controlled.

We have never quite appreciated hare as the continentals do and until recently it was cheap meat; you can feed up to 8 from a good hare and the meat is tasty, lean and healthy and a young animal is very tender. It lends itself to all sorts of lovely recipes and sauces and many venison dishes can be adapted to hare very successfully.

Young hares have short claws set in the fur of their slender paws and a pronounced knobble on the bone under the leg joint which disappears as they become mature. They have soft ears that tear and a smooth coat; the teeth are white and the cleft above the teeth is short; females will remain tender into their second year but this may be difficult to judge. Old hares are heavier, have wavy greying coats, the claws are longer and protrude beyond the fur. The teeth are yellow, the cleft longer and the ears are tough.

The English brown hare (*Lepus europaeus*) is larger and considered better than the Scottish blue or mountain hare (*Lepus timidus*), though some people (probably Scots!) find these better. Hares are best from well-drained downland. Instructions for skinning hare may be found under Rabbit, only carefully collect the blood, most of which is in the rib cavity if you want it for a dish; and mix it with a little vinegar to prevent it clotting.

Roast Saddle of Hare with Mustard

Choose a leveret or young hare for this dish though more mature fellows can be marinated. You can also lard the saddle, which helps it to be more succulent, but the coating with mustard and butter is designed to stop the saddle drying out.

Ingredients	Marinade	Serves 2–3
1 saddle of hare	1 glass red wine	
1 tbs good French mustard	1 carrot, finely chopped	
2 oz (50 g) butter	1 onion, finely chopped	
¼ pt (150 ml) cream	2 tbs olive oil	
	4 juniper berries, crushed	
	4–5 peppercorns, crushed	

Mix all the ingredients for the marinade and marinate the hare for 2–12 hours. If you know it is a leveret, it is not necessary to marinate it. Remove from the marinade and dry well. Spread with mustard and butter and roast in a hot oven (450°F/230°C/Gas 8) for 30 minutes, basting from time to time with 1 tbs of strained marinade. Remove the hare to a serving dish and add ¼ pt (150 ml) of cream to the juices in the roasting pan. Stir all together, heat until the sauce thickens and pour through a sieve into a sauceboat.

Carve the hare lengthways into fine fillets and serve with the sauce.
Suggested Wine. Best red.

Hare Fillets and Sherry Vinegar or Balsamic Vinegar Sauce

Tender back fillets of hare can be one of the finest dishes that a good game cook can produce and so much easier to carve than a saddle.

Find a really high-quality sherry vinegar to make this reduction sauce. Italian balsamic vinegar is just as good but it also should only be discreetly added at the end to flavour the sauce. The wine connoisseur, worried about the vinegar, can use a little less or make a stock and wine reduction sauce, finished with cream and redcurrant jelly or adapt either of the preceding sauce; you can even serve it with just the pan juices.

Ingredients   *Serves 2–3*

1 saddle of hare
2 oz (50 g) shallots
3 fl oz (75 ml) sherry vinegar or white wine
¼ pt (150 ml) strong hare, game or chicken
   stock

1–3 teasp sherry vinegar or balsamic
   vinegar (to taste)
2–3 oz (50–75 g) good butter
2–3 tbs olive oil
salt and pepper

Marinade

3 tbs olive oil
3 tbs sunflower oil

3 tbs strong red wine
1 tbs sherry vinegar

Bone out the saddle of hare, removing all the bluish membrane and tendons. Place the fillets and both tiny filets mignon from under the saddle in a glass or china bowl and pour the marinade ingredients over them; mix well and marinate in the fridge for 2–3 days.

Chop the shallot finely and place in a small pan with the 3 fl oz (75 ml) of sherry vinegar; simmer until the shallot is absolutely tender and the vinegar almost gone. Set aside. Take the hare fillets from the marinade, pat dry, and season with pepper. Heat a frying pan and, when hot, add the oil and heat until just hazing; sauté the fillets for about 2–3 minutes, rolling over and over in the pan until brown on the outside but still pink in the middle; the tiny filet mignons will take even less time and they should still be squishy under your finger when you press them; remove and keep warm. Add the marinade, the shallot reduction and the stock to the pan and boil down very fast to reduce by nearly half and to amalgamate the oil and stock. When reduced, season, add sherry vinegar or balsamic vinegar to taste if necessary, then, off the stove, swirl and whisk in the butter in little pieces and serve at once, though the sauce will not separate if kept warm for a little while.

Slice the meat in thin slanting slices and arrange on warm plates; add the sauce and serve at once. Buckwheat Noodles (p. 120) or Spätzle (p. 210) go well with this.
Suggested Wine. Best or French provincial red, depending on the occasion.

Jugged Hare

illustrated opposite

To jug is to cook in a jug or deep earthenware casserole, set in a pan of water, either on the stove or in the oven. It's like the Chinese double-boiling technique, the outer water bath tempering the heat so the dish cooks very gently. The seasoning is usually very simple and the liquid copious and thin, though it can be thickened at the end with the hare's own blood; in this case, the sauce must *not* then be boiled or it will curdle.

It's not always easy to tell the age of a hare and I have found myself prodding an unrelenting hare for 6 to 8 hours. This protracted waiting for dinner can be bad for tempers so I usually cook a jugged hare a day ahead and re-heat it and then my nerves don't suffer!

Ingredients   *Serves 4–6*

1 hare, jointed
4–6 shallots or small onions
4 cloves
4 oz (100 g) thick-cut streaky bacon, in lardons
bouquet garni of parsley stalks, sprigs thyme, 2 bay leaves and strip lemon rind

stock made from the hare trimmings (optional)
potato flour to thicken (optional)
blood of the hare mixed with a little vinegar (optional)
3–4 fl oz (75–100 ml) port
salt, pepper and cayenne

Marinade
8 fl oz (225 ml) red wine
2 fl oz (50 ml) wine vinegar
2 bay leaves
3 cloves
good pinch quatre-épices (optional)
salt and pepper

Wipe the hare joints and marinate for 12–24 hours in the mixed marinade ingredients. Turn from time to time, or place in a plastic bag so the marinade is in full contact with the hare. Pack the hare joints into a deep earthenware casserole or jug with the onion, each stuck with a clove, the lardons of bacon, the bouquet garni and plenty of seasoning. Pour over the strained marinade and add stock or water just to cover. Cover the casserole or jug tightly and stand in a pan of water to come almost up to the top of the casserole or jug. Simmer gently, or cook in a slow oven (300°F/150°C/Gas 2) for about 3 hours or until the hare is tender. I like to allow plenty of time for the hare to cook; it will keep warm or re-heat perfectly but is not nice if underdone.

Strain off the gravy and boil down to reduce. You can thicken the gravy with a little potato flour mixed with the port and, if you like, with the reserved hare blood; whisk it well and gradually add some of the hot but not boiling hare sauce; then return this carefully to the sauce but do *not* let the sauce boil once the blood is added or it may curdle. A little redcurrant jelly can also be added if you wish, or it can be served separately.

Return the sauce to the casserole and serve or keep warm.

Suggested Wine. Big red, if you have included the blood, or French provincial red.

Hare in an Italian Way (Lepre alla Boscaiola)

Susannah Braithwaite, a great lover of Italy, gave me a sheaf of Tuscan recipes some years ago and this one is excellent and tasty. I include some dried *cèpe* mushrooms as that is undoubtedly what would have been used in Tuscany. It's a good recipe for using up the legs when you have already treated yourself to the fillets or saddle separately and is excellent either as a braise or served with pasta to produce the classic Tuscan dish of Pappardelle con Lepra; home-made noodles (p. 120) cut into ½ inch (1 cm) widths is what is required. I like to cook the hare in a heavy earthenware casserole which can go on the top of the stove. The Italian method of cooking gives the authentic rich flavour. I find 3–4 days' marinading not at all too long, and it allows you to have it fresh, yet quite a few days after you have enjoyed the saddle.

Ingredients

The front and back legs will do a braise for 4 or a pasta sauce for 8 or so.
A whole hare will do a braise for 8 and pasta sauce for 12 or more

front and back legs of a hare (or use the
   whole hare and increase the wine a little)
4–6 pieces or a small sachet of dried *cèpe*
   mushrooms
2–3 tbs olive oil
1 carrot, diced
½ onion, diced
1 stick celery, diced
1 clove garlic, roughly chopped
1 oz (25 g) plain flour
2–3 tbs spiced vinegar
6–8 fl oz (175–225 ml) dry white wine

1 tbs tomato purée
8–10 fl oz (225–300 ml) good stock
1 oz (25 g) butter)
4 oz (100 g) thick-cut smoked bacon
½ lb (225 g) mushrooms
squeeze of lemon (optional)
grated nutmeg (optional)
salt and pepper

Marinade
3 tbs olive oil
3 tbs sunflower oil
1 onion, finely chopped
1 clove garlic, chopped

sprigs rosemary, lemon thyme and fresh
   sage
1 bay leaf
3–4 tbs spiced vinegar

Cut the hare into joints and marinate with all the marinade ingredients, turning daily, for 1–4 days; keep in a cool larder or the fridge. Drain from the marinade (if I'm using for a pasta sauce, I usually cut the fat thigh joint into 3 or 4 pieces and discard the bone; the shoulder and lower leg pieces are easier de-boned once cooked either whilst still hot or once cooled).

Soak the dried *cèpe* mushrooms in about ½ pt (300 ml) water for 15–20 minutes then simmer until the liquid is well reduced. Heat the oil in a heavy casserole, add the diced carrot, onion, celery and garlic and allow to brown over moderate heat; then turn the heat up high and add the pieces of drained hare, salt, pepper and flour; turn until sealed then add the vinegar and wine and reduce by boiling. Add the tomato purée and the dried mushrooms and their liquid, straining it off carefully to leave any sand behind. Add some stock and cook over moderate heat, keeping at a steady gentle bubble for 2½ hours or longer, adding a little more stock if it dries out (you could cook it in the oven but the sauce must reduce significantly). Meanwhile, dice the bacon and brown gently in the butter in a frying pan; turn up the heat, add the mushrooms cut in halves or quarters and sauté briskly for a few moments. Add these to the hare and cook together for about 30 minutes; then correct the seasoning, add a squeeze of lemon and grate of nutmeg if you like and serve. It's good with Polenta (p. 118).

For a pasta sauce I leave until cool (or overnight), remove all bones and cut the meat small. Re-simmer for it needs to be very thick and velvety to make a good sauce for pasta. Once ready to eat, cook your pasta (p. 120), drain, but not too much, then add to a hot dish with some melted butter in the bottom; add a few more pats of butter, a grate of nutmeg and few turns of pepper and most of the hare sauce; toss well together and pile the remaining hare in the centre. Serve at once on very hot plates.

Suggested Wine. Chianti Classico.

Hare with Honey and Prunes

So many of the dark game meats can take a little or even quite a lot of sweetness; this Moroccan dish is decidedly sweet, including honey, prunes, saffron and a hint of hotness from the ras el hanout or chilli, but the dark rich hare meat can take it and gives a lavish, fragrant casserole. It is not always easy to be certain of a young hare but with this dish you can just continue the gentle simmering until it *is* tender. I usually prepare it a day ahead so I can allow it all the time it needs and anyway the flavour is all the better on re-heating. One important point; hare meat will darken and dry out if not covered in sauce so reduce the sauce only when ready to serve, keeping the hare well covered.

Ingredients   *Serves 6–8*

1 hare jointed	a good pinch of ras el hanout (Moroccan
a good pinch of saffron threads or small	seasoning (optional)) or chilli powder
packet of powder	1 stick cinnamon
¾–1 pt (450 ml–600 ml) good stock,	6 oz (175 g) large plump prunes
heated	1 teasp powdered cinnamon
2 oz (50 g) butter	6 tbs thin honey
1 teasp oil	½–1 teasp potato flour
2 onions, diced	1 oz (25 g) flaked, browned almonds
	salt and pepper

Soak the saffron in the hot stock for about 15 minutes. Meanwhile heat the butter and oil in a heavy frying pan or casserole and brown the pieces of hare. Remove the meat and gently fry the onion until soft and golden; return the meat and season heavily with salt, pepper and if you wish, the pinch of ras el hanout or chilli; add the cinnamon stick and saffron stock to cover. Cover very closely and simmer very gently (or cook in a slow oven at 300°F/150°C/Gas 1½–2 for 1–1½ hours or until the hare is nearly tender). Remove the pieces to a tightly covered container and keep warm. Add the prunes to the sauce and simmer, uncovered, for about 15 minutes; then add the powdered cinnamon and honey and boil down to reduce until syrupy and tasty. Thicken lightly with a little potato flour mixed with cold water and return the hare pieces. Simmer all together gently (or return to the oven, or reheat the next day) until the hare is very tender and the flavours are well blended.

Scatter with flaked, browned almonds. Serve with rice pilau or noodles.

Suggested Wine. Big red, though I might be tempted occasionally to try a big white with lots of flavour and power, like a Rhône or Rioja, or even a rich Gewürztraminer from Alsace or a Spätlese from the Palatinate.

Wild Boar

The wild boar became extinct in Britain during the seventeenth century but it still makes exciting hunting on the continent. The families, with their stripy brown offspring, were a charming sight that I often used to see when riding on the ranges of north Germany. Only young animals make good eating; the French call those up to the age of six months Marcassin and these are excellent. From six months to one year they are known as *bête rousse* and make good eating. Between 1–2 years they become a *bête de campagne* and are more mature, needing marinating and careful treatment. They can live to thirty years, becoming utterly inedible but extremely fierce; in fact in Kashmir they can weigh up to 660 lb (300 kg) and take on a tiger, so it's not surprising that they are classed as ferocious beasts.

But in Britain there are now a few enterprising people who breed and farm boar, letting them roam and eat acorns, beechmast, reeds and crab apples, culling them at about eighteen months for good mature yet still quite tender meat. Not being bled as is pork, the meat is dark and is usually best marinated to bring out its gaminess and to tenderise the older beasts. It is generally better braised or roasted though I like to take a piece of rib or belly, cut a pocket, stuff it with apple and sultanas, sew up and pot roast until very well cooked. It's a simple German way for pork or boar.

Producer of Wild Boar. Robert Spencer Bernard Esq, Estate Office, Nether Winchendon, Aylesbury, Buckinghamshire HP18 0DY (Tel: 0844 290101).

Roast Wild Boar with Chocolate and Wild Cherry Sauce
illustrated opposite

I have a passion for Italian wild cherries, Amarena Fabbri, available from I. Camisa, or Valvona and Crolla (see pp. 138–9). This is a classic sauce, finished with chocolate, that can be used for venison as well as wild boar, with or without the addition of the cherries and pine nuts.

Ingredients   *Serves 8–10*

around 8½ lb (3.8 kg) leg of wild boar,
  skinned

Seasoning Mix

1 teasp sea salt
½ teasp peppercorns
1 clove garlic
6 juniper berries
1 sprig sage, rosemary or thyme

Marinade

1 onion
1 carrot
1 stick celery
6 juniper berries
bouquet garni
1 pt (600 ml) red wine
2–3 tbs olive oil
salt and pepper

Chocolate and Wild Cherry Sauce

1 onion, finely chopped
1 large carrot, finely diced
1 stick celery, finely diced
2 tbs olive oil
3 tbs flour
2 pts (1.2 l) good stock
bouquet garni of parsley stalks, thyme, bay
  leaf, 4 juniper berries and 6 peppercorns
3 tbs soft light brown sugar
3 tbs red wine vinegar
¼ pt (150 ml) dry white wine
a small handful large raisins
12–18 tinned wild cherries (Amarena
  Fabbri) or glacé cherries
2 cubes dark chocolate
1–2 tbs browned pinenuts (optional)
salt and pepper

Pound all the ingredients for the seasoning mix together to form a paste and rub well into the meat and leave overnight.

Marinade. Dice the onion, carrot and celery and combine with the remaining ingredients. Place the seasoned leg of wild boar in the marinade and marinate for 2–3 days, turning daily.

To Cook the Boar. Take out and pat dry, and slow roast, in a very moderate oven (325°F/170°C/Gas 3) allowing 30 minutes to the pound and 15 minutes over.
  Baste well and add spoonfuls of marinade to the pan as necessary.

Chocolate and Wild Cherry Sauce. Fry the onion, carrot and celery in the oil until they are a good brown colour; add the flour and brown that gently. Draw the pan off the stove, add the stock and bring to the boil, whisking hard. Add the bouquet garni and simmer the sauce for about 2 hours, skimming from time to time until reduced to about 12 fl oz (350 ml). Strain into a small saucepan.
  Meanwhile, in a small pan, dissolve the sugar in the vinegar and boil to a dark caramel; heat the wine and add carefully and quickly to dissolve off the caramel. Add the raisins to this mixture and simmer gently until the raisins are plumped and the mixture reduced by half. Add the chocolate to the sauce and stir well until it has melted; then add the wine-raisin mixture, the cherries, and correct the seasoning. Simmer down to a good flavour and consistency and keep warm in a bain-marie. Add the browned pinenuts, if used, only shortly before serving the sauce with the boar. The deglazed, defatted and strained roasting pan juices can be served as a separate gravy or added to the sauce, depending on their quantity.

Suggested Wine. Difficult and rather according to your taste. I'd be inclined to suggest a big red or a French provincial red or a big white.

Wild Boar Casserole in a Rich Italian Style (alla Diavola)

The marinade brings out the gamy flavour and the cooking produces a tender, rich almost sauceless dish with very intense flavours. Serve it with Polenta (p. 118) or with Noodles (p. 120). It will be very well received even if you just do it with a mature piece of pork; turn it in the marinade a day or two longer to bring up the flavour.

Ingredients   *Serves 4–6*
2 lb (900 g) generous cubes trimmed wild
    boar shoulder or mature pork
2–3 tbs oil (or butter)
1 tbs flour
½ pt (300 ml) robust red wine

Marinade
1 onion, diced
2 cloves garlic
3–4 sage leaves, chopped
good sprig rosemary leaves, finely cut
2–3 cloves
2–3 crushed juniper berries
2 tbs spiced vinegar (p. 27) or wine
    vinegar

2 tbs spiced oil (p. 25) or olive oil
2 tbs Marsala (optional)
2 tbs robust red wine
1½ teasp salt
plenty of pepper

Mix the meat with all the marinade ingredients and marinate in a cool place for 24 hours or up to 5 days. Drain from the marinade and pat dry. Heat the butter or oil in a heavy frying pan and fry the meat until brown all over, sprinkling the flour over to brown a little too. Do not overfill the pan or the meat may stew, not brown, and you must keep the heat up. Remove to a casserole, preferably earthenware. Deglaze the pan with the marinade and wine and pour over the meat. Cover closely, a layer of tinfoil or Bakewell under the lid, and cook in a very slow oven (250°F/130°C/Gas 1) for about 2½–3 hours until the meat is very tender and the sauce well reduced. Cook with the lid off if not well reduced for the sauce should be little more than a sticky substance that coats the meat. Degrease any excess fat and serve over polenta or with noodles. This of course re-heats and gets better and better.

Alternatively, here is an excellent German way of cooking boar that I have from an old German book belonging to Robert Spencer Bernard who rears wild boar. Take onions to half the weight of the meat and slice and brown them gently and well in fat; cube the meat, say 2 lbs (1.8 kg) and roll in about 2 teasp paprika and 1 tbs flour; fry with the onions until browned then add about ½ pt (300 ml) beer, 1 teasp sugar, ¼ teasp caraway seeds and seasoning. Cover and cook in a slow oven for 2½–3 hours. It's very tasty and good but without quite the rich gaminess and intensity of the Italian style – nice for a change and also good with mature pork.

Suggested Wine. A good Italian red wine, probably a Barolo, Barbaresco or Chianti Classico.

PIES AND MIXED GAME

I have gathered nearly all the pastry dishes and those made with a mixture of game into this section. Game mixes and combines well and so often the bag may contain a variety of game, perhaps not quite enough for any one dish. Game of doubtful age responds well to long gentle cooking and turning into a pie or pudding.

Good strong stock made from the carcasses can often improve these dishes and can be made while the meats marinate. Don't hesitate to marinate for longer and to continue cooking until tender when you know you have an aged creature; often it will turn out to have wonderful flavour.

Some of these dishes take some time to make but are excellent for a large party, buffet or shooting lunch.

Game Pithiviers

illustrated opposite

I have to thank Julia Child for the idea of this quick puff pastry and glorious hot vol-au-vent-like creation. It makes a wonderful dinner party dish and can be filled with all sorts of combinations of game. I only use the breast and thigh meat and cook the game in a way to keep it very succulent. (This method is particularly successful for any game to be served cold or used in made-up dishes). All the preparation and assembly can be done ahead, leaving the Pithiviers ready for 40–50 minutes in the oven before serving.

Ingredients

Serves 6–8

1 pheasant ⎫ or any other individual or
1 grouse ⎭ combination of game
1 onion, roughly chopped
1 carrot, diced
1 stick celery, diced
1 oz (25 g) butter
1 tbs oil
3 tbs wine
egg wash

Fast Puff Pastry

12 oz (350 g) firm butter
1 lb (450 g) strong white flour
1 teasp salt (if using unsalted butter)
8–10 fl oz (200–300 ml) iced water

Sauce

¾ oz (20 g) butter
¾ oz (20 g) plain flour
3 fl oz (75 ml) strong stock from cooking
   the game
2 fl oz (50 ml) cream
1 egg yolk
1 tbs Dijon mustard
a shake Worcestershire sauce
a few drops Tabasco or chilli sauce
a little finely chopped tarragon or lemon
   thyme
salt, pepper and ground mace

To Cook the Game. Dry the birds. Heat the butter and oil in a heavy casserole and brown the birds carefully all over, adjusting the heat so the butter does not burn. Brown the onion, carrot and celery in with the birds then add the wine, cover closely (a sheet of tinfoil under the

lid) and cook gently, either on top of the stove or in a very moderate oven (325°F/170°C/Gas 3) for 20–35 minutes until just done and the breast no longer feels squishy, removing each bird as it is done. Leave to cool before carving. Strain the cooking juices into a measuring jug and remove the fat from on top when cold; if the juices have evaporated away (too high a heat), deglaze the pan with stock, wine or water, stirring in all the tasty bits, and set that aside for the sauce. Once cold, remove the skin, take off the breasts and slice into thin slices. Also skin and thinly slice the tender thigh meat; set aside. Set aside the drumsticks for another use.

Fast Puff Pastry. Dice the butter into ½ inch (1 cm) dice and chill. Sift the flour and salt, if used, into a bowl, add the butter and rub in only until the butter is in large pea-sized pieces. Sprinkle the water over it gradually, drawing the mixture together until it forms a rough mass. Turn on to a floured board and form into a rectangle; don't worry if it looks an awful mess because it will draw together in the rolling. Roll the pastry to about 1 inch (2.5 cm) thickness then fold the top third down, bottom third up, as in making puff pastry. Turn a quarter turn to your right and roll and fold again. Roll and fold twice more, rolling progressively thinner as the pastry allows. Now rest the pastry for 40 minutes, wrapped, in the fridge. Roll and fold twice more by which time it should be smooth and even.

Sauce. Melt the butter, add the flour and cook, stirring, over moderate heat for 2–3 minutes. Draw the pan off the stove, wait for the sizzling to cease then add the stock, cream and egg yolk and bring to the boil. Simmer for 1–2 minutes by which time the sauce should be pretty thick. Then season quite highly with mustard, Worcestershire sauce, Tabasco or chilli sauce, tarragon or lemon thyme, mace and salt and pepper. Fold the game meat into the sauce, adjust the consistency and flavour and set aside to cool.

To Assemble. Roll the pastry to an 18 × 9 inch (45 × 22 cm) rectangle and cut into two slightly unequal parts. Roll the smaller to a 12 inch (30 cm) square then, using a tart base or cake tin, cut out an 11 inch (28 cm) circle. Turn this over on to a damp baking sheet and prick firmly with a fork all over. Spread the cold game filling in the middle, leaving a 2 inch (5 cm) border of clear pastry all around. Paint this with cold water. Roll the remaining piece of pastry to a 12 inch (30 cm) square and cut a second 11 inch (28 cm) round. Carefully lay this on top of the filling, matching the edges and press the top in place; cut a little hole in the middle to let steam escape. Scallop the edges of the Pithiviers at 2 inch (5 cm) intervals by indenting firmly with the blunt back of a knife. Chill until firm before cooking. Once ready to cook, paint the top over twice carefully with egg wash, not allowing any to drip down the edges which would prevent the Pithiviers from rising. Finally, with the point of a small knife, cut decorative lines 1/16 inch (¼ cm) deep into the top of the pastry. Bake in a very hot oven (450°F/230°C/Gas 8) for about 20 minutes until well risen and browned. Lower the temperature to 400°F/200°C/Gas 6 and continue to bake for 20–30 minutes, covering loosely with tinfoil when brown enough. Cook until the pastry is full cooked then serve, cut in wedges like a pie. The pastry tends to go soft if the Pithiviers are kept warm for too long.

Serve well-coloured vegetables such as sprouts, beans, courgettes and baked or stuffed tomatoes (these could be stuffed with a farci made up of the minced leg meat, breadcrumbs and herbs) or a soft celeriac and watercress purée. You could serve a rich gravy sauce, made from all the bones, with this if you wish.

Suggested Wine. Light or French provincial red.

Raised Game Pie

How handsome these look in the traditional waisted shape (what a pity the moulds are so expensive) but you can of course use a removable base, round cake tin as a substitute. Any variety or mixture of game can be used, and if you just use prime meat, you can layer it in pieces rather than mince it but then I think you need to top up after it's cooked with good game aspic. Read carefully to see how to fit the pastry to the mould because demonstrating this dish is so much easier than explaining it! I use a French pastry that can take the long cook without spoiling yet still tastes very good cold. Use any mixture of game, but include something tasty like grouse or hare if you can and do include enough pork fat to keep it succulent for dry pie is very sawdusty. Watch that little 'chimneys' don't form, up which juices can escape, where there are folds in the pastry around the edge of the mould; press them out or seal with water. It's such a pity if a hole appears because not only does the juice escape but the pastry also goes soggy. A meat thermometer is useful as it indicates when the centre is cooked and it is so much nicer just cooked, rather than well cooked; but do leave it in place until the pie is cold or hot juices bubble up, ooze out and run down the pastry to make it soggy. These pies are always best after several days when the flavour has matured and blended.

Serve with Cumberland Sauce (p. 202) or Spiced Grape Jelly (p. 199) if you wish.

Ingredients
Serves 10–12

1 pheasant's breast or 8 oz (225 g) game
   fillets kept whole

Pâté Mixture

8 oz (225 g) boned flesh of pheasant,
   partridge, rabbit, hare or grouse etc
4 oz (100 g) lean pie veal }
4 oz (100 g) lean pork } or use all pork
8 oz (225 g) pork back-fat
4 oz (100 g) streaky bacon
½ teasp allspice or quatre-épices
4 tbs brandy
2 eggs
1½ teasp salt
black pepper

Raised Pie Pastry

1 lb (450 g) flour
8 oz (225 g) butter
2 egg yolks
3 fl oz (75 ml) cold water (approx)
1 teasp salt

Pastry. Sift the flour and salt into a bowl, rub in the butter and work up to a stiff paste with the egg yolks and some water (in a food processor make half at a time). Rest, preferably for 12–24 hours.

Pâté Mixture. Mince, or preferably chop finely in a food processor with the metal blade, the game, veal, pork, pork fat and streaky bacon and beat in the seasoning, brandy and eggs. Fry a little bit of the mixture and taste it to check the seasoning.

Grease well a 2–3 pt (1.2–1.7 l) hinged pâté mould or removable base cake tin. Take three-quarters of the pastry and roll out into an oval, keeping the middle thicker than the edges. Flour well and fold in half, edges towards you. Roll into a bag shape by drawing the edges towards you and rolling out the thicker centre. Fit into the mould, pressing well into all the corners and making sure no holes appear. Leave 1 inch (2–3 cm) overhang all round the mould. Pack with half the pâté mixture, then lay in strips of the pheasant breast or game fillets. Cover with the remaining pâté mixture, doming slightly in the centre; if the mould is too full, juices bubble out during cooking. Cover with the remaining pastry to fit the top and nearly ½ inch (1 cm) thick. Seal the edges with water. Decorate and brush with beaten egg. Make a hole and insert a tinfoil 'chimney' for steam to escape, and a meat thermometer if you use one. Bake in a moderately hot oven (375°F/190°C/Gas 5) for 20–30 minutes until the crust sets and colours, then turn down to moderate (350°F/180°C/Gas 4) for 1–1½ hours until the meat is cooked (160°F/75°C on a meat thermometer). Cover with tinfoil or brown paper if it is getting too brown. Leave to cool completely before unmoulding.

Setting aspic can be poured through a funnel into the pâté to fill any empty corners and helps to keep it moist, but to my mind it is not really necessary.

Keep 2–3 days for the flavour to mature before serving.

Suggested Wine. French provincial red.

Hot Pâté en Croûte

It's nice sometimes to serve a pâté hot although it won't go quite so far. In this recipe, which can equally well be served cold, the pastry forms a free-standing rectangular case around the filling and needs no pie dish or terrine. You can make it as long as your oven will hold and it's good for large parties; the pastry, which is a melting and crisp shortcrust, gets nice and brown by not having been enclosed in any mould. Serve it hot with Sweet Red Cabbage (p. 207) and a lentil or Chestnut Purée (p. 207). Serve it cold with salads and Cumberland Sauce (p. 202) or one of our interesting spiced jellies (p. 199).

Ingredients   *Serves 6–8*

¾ lb (350 g) lean game meat such as hare,
  venison, pheasant etc.
½ lb (225 g) pork back-fat
½ lb (225 g) pork sausagemeat or minced
  and seasoned belly of pork
1 onion   *Shortcrust Pastry*
1 clove garlic   1 lb (450 g) plain flour
6 juniper berries   5 oz (125 g) firm butter
¼ teasp ground mace   3 oz (75 g) lard
¼ teasp quatre-épices or a good pinch of   2 eggs
  cloves, nutmeg, cinnamon and ginger   2–3 tbs water
2 tbs brandy   ½ teasp salt
1 egg   egg wash

Pastry. Mix the egg with a little cold water. Sieve the flour and salt into a bowl and add the butter and lard, cut into hazelnut-sized pieces; rub in the fats, adding egg and water as you do so to make a paste; then roll and turn three times. Or place flour, salt and fats in the food processor with metal blade and process, adding eggs and water at once. Roll and turn three times and set aside to rest in a plastic bag in the fridge for 2 hours.

Pâté. Mince the game meat and fat with the onion and garlic, or process in the food processor which gives a moister and better pâté; combine with the sausagemeat, spices, brandy and egg and beat well. Fry a little of the mixture to check the seasoning. If possible, leave in a cool place for 2–3 hours or overnight for the flavour to blend before cooking.

Cut off one-third of the pastry for a lid. Roll the remainder into a 10 × 14 inch (25 × 36 cm) rectangle and trim the edges. Spread the pâté down the centre of the pastry, leaving a 2 inch (5 cm) margin all round. Turn up the pastry all round and mitre the corners, moisten with cold water and press together. Roll out the remaining pastry to a rectangle for the lid, moisten the edges and fix in place. Decorate with pastry leaves and brush with egg wash. Bake in a hot oven (400°F/200°C/Gas 6) for 15 minutes until pastry is brown and set, then turn down to very moderate (325°F/170°C/Gas 3) and bake for a further 1–1¼ hours until cooked (170°F/75°C on a meat thermometer). Cover the top if getting too brown.

Serve hot or cold; if serving cold you can leave it for a day or so for the flavour to mellow.

Suggested Wine. Light red.

Mixed Game Torte

This lovely mixed game pie with simple flavourings is based on a recipe from the valley of Munster in Alsace, only they do it just with pork. It can of course be made with just one sort of game (such as pheasant), or a variety. I often use the breasts only, keeping the legs for Devilled Game (p. 198). It's handsome hot for a party or taken, wrapped in tinfoil and newspaper, out on shooting lunches or picnics. But of course it eats well cold too. The way of sealing the edges is very Alsatian and good and so is the centre cut-out and decoration. You can vary the flavourings and marinate the meat in port and brandy if you want a stronger gamy flavour (especially if you use hare, venison or grouse or wild goose breast). I enjoy its clean, light flavour and often use just pheasant for it.

Ingredients   *Serves 6–8*

2 lb (900 g) boned, skinned game meat (pheasant, wild duck, grouse, hare, venison or wild goose breast)
8–10 oz (225–275 g) pork back-fat
5 oz (125 g) stale brown or white bread
8 tbs milk
2 onions, finely diced
1 oz (25 g) butter
2 cloves garlic, finely chopped
¼ pt (150 ml) dry white wine or good cider

1–1½ teasp herbes de Provence crushed fine (or use a variety of fresh herbs like parsley, lemon thyme, or rosemary)
2 eggs, whisked
½ teasp grated nutmeg
1½–2 teasp salt
plenty of peppermill mixture or pepper
¾ batch of Fast Puff Pastry (p. 182) using 9 oz (250 g) butter, 12 oz (350 g) flour, ¾ teasp salt and 6–8 fl oz (175–225 ml) iced water

Soak the bread or breadcrumbs in milk. Soften the onion gently in the butter without browning, add the garlic, wine and herbs and boil hard until reduced by half; cool.

Dice the game meat and pork fat and process in the food processor with metal blade, or mince, coarsely. Change to the plastic blade or turn into a bowl and process or beat in by hand the soaked bread, reduced wine, onion and herb mixture, the eggs (keeping back enough to egg wash the pastry), nutmeg and seasoning. Fry a little of the mixture to check the seasoning (too sad to make it and have it under-seasoned). Preferably leave for the flavouring to blend for a few hours or overnight.

Roll the pastry a little and cut into two unequal pieces. Roll the smaller piece thinly and line a 9 inch (22 cm) removable base sandwich tin, allowing at least 1 inch (2.5 cm) of pastry to hang over the edge all round. Pack in the mixture, doming it in the centre. Roll the remaining piece of pastry for a lid, leave it quite a lot thicker than the base but 1 inch (2.5 cm) extra all round. Using a fluted 1½ inch (4 cm) circular cutter remove the centre; moisten the pie edges with water; lay the pastry over the game filling, press the two edges firmly together; and trim the edges still leaving ½–¾ inch (1–1½ cm) extra all round; now turn this extra rim up to form a rolled border, looking like a rope all round the edge of the pie. Paint the pie with egg wash then, with a small sharp knife, cut just into the pastry to form a decorative whorl or curly sunburst design from the centre to the edge of the pie. Bake in a hot oven (400°F/200°C/Gas 6) for about 30–40 minutes until well risen and browned then reduce the heat to moderately hot (350°F/180°C/Gas 4) for a further 30–40 minutes until golden brown all over and the meat is cooked. The base pastry must cook (it would have originally been cooked in a baker's oven with bottom heat). Place near the bottom of an Aga for bottom heat or turn on bottom heat in oven; otherwise cover the top lightly with tinfoil and keep cooking until the bottom is brown and crisp. (Quality tins such as Pullman's pans also help to bake crisply).

It should be left in a low oven or at room temperature to rest for ½ hour before serving. It is good hot, warm or cold.

Suggested Wine. Light red or big white.

Game Suet Pudding

Lesser quality game with plenty of flavour makes a splendid steamed suet pudding. Venison, grouse, hare and partridge or pigeon can all be used. Steak can be included, cooked with ancient but tasty grouse that can then be discarded. I like to cook the game (keeping it a little underdone) and make a rich sauce before putting it in the suet, not having had quite so much success with puddings prepared with raw game, though you can just layer game joints, herbs, mushrooms and good stock and let it steam for 4 hours or so. I also prefer to make quite a large pudding as small ones seem to be all pastry and no filling!

Ingredients   *Serves 6–8*

approx 3½ pt (2 l) cooked game in rich
    thickened sauce as in the Hot Venison Pie
    (p. 190) or Venison Casserole (p. 160)

Suet Crust
8 oz (225 g) chopped beef suet
1 lb (450 g) self-raising flour
½ pt (300 ml) cold water approx.
2–3 tbs finely chopped herbs (optional)
1 teasp salt

Suet Crust. If you are using real suet, not a packet, pull it apart, discarding the membranes and thready bits, then chop finely and weigh. Sift the flour and salt into a mixing bowl, stir in the finely chopped suet and herbs and mix to a medium soft dough with the water, using a knife. Knead briefly into one lump, cut off a quarter of the pastry and set aside. Roll the remainder on a well-floured board into a round of 9 inches (23 cm) diameter and thicker in the middle than round the edges. Sprinkle well with flour and fold in half with the fold away from you. Draw the edges towards you a little and carefully roll out the centre to form the pastry into a bag which will fit the pudding basin.

Grease a 3½–4 pt (2–2.25 l) basin well and set the pastry in it, pressing out evenly. Spoon in the cold game stew mixture which should be tasty, juicy and quite well thickened. Moisten the edges of the pastry with water, roll the remaining quarter of pastry for a lid and fit in place. Cover with greased paper and tinfoil or a securely tied-on cloth, leaving space for the pastry to rise. Place the bowl in a steamer or in a saucepan with boiling water to come halfway up the outside of the bowl. Cover closely and boil or steam for 2½–3 hours. Top up with boiling water when necessary.

To Serve. Remove the cloth or tinfoil and paper and carefully run a knife between pastry and bowl. Place a deep serving plate on top of the bowl and invert. Remove the bowl and serve.

Suggested Wine. Big red.

Pheasant and Celeriac Pie

This has a lovely creamy filling, flavoured with celeriac or salsify, to which you add cubes of cooked game, usually the pale meats such as pheasant, rabbit and partridge, but try it with whatever you have got. I top it with a variety of pastries but really prefer home-made puff or Fast Puff Pastry (p. 182).

Ingredients   *Serves 4–6*

¾ lb–1 lb (375–450 g) cooked, cubed
   pheasant, rabbit or chicken
1½ oz (35 g) butter
1 small onion, finely chopped
1 small carrot, finely diced
1½ oz (35 g) flour
10 fl oz (300 ml) game or chicken stock
8 fl oz (225 ml) milk

1 tbs Dijon mustard
8–12 oz (225–375 g) cooked cubed
   celeriac or salsify
salt and pepper

6–8 oz (175–225 g) puff, fast puff, cheesy
   flaky, flaky or shortcrust pastry
egg wash

Melt the butter in a saucepan and gently soften the finely diced onion and carrot. When soft, add the flour and cook over moderate heat, stirring, for 1–2 minutes; then draw the pan off the stove and wait for the sizzling to cease. Add the stock and milk to the pan and bring to the boil, whisking hard. Simmer for 2–3 minutes. Stir in the mustard, season with salt and pepper and fold in the meat and celeriac. Simmer for several minutes so the meat is brought through the boil before turning into a 1½–2 pt (900 ml–1.2 l) pie dish with pie funnel in place. Leave until cold.

Roll the pastry thinly, cut a ½ inch (1–2 cm) strip from round the edge, moisten with cold water and set in place round the rim of the pie dish. Moisten this with cold water and set the pastry cover in place. Trim the pastry, knock up the edges and decorate the pie. Paint with egg wash and cook in a hot oven (425°F/220°C/Gas 7) for about 10–15 minutes until a good brown, then lower the temperature to moderate (350°F/180°C/Gas 4) and continue cooking for a further 30–40 minutes or so until the pie is heated through and the pastry is crisp and a good brown. Cover loosely with tinfoil if the top gets too brown. Serve at once.

I sometimes add mushrooms or cooked pasta to the pie.

Suggested Wine. Light red or big white.

Hot Venison or Mixed Game Pie

A rich tasty pie that jazzes up farmed venison quite well or will tenderise hill beasts (increase the marinating time to 3–5 days). It is also excellent using any mixture of game and I always like to include some dark meat like grouse, hare, venison or pigeon. You can also use it for grouse and steak (a really old grouse can be cooked in it for flavour then discarded) or pigeon breasts mixed with steak. Fast Puff pastry (p. 182) makes an alternative topping. The hazelnut forcemeat balls can be fried and served with any dish like Jugged Hare (p. 174), Pigeon with Mediaeval Flavours (p. 127), around Roast Rabbit (p. 166) or where you will.

Ingredients *Serves 4–6*

1½–2 lb (675–900 g) boned trimmed
   venison, hare or mixed jointed game
1 oz (25 g) butter
2 thick rashers fat bacon, diced into lardons
1 onion, thickly sliced
4 oz (100 g) mushrooms, whole or
   quartered
½ oz (12 g) seasoned flour

Marinade

1 tbs redcurrant jelly
1 fl oz (25 ml) shallot, spiced or wine
   vinegar
2 fl oz (50 ml) port
¼ pt (150 ml) red wine
3 fl oz (75 ml) mushroom ketchup

1 small onion, finely chopped
1 teasp mixed fresh chopped thyme and
   marjoram
4 bruised juniper or allspice berries
1 tbs olive oil
salt and pepper

Flaky Pastry
5 oz (125 g) plain strong flour
squeeze lemon juice
3½ oz (90 g) butter
2–3 fl oz (50–75 ml) iced water
pinch salt
egg wash

Hazelnut Forcemeat Balls
4 oz (100 g) sausage meat or minced pork
2 slices brown bread
2 tbs ground hazelnuts
grated rind ½ lemon
a little fresh chopped parsley and chives
1 egg yolk
salt and pepper

Marinade. Make the marinade by melting jelly and adding all ingredients. Cut the meat into 1–1½ inch (2–4 cm) cubes and marinate for 24–48 hours.

Flaky Pastry. Sieve flour and salt into a bowl or food processor with metal blade and add a squeeze of lemon juice. Divide firm but malleable butter into quarters. Rub in one quarter until the mixture is like breadcrumbs, then add enough iced water to form a medium firm dough. Knead briefly until smooth and roll into an oblong ¼ inch thick. Take one quarter of butter and, with the point of a knife, place dabs of butter on the top two thirds of pastry leaving an inch margin all round. Sprinkle with flour and fold bottom third up, top third down, press edges to seal and turn pastry one turn to your right. Repeat process with remaining portions of butter. Refrigerate if pastry becomes too soft. Rest in fridge overnight or for 1–2 hours before using.

Meat. Drain the meat well from marinade and pat dry. Melt the butter in a frying pan and gently fry the fat bacon; remove to a casserole. Add the onion to the fat and soften, then toss in the mushrooms, fry to brown and add to the bacon in the casserole. In the remaining fat (adding a little dripping or oil if necessary) sauté the meat, tossed in seasoned flour at the moment of frying, over high heat to a good brown. Turn the meat into the casserole and add the marinade. Cover closely and cook in a very moderate oven (325°F/170°C/Gas 3) for 1½–2½ hours or until just tender, adding a little stock or water if the meat becomes too dry. Check seasoning and taste, adding redcurrant jelly if necessary and turn the meat and forcemeat balls (see below) into a 2½ pt (1.5 l) pie dish with a funnel. Leave to cool.

Hazelnut Forcemeat Balls. Mash the sausage meat, add the soft breadcrumbs, hazelnut and lemon, parsley, chives and seasoning and bind with the egg yolk. Form into marble-sized balls and lightly brown in fat.

Roll the pastry 1 inch (3 cm) too large and cut a half inch strip to fit round the rim. Moisten the rim of the pie dish with cold water and fit on the strip. Moisten it with water and cover with the pastry but do not stretch. Press into place, trim and decorate; make a hole in the crust and brush with egg wash. Chill before cooking if you can. Bake in a hot oven (425°F/220°C/Gas 7) for 15–20 minutes, until a good brown then turn down to 350°F/180°C/Gas 4 and continue to cook for 30–40 minutes until the pie is heated through and the pastry is a good crisp brown (cover lightly if necessary).

Suggested Wine. Big red.

Great Game Pilau

I evolved this recipe for one of the recent Game Fairs, knowing how useful it is to have a dish that is all prepared ahead, keeps warm well, can be used for a buffet or shooting lunch and is suitable for large numbers. It uses odds and ends of different game or can be used to clear the freezer of the remaining inhabitants!

In all these ways it is a paragon of a dish.

Lightly spiced and richly flavoured like a fine biriani, it is a bit of work to prepare but then you can sit back and enjoy it.

Ingredients *Serves 4–6*

game enough to furnish about 1½ lb
    (675 g) cooked meat (say 2 grouse and
    1 wild duck, or 1 pheasant and 1–2
    partridge or any combination or single
    game if you prefer)
1 tbs roasted crushed coriander seeds
2 oz (50 g) butter
2 tbs oil
1 carrot, roughly diced
1 onion, chopped
1 stick celery, roughly diced
3–4 tbs white wine
salt and pepper

Pilau Rice

12 oz (350 g) Basmati, long grain or Patna
    rice soaked in salted water for 3 hours
a few pieces dried *cèpe* mushrooms, soaked
    in warm stock
1 pkt or large pinch, saffron
2 tbs oil
2 inch (5 cm) stick cinnamon
8 cloves
6–8 cardamom pods
4 oz (100 g) butter
1 onion, finely chopped
1¼ pt (750 ml) strong game stock (see
    method below)
¼–½ teasp grated nutmeg
3 tbs sultanas
3 tbs flaked almonds
salt and pepper

Stock for Pilau Rice

All the carcasses, having cooked the game
3 cloves
4 cardamom pods
4 allspice berries
8 black peppercorns
1 inch (2.5 cm) stick cinnamon
2 cloves garlic
2 small slices ginger
bouquet garni of parsley, thyme and bay
    leaf
2 thin pared strips lemon zest
¼ pt (150 ml) white wine
3 pt (1.7 l) light stock or water

Wipe the game and season inside with salt, pepper and crushed coriander. Heat the butter and oil in a heavy casserole and brown the game gently on all sides (which will take about 10–15 minutes) adding the chopped carrot, onion and celery about half way through. Once brown, set the birds breast up, add the wine and cover tightly with a sheet of foil and a lid.

Cook young game gently on top of the stove or in a moderate oven (350°F/180°C/Gas 4) until just cooked. Older or tougher game is best cooked, hermetically sealed, covered in stock in a very slow oven (200°F/100°C/Gas ¼–½) for up to 6–8 hours so it will become tender. Remove each bird when cooked and leave to rest for at least 10 minutes or until cold. Remove all flesh carefully, cut into generous pieces and set aside.

To Make the Stock. Break the bones of the carcasses and return to the casserole; fry up, adding all the remaining stock ingredients, except stock or water, and reduce until the wine has evaporated and the mixture is frying again. Now cover with 3 pints (1.7 l) stock or water and simmer, uncovered, skimming from time to time, for 3–4 hours until the stock is strong and reduced (or cook, covered, overnight in a low oven, then strain and reduce). Strain through muslin and you should have about 1¼ pints (750 ml) left for cooking the pilau.

Pilau Rice. Soak the rice in plenty of salted cold water for 1–3 hours then drain well and dry. Soak the dried *cèpe* pieces in a little hot stock for about 30 minutes (or boil up for about 10 minutes adding a little sherry) and soak the saffron in a little hot stock for about 15 minutes. Heat the oil in a heavy casserole; once smoking, tip the casserole and drop in the cinnamon, cloves and cardamom which will swell up and pop a little. Now add half the butter and the onion and cook gently until soft and translucent. Add the drained rice, fry whilst stirring for several minutes and then pour in the stock. Add the mushroom and their liquid (watch out for sand at the bottom), the saffron, a little grated nutmeg, sultanas, almonds and seasoning. Cover and cook gently for 15 minutes. Leave to stand for another 10–20 minutes before assembling.

To Assemble. Into a deep serving dish or casserole, spoon a layer of rice (the whole spices are left in but warn people not to eat them); cover with a layer of cooked game, season and add flakes of butter; continue layering rice and game, finishing with rice and flakes of butter. Bake, covered, for 30 minutes (if hot) or about 1 hour (if cold) in a moderate oven (350°F/180°C/Gas 4) before serving.

Serve with a colourful vegetable, such as carrots or beans, peas or courgettes.

This recipe can be adapted to use cubed game pie mixture. Brown and braise with flavouring in stock. Use stock to cook rice and assemble as above.

Suggested Wine. Big or French provincial red.

SAVOURIES AND EATUPS

Game can be used up in all the usual ways, but here are a few recipes we find especially useful or successful. Don't forget that good cooked game can be diced, marinated in a tasty vinaigrette and tossed into a salad; or wafer slices of fine venison or goose breast can be marinated in spiced oil and served just with pepper and lemon juice. Trout and salmon, especially home-smoked, make lovely kedgeree; add lots of parsley, butter and hard-boiled eggs or try Basmati rice and a touch of curry powder for a change.

Mousses, quenelles and soufflés also turn your leftovers into new and exciting dishes like Salmon Rillettes (p. 46) and Little Salmon Creams (p. 45). After breaking down a venison carcass, I pack all the scraps into a pot with a little water, herbs and light seasoning; seal, cook very gently for 6–8 hours and pour off the wonderful consommé (not much – but good); if decent meat went into the pot, you can make some Game Pâté with Green Peppercorns (p. 49) too. Quite a number of recipes like rillettes, pâtés, terrines and braises and Devilled Game (p. 198) use up the leg meat, the prime meat being used elsewhere. Nothing need be wasted; hearts and gizzards make confit, livers make pâté, carcasses make stock and a pot of pheasant, duck or goose dripping (not venison fat which is horrid) is wonderful for frying croûtes, noodles, spätzle or potatoes. My definition of a good cook is someone who can make something really delicious from what is left over.

Savoury Woodcock Croûtes

One strongly flavoured little woodcock can make a tasty savoury for 4–6 people if prepared in this way, or a supper for two! Mature woodcock have much darker flesh than young birds and can take very high seasoning.

Ingredients   *Serves 4–6*
1 mature woodcock
bard of pork fat
2½ oz (65 g) best butter
2–3 tbs Cognac
2–3 tbs stock
¼–½ teasp Dijon mustard
1 tbs Madeira
4–6 thick slanting slices stale French bread
salt and crushed coarse black pepper or
      peppermill mixture

Remove the crop and gizzard only (p. 128). Bard with pork fat and tie on. Heat the butter in a small heavy pan or cocotte and brown the bird gently all over for 15 minutes or so. Pour 2 tbs Cognac over it and flame; cover and cook very gently on the edge of the stove or in a slow oven for 2 hours, adding 1 tbs stock as necessary. Remove all the meat, which by now should fall off the bird, and process it with the scraped out trail (innards) and the pork bard. Add the mustard, Madeira and remaining brandy and a spoon or two of the cooking juices to make a smooth pâté, season highly and keep warm or re-heat.

Toast the stale bread on both sides, spoon some of the hot buttery cooking juices over each and spread with the woodcock mixture. Pop into a hot oven for a few moments and serve sizzling hot.

Suggested Wine. Rather a gourmet dish so suitable as a savoury on some occasion when you are already drinking a good claret.

Baked Brown and Wild Rice with Game

An invaluable dish for using up any leftover game and I love brown rice, such a comfortable dish. Mix it with a little wild rice for extra style and crunch for a party if you wish or serve it plain to accompany roast game. Fry the onion and rice in a little duck or goose fat if you have it but then be rather spare when using up fatty duck or goose or it can become a bit greasy. You can vary the flavouring endlessly with, for instance, a little curry with venison, diced lime pickle with rich duck or other game or again a pinch of coriander, cumin or celery seed with pheasant and caraway with wild boar.

Ingredients   *Serves 4–6*
8–12 oz (225–350 g) cooked game, diced
10–12 oz (275–350 g) long grain brown
    rice
1–2 oz (25–50 g) wild rice (optional),
    covered in boiling water and soaked for 1
    hour and drained
1 finely chopped onion
1 stick celery, diced
4–6 oz (100–175 g) mushrooms, sliced
2 tbs fat, dripping oil or butter
1 tbs tomato purée
1 tbs currants
about 1 pt (600 ml) good game stock
salt and pepper

Fry the onion, celery and mushrooms in the fat in a casserole until softened, then add the brown rice. Fry for another 2–3 minutes to seal the starch on to the grains of rice then stir in the soaked wild rice, if used, tomato purée, meat, currants and hot stock. Season, stir once, cover closely and cook in a slow oven (300°F/150°C/Gas 2) for about 1½–2 hours, or simmer very gently until tender. Taste a few grains of rice taken from the middle to see if they are tender but still a bit chewy. If all the stock has not gone, boil fast for a moment or, if the mixture is dry before the rice is tender, add a little more boiling stock or water. Toss lightly with a fork before serving. This dish will keep warm in a very slow oven or re-heats well.

Suggested Wine. French provincial red.

Hot Game Soufflé

This is such a useful dish if you either only have a small quantity of some tasty game or some bits and pieces too small to offer on their own. Make sure you use flavourful game and season it highly. I am a great believer in both anchovy and cayenne as flavour-heighteners though they were more often used in the old days.

You will note that I use a moderate oven for cooking soufflés; they rise just as well as in a hot oven but you have a little more time to serve them while they are at perfection which is easier for the home cook.

Serves 4–6 as a first course
or 3–4 as a main course

Ingredients

To cook the game

1 grouse, or use other tasty game meats
2 tbs oil
1 small onion, sliced
1 carrot, sliced
½ stick celery, sliced
1 clove garlic
1 sprig lemon thyme
¼ pt (150 ml) good red wine
salt, pepper and mace

Soufflé

4–6 oz (100–175 g) cooked game meat
vegetables with which the game was cooked
1 oz (25 g) butter
1 oz (25 g) flour
6–8 fl oz (175–225 ml) reduced game stock
1 tbs Madeira or Marsala
½ teasp anchovy paste
a few drops Worcestershire sauce
4 whole eggs
2 egg whites
salt, pepper and cayenne

To Cook the Game. Season the bird inside with salt, pepper and mace. Heat the oil in a casserole and brown the bird gently all over, adding in the onion, carrot and celery to soften and become golden. Once brown, add the garlic, lemon thyme and wine. Cover tightly with tinfoil and a lid and cook in a slow oven (300°F/150°C/Gas 2) until tender; a young bird will be ready in an hour or so, an old one may take all day! Leave to cool a little then remove all flesh, discarding the skin and set aside with the vegetables, but not the lemon thyme, for the soufflé. Either use the strong pan juices, supplemented with a little strong game stock for the soufflé base, or break up the bones of the carcass and boil up with a little wine, water and usual stock ingredients to make a little strong stock.

Soufflé. Melt the butter, add the flour and cook gently, stirring, for 2–3 minutes; then draw the pan off the stove, wait for the sizzling to cease and add the strong stock. Bring to the boil, whisking hard, and simmer for 1–2 minutes. Process the game meat and vegetables to a purée and add in the sauce; add the Madeira, the anchovy and Worcestershire sauce and season highly. Return all to the saucepan, cover and set aside until ready to cook. Generously butter a 1½ pt (900 ml) soufflé dish. Warm the mixture and beat in the egg yolks. Whip the whites until just holding a peak, then fold one-quarter of the whites into the mixture to lighten it. Now fold in the remainder and turn into the prepared dish. Cook in a moderate oven (350°F/180°C/Gas 4) for about 25–35 minutes until the centre just quakes when you shake the dish. Serve at once. If used as a main course, you could serve spinach *en branche*, broccoli or glazed carrots and onions.

Suggested Wine. Light red.

Baked Noodles with Game

This is a nice way to poach game in a slightly spicy Chinese stock, but you can also use leftover cooked game. Home made noodles have a very tender texture but bought ones can equally well be used. Season the sauce highly and keep everything very moist because it's surprising how it dries out as it bakes. A few dried mushrooms added will give extra flavour. A pheasant will give you about 12 oz (350 g) meat, a pigeon only about 4 oz (100 g).

Ingredients   *Serves 6–8*

1 batch home-made noodles (p. 211)

To Poach Game

1 pheasant
2 pigeon
4 pt (2.25 l) stock
4 tbs sherry
2 carrots, sliced
3 slices fresh root ginger
1–2 chillies
bouquet garni of parsley stalks, thyme and
   bay leaf
1 teasp black peppercorns
salt

Sauce

1¼ lb (550 g) diced cooked game meat
   from the birds
2½ oz (65 g) butter
6–8 oz (150–225 g) mushrooms, sliced
2½ oz (65 g) plain flour
½ pt (300 ml) strong stock
1 pt (600 ml) milk
1 teasp tomato purée
3–4 tbs Marsala
3 oz (75 g) Parmesan or strong cheese
good pinch cinnamon
salt and pepper

Topping

4–6 oz (100–175 g) dryish breadcrumbs
2–3 oz (50–75 g) grated Parmesan or
   strong cheese

3–4 tbs sunflower seeds
2 tbs olive oil
a few dabs butter

To Cook the Birds. Wash birds well to remove blood from their cavities. Place all in a pan and simmer very gently (I prefer to put in a slow oven) for about 1–2 hours until tender. Cool, remove and dice the meat; preferably add the carcasses to the stock and simmer until very strong, or just reduce cooking stock for the sauce.

Sauce. Melt the butter in a saucepan, add the mushrooms and cook over moderate heat until they brown and the moisture has all gone. Sprinkle over the flour and cook for a minute or two; draw the pan off the stove, wait for the sizzling to cease then add the stock, milk, tomato purée, and Marsala and bring to the boil, whisking. Let the sauce simmer for 10–15 minutes then add cheese, cinnamon, diced game and seasoning and simmer for about a further 5 minutes.

Meanwhile cook the pasta in plenty of boiling salted water; drain and mix with the sauce, keeping very sloppy. Turn into a greased gratin dish. Sprinkle with mixed breadcrumbs, cheese and sunflower seeds, tossed with a little oil and top with a few dabs of butter. Bake in a moderately hot oven (375°F/190°C/Gas 5) for 35–45 minutes until brown and bubbling. It's nice served with a salad and is a useful dish to prepare and leave all ready for the oven; make sure the game simmers when it is added to the sauce.

Suggested Wine. French provincial or light red.

Devilled Game

Devilled bones were greatly appreciated in Regency times. Young blades would often drop in at their clubs for a late night dish of devilled game, the bitter backbones of game birds being especially enjoyed. The influence of India in these recipes is very noticeable and many gentlemen travelled with their own bottle of strong sauce with which to douse the dubious post house food! This version from Meg Dods is wonderfully tasty and should not be missed by anyone who enjoys a piquant dish, though I have never come across either truffle or mushroom powder (the elusive taste of truffle would surely have been wasted anyway); a crumbled dried *cèpe* mushroom works well. I use this recipe for the accumulated legs of grouse or wild duck, both birds being in some ways better served legless (like the Regency blades) to let the breasts be cooked rare. Devilled game is best eaten in the finger with napkins or fingerbowls available and I usually serve it as a tasty supper for friends though it used also to be a traditional breakfast dish. Sometimes the brains and entrails or a hard-boiled egg was crushed into the sauce, something you could do with woodcock (though personally I find it a bit much).

Ingredients   *Serves 3–4*
6–8 grouse or wild duck legs or other joints
    of game

Seasoning Mix
½–1 teasp salt
½ teasp cayenne or just a shake if you don't
    like it too hot
½ teasp curry powder
1 teasp mushroom or truffle powder
    (optional, if available) or crumbled dried,
    cèpe mushroom

Sauce
good pinch ground mace or nutmeg
grated rind ½ lemon
2 teasp soy sauce
1 tbs mushroom or tomato ketchup
4 fl oz (100 ml) Madeira
juice of ½ orange and ½ lemon (or 2 Seville
    oranges)
½–1 oz (12–25 g) butter or 1 tbs oil

Slash the duck legs and rub in the seasoning mix.

Mix all the sauce ingredients, except the butter or oil, in a pan that will hold all the legs in one layer. Add the legs and simmer, very gently and covered, until the legs are tender, turning from time to time. They can take anything from 30 minutes to 1 hour or more. Then remove the lid and boil fast to reduce the sauce until thick and sticky and adhering to the legs; add the butter or oil and serve very hot. Best served on its own, perhaps with an interesting pilau and vegetables to follow.

Suggested Wine. Big or French provincial red or a pint of best bitter if it's a late evening snack after the gaming-house!

ACCOMPANIMENTS

Game needs to be created as a composition with the right accompaniments, balancing background and highlighted notes. Here are a few of my favourite dishes to accompany game, some of which may be a little unusual to you but all of which complement game in one way or another. As well as these recipes you will find many others throughout the book and well indexed.

Jellies and Conserves

Spiced Grape Jelly

Make this spicy jelly to serve with your game or to add to your marinades and sauces to give that sweet hint which so enhances the flavour of most game. This sets only to a flowing sauce so, if you want the jelly set more firmly, add apple or crab apple peelings and cores to the grapes as they boil to get more pectin.

Ingredients   *2–3 small jars*

2 lb (900 g) grapes (sour outdoor variety   5–6 whole cloves
   are good) to make approx. ¾ pt (450 ml) juice   ¼ teasp ground cinnamon
¾ lb (350 g) sugar   1–2 bits cinnamon stick
1–2 finely shredded fresh red chillies   1 teasp pink pepper berries
¼ teasp ground cloves   2 fl oz (50 ml) white wine vinegar

Wash the grapes and pull from their stems. Crush roughly, using a potato masher or giving them a whirl in the food processor with plastic blade. Turn into a large pan and boil fast for 10 minutes. Strain off the juice and measure (2 lb should make about ¾ pt). To each ¾ pt (450 ml) add ¾ lb (350 g) sugar and the chillies, spices and vinegar. Stir over gentle heat until the sugar has dissolved then boil fast at a good rolling boil for about 5 minutes. Test for a set on a saucer and pot up in clean warm pots. Cover and label when cold.

Redcurrant and Green Peppercorn Jelly

This can be made with a jar of bought redcurrant jelly. It is nice to serve with venison and other game, terrines and pâtés as well as using in marinades and sauces.

Ingredients   grated rind of ½ lemon   *for 8 oz (225 g) jelly*

8 oz (225 g) redcurrant jelly   juice 1 lemon
grated rind of ½ orange   1–2 teasp green peppercorns in brine

Place the redcurrant jelly, orange and lemon rind and the lemon juice in a little pan and heat gently until the jelly melts. Add the green peppercorns with a little of their juice and boil the mixture fast for 1–2 minutes. Draw the pan off the stove and place a drop or two of the jelly on a saucer to test for a set (once cooled it should set or at least wrinkle when you push the surface with your finger). Boil for a minute or so more if it does not set first time, but don't boil for too long or it can go over the set and turn syrupy. Turn into a clean, warmed jar and cool before covering. Stir with a fork before serving with game, pâtés, lamb or ham.

Spiced Drambuie Jelly

A lovely spicy jelly that will keep for a year once made and can be served with all sorts of game or included in marinades. It's quite full flavoured so don't use with delicate game.

Ingredients

1 × 12 oz (350 g) jar redcurrant jelly
julienne shreds of 1 lemon, blanched for
    5–10 minutes
juice 1 lemon
1 stick cinnamon

4 cloves or pinch ground cloves
2 cardamom pods
2–3 tbs Drambuie
a little pepper
¼–½ teasp pink pepper berries

Gently melt the redcurrant jelly and add the lemon shreds, juice, spices, pepper, Drambuie and pepper berries. Boil fast for about 4–5 minutes, test for setting and turn into a jar.

    Serve with cold ham or game pie, or Drambuie Flamed Venison Kebabs (p. 157).

Rowan Jelly

The slight austerity of this jelly makes it a good partner for venison and a good addition to sauces and marinades.

Ingredients

1½ lb (675 g) ripe rowan berries, stripped
    from their stems
1½ lb (675 g) cooking apples

4 tbs lemon juice or 1 teasp citric acid
2½ pt (1.5 l) water
sugar (see method)

Roughly cut up the apples, leaving pips and skin; place in a pan with the rowan berries, lemon juice or citric acid and water. Simmer very gently until absolutely tender or place in a very slow oven (250°F/120°C/Gas ½) for about 4 hours.

    Strain off the liquid using a jelly bag; do not press but just leave to drip for several hours or overnight. Measure the juice and, to each pint, take 1 pound of sugar. Place juice and sugar in a large jam pan or saucepan and heat gently, stirring until all the sugar has dissolved. Boil fast for a few minutes then test for a set by spooning a little mixture on to a saucer, chilling and seeing if the top wrinkles when you push it with a finger. Boil up again and re-test until it does. Pot up the mixture into small, warm, clean pots; cover and label when cold. Serve the jelly, turned into a glass dish, to accompany game dishes especially venison, wild duck and goose.

Mulberry Conserve for Game

The best mulberries I ever tasted were on a great tree I came across while walking in the Dordogne. Never have I tasted such flavoursome and juicy berries and as I sampled them, with brilliant juice trickling down my arms, the farmer's wife appeared; I chatted nonchalantly to her terribly aware of my brilliant crimson fingers, but she didn't seem to mind. Our mulberry at Farthinghoe never has such luscious juicy fruit, but it does make a good conserve for game and the fruit don't have to be too ripe. The only problem is ever getting enough at the same moment.

Ingredients   *5–6 small pots*

2 lb (900 g) mulberries
1 thick-skinned, squeezed lemon shell (for added pectin)
¼ pt (150 ml) water
4 tbs lemon juice
2 lb (900 g) sugar

Prepare your jars by washing them well, rinsing with boiling water and drying out in the oven.

Thinly peel off the outer yellow zest from the squeezed lemon shell (you can leave it on if you prefer your conserve more lemony), cut the white pectin-rich pith into 2–3 pieces and soak in the water, preferably for 2–4 hours. Place mulberries, water, lemon juice and lemon pieces in a heavy covered pan and simmer very gently for about ½–¾ hour (low Aga oven for longer is even better). Once the fruit are soft, add the warmed sugar and boil fast, stirring, until a light set is obtained (a little on a saucer, cooled, wrinkles when pushed with a finger). Remove the lemon pith and leave for a few minutes for the fruit to settle. Pot up in the usual way. Serve with venison, grouse, wild duck, terrines or ham.

Spiced Cherries

Many times in the book I have used a wonderful Italian conserve of wild cherries (Amarena Fabbri) which you may not easily be able to get, so here are some spiced cherries that would do instead. Make them when Morellos are ripe at the end of July.

Ingredients   *1–2 jars*

2 lb (900 g) Morello cherries
1 lb (450 g) sugar
½ pt (300 ml) wine vinegar or cherry vinegar
1 inch (2.5 cm) stick cinnamon
good pinch cloves
good pinch dried ginger

Stone the cherries. Dissolve the sugar in the vinegar over gentle heat and add the cherries and spices. Simmer very gently until the cherries are tender then remove to a sieve. Keep simmering the liquid, adding any juice that drips from the cherries, until you get a very heavy syrup. Remove the cinnamon and return the cherries. Boil up and pot up in clean warm jars. Cover when cold and keep for at least 2 weeks before using. Will keep, even opened for a year or more. Excellent with game.

Sauces

Cumberland Sauce

This classic recipe for a sauce to serve with venison, game pies, some game pâtés or hams comes from my great-great-grandmother's book. It is tasty and zesty and will keep well.

Ingredients

6 shallots
5 tbs white wine vinegar
2 oranges
2 lemons
3 sugar lumps
1 teasp potato flour or arrowroot
5 tbs sherry

1–2 teasp made English mustard
2 teasp ground ginger or grated fresh root ginger
8 oz (225 g) redcurrant jelly
2 tbs Grand Marnier
salt

Dice the shallots finely and simmer in vinegar with a pinch of salt. Take julienne strips from the oranges and lemons and blanch in plenty of water for 15 minutes. Rub the sugar lumps on lemons for zest. Squeeze ½ a lemon and ½ an orange. Mix the potato flour with 1 tbs sherry. Add everything to the shallots, bring to the boil and simmer for 3–4 minutes. Pour into a jar and keep tightly stopped. It is best kept for a few days before serving and it improves with keeping.

Seville Orange Sauce for Duck

This lovely sauce for roast wild or farmyard duck is based on another old recipe I have in my great-great-grandmother's book. It's not difficult to have good duck stock available from the freezer when you need it but Seville oranges are in the shops for such a very short time you must not miss them. Put some away into the freezer and when you come to use them, strip off the zest when the oranges are barely thawed; then microwave or leave to thaw fully before squeezing out the juice but also keep a few in a cool larder or fridge; they will keep for a month or so and longer. Their flavour is so true and intense they are worth seeking but if you can't get them, use mixed orange and lemon for the right effect.

Ingredients   *for 1 duck*

1–1½ pts (600–900 ml) good duck or game stock
2 Seville oranges
¼ pt (150 ml) good red wine
1 tbs honey

1 tbs wine vinegar
a little potato flour or 1–2 oz (25–50 g) butter to thicken or the heart and liver of duck and 1 tbs brandy

Set the stock in a wide pan to boil down by half, skimming if necessary.

With a peeler but leaving the white pith, strip the skin carefully from the oranges. Pile the strips together, cut with a sharp knife into pine needle strips and place in plenty of cold water; bring to the boil and boil for 5–8 minutes until no longer bitter. Drain and refresh under the cold tap; set aside. Add the wine to the stock and continue to reduce until strongly flavoured and less than ½ pt (300 ml) remains. Add honey, vinegar and the strained juice of the oranges to taste. Add in the orange strips and simmer to marry the flavours and to reduce again. Once well flavoured and balanced, you can serve it as it is or thicken it with a tiny bit of potato flour, mixed with cold water, or beat in a little butter, off the stove; or for a darker, gamy sauce, process the liver and heart of the duck until absolutely smooth, adding 1 tbs of brandy, then whisk this in, off the stove, and keep in a bain-marie. *Do not boil or it will curdle.*

Bread Sauce and Gourmet Breadcrumbs

Bread sauce is a real old British sauce (there used to be others; bread, wine, stock and raisins for venison, but none so good) and still a great favourite. Try to use good bread, staled for 4–5 days. I keep bags in the freezer, white for bread sauce, coarse brown and white for fried breadcrumbs and it's then easy to prepare either. If you use fresh modern bread it tends to turn to slimy pap. Good fried breadcrumbs are one of the best accompaniments for game yet often forgotten.

Allow at least ½ hour in a good heavy pan for them to become golden and crispen gently. The addition of shallot and walnuts gives them a very special flavour and I think crumbs are best fried in a mixture of butter and olive oil or good game dripping.

Ingredients   *Serves 4–6*

Bread Sauce

1 small onion	4 oz (100 g) white breadcrumbs
½ pt (300 ml) milk	1–2 oz (25–50 g) butter
3–4 cloves	salt and pepper

Bread Sauce. Finely chop the onion and put it in a saucepan with the milk and cloves. Cover and simmer gently until the onion is tender (about ½ hour). You can do this ahead, if you like, and have the breadcrumbs ready in a bag or from the freezer.

Shortly before serving, fish out the cloves and sprinkle in enough breadcrumbs to make a fairly thick sauce. Don't forget that they swell up so that the sauce gets thicker after a while, and it should not be too solid. Season with salt and pepper and stir in a little butter in small pieces. Keep warm, turn into a sauceboat and hand with the game.

Gourmet Breadcrumbs

7–8 tbs coarse dry breadcrumbs, brown or white	1–2 tbs shallot, very finely chopped (optional)
1 tbs olive oil	2–3 tbs fresh walnuts, roughly chopped (optional)
½–1 oz (12–25 g) butter	

Gourmet Breadcrumbs. Heat the oil and butter in a heavy frying pan and add shallot, bread and walnuts. Toss until bread has evenly absorbed the fat then cook slowly, turning from time to time until dried and crisp and pale golden in colour. Serve with roast grouse, pheasant, partridge, quail, woodcock or snipe.

French Canadian Roast Apple Sauce

This is delicious, and a first-rate choice for wild goose or duck and wild boar, not to mention the domestic varieties.

Ingredients   *Serves 4–6*

1½ lb (675 g) tart cooking apples   1 tbs dark rum (optional)
2 cloves   ⅛ teasp ground cloves
some Demerara sugar   ¼ teasp ground cinnamon
1 lemon

Peel, core and cut apples into quarters or thick slices to fill a baking dish. Add 2 cloves, 2 tbs of Demerara sugar, some grated rind and the juice of 1 lemon; add a tablespoon or so of water and bake in a moderate oven (350°F/180°C/Gas 4) for ¾ hour until tender. Now add rum and sprinkle with the ground cloves and cinnamon and plenty of Demerara sugar. Pop under a grill until the top caramelises and serve.

Cranberry Sauce

We like cranberries lightly cooked, fresh tasting and holding their shape so cook very gently or use a microwave.

Ingredients   *Serves 4–6*

8 oz (225 g) fresh cranberries   a little grated orange rind
juice 1 orange   3–4 oz (75–100 g) sugar

Place the orange juice and rind with the sugar in a pan. Heat, stirring, to dissolve the sugar. Add the cranberries and cook very gently until they are tender but hardly broken up; cool quickly: or place everything in a bowl and microwave, on full power for 1–2 minutes, watching carefully and stopping before they collapse. Leave overnight for the sugar to penetrate the fruit and serve in a sauceboat.

Trenchers, Croûtes and Croûtons

One of the best and most traditional game accompaniments is a slice or crust of bread, toasted or fried for the bird to be set on and for its juices to soak into. Much modern English bread is soggy and disappointing so choose bread from a good baker or use French or Italian bread. (I bring stale bread back from France and freeze it!) Let it get stale for 4–5 days; cut quite thick slices then cut ovals to suit the bird and fry carefully in mixed butter and olive oil or tasty game dripping. Set beneath the bird while it rests to catch the juices. A large slice of bread or trencher toasted then set beneath a pheasant while it roasts is always wonderfully tasty and bread should be set under spit-roast or spatchcock-grilled birds to catch the drips. The liver of the bird can be fried with onion, herbs and sherry to make a *farci* to spread on the croûtes, or in the Woodcock recipe (p. 194), the trail is used. Serve heart-shaped or diamond croûtes with your venison steaks or fry small croûtons to accompany your venison casserole and rabbit or hare dishes. Good fat, proper stale bread cut thick and careful frying are the secret.

Vegetables and Accompaniments

Beetroot with Sherry Vinegar and Caraway

Spicy beetroot is very good with rich game meat, especially hare and venison.

Ingredients   *Serves 4–6*

1–1½ lb (450–675 g) peeled and
   generously diced or segmented beetroot
1 large sweet red onion, diced
1–2 tbs walnut oil
¼ pt (150 ml) red wine or cider
3–4 tbs sherry vinegar or cider vinegar
2–3 teasp sugar
¼–½ teasp caraway seeds
1 clove garlic, finely chopped
salt and pepper
shreds of lemon zest for garnish
coriander leaves for garnish

Gently soften the onion in the oil in a casserole then add the beetroot pieces and fry gently. Stir in the wine or cider, sherry vinegar, sugar, caraway and garlic. Season and cook, covered, either on low heat or in a very moderate oven (325°F/170°C/Gas 3) for about 1–1½ hours or until the beetroot are tender; then remove the lid and boil fast until the sauce is only a syrupy glaze. Correct seasoning and serve scattered with fine shreds of lemon zest and a few coriander leaves for garnish.

Chou Bonne Maman

A simple recipe whose taste belies its simplicity, sent to me by Fafa Randag and coming from her mother-in-law. You can set roast quail or partridge on the cabbage, or half cook birds, cover them with the cabbage and cream and finish cooking them together.

Ingredients *Serves 4–6*

1–1½ lb (450–675 g) cabbage, finely
    shredded
2 tbs butter, fat or oil
1 clove garlic, very finely chopped or
    crushed
1 teasp paprika
8–10 fl oz (225–300 ml) whipping cream
squeeze lemon if necessary
½ teasp salt

Sauté the cabbage in the butter in a large saucepan. Add the garlic, paprika, and salt then turn into a shallowish baking dish; pour over the cream and bake in a moderate oven (350°F/180°C/Gas 4) for about 25 minutes.

Lentils with Butter or Coconut Cream and Parsley

Lentils make a very good accompaniment for rich game dishes such as wild duck and goose or wild boar. You can make a rich sieved purée, beating in butter or fat to go with drier game dishes, saddle of hare, rabbit or grouse.

Ingredients *Serves 4–6*

8 oz (225 g) brown lentils – use brown
    lentils or the little greeny lentils du Puy –
    not the split orange jobs – and not ones
    that have sat in the cupboard for years!
1 small onion, chopped

2 oz (50 g) butter or nut of coconut cream
    (or a bit of both or tasty game fat)
2–3 tbs parsley, finely chopped, or
    coriander
salt and pepper

Wash the lentils well, picking out any stones or grit that may be amongst them. Cover with about 2 pts (1.2 l) of fresh water, add the finely chopped onion and a grind or two of pepper and simmer gently for 1–1½ hours, covered, until tender, adding a little more boiling water should they get too dry. When tender but not mushy, season with salt and more pepper; boil away or drain off excess liquid, if any, stir in butter or coconut cream and parsley or coriander and cook together for a few minutes before serving with game dishes.

For a Lentil Salad. Drain off cooking water and dress with vinaigrette while still warm; serve heavily dusted with parsley.

Chestnut Purée

This is a lovely accompaniment for game, especially the dark, firm meats like hare, pigeon and venison. Buy early chestnuts when they are really plump and fresh (for by Christmas they are often drying and shrivelling) and freeze them for later use.

I am sure my way of peeling them is the best. Follow it carefully and they really don't take long. But if, on sudden whim, you wish to serve chestnut purée with a dish, then it can be ready in about 5–10 minutes from a tin, and nearly as tasty. Make sure you use the un-sweetened purée! See (p. 87) for whole cooked chestnut accompaniment.

Ingredients *Serves 4–6*

1 lb (450 g) (24 or so) large firm chestnuts
1 onion, finely chopped
1 stick celery, finely chopped
2 tbs tasty fat or oil
¾ pt (450 ml) stock (game for choice) just
  to cover
1 oz (25 g) or so butter
salt and pepper

Quick Chestnut Purée

1 tin chestnut purée
1 onion, finely chopped
1 tbs tasty fat or oil
a few tbs stock or sauce to thin
knob butter
salt and pepper

To Shell Chestnuts. I think I have finally found the ultimate in easy chestnut peeling. The trick is carefully to cut halfway round the circumference of each nut, midway on the rounded side between tip and base, and just through the shell and skin. Drop the nuts, a few at a time, into boiling water for 2–3 minutes, then remove them one at a time with a slotted spoon; take them in a kitchen cloth in your hands and push off the top half of the shell and skin (like the top of a boiled egg); then squeeze from the bottom and out should pop the whole nut, leaving the inner skin and shell behind.

To Cook. Soften the onion and celery in the fat or oil, add the chestnuts and just cover with stock; season lightly and simmer gently for about 1 hour until tender; then remove from the stock and process smooth, adding just enough stock to moisten it and a knob of butter at the end; it should have a soft dropping consistency. Correct seasoning and keep warm. Serve as an accompaniment for venison, hare, pigeon or grouse.

Whole chestnuts can be roasted round the joint or bird or served braised (p. 87).

To Make a Quick Chestnut Purée. Cook the onion in the fat or oil until soft and golden; then stir in the tin of purée, adding a little stock or sauce as you beat it smooth. Season with salt and pepper and stir in the butter at the end. Keep warm and serve as above.

Sweet Red Cabbage

A slow cooked dish of red cabbage is very good with game, especially this quite sweet version; serve it in particular with venison, hare and pigeon. When in a hurry I sometimes use cheaty tins of red cabbage, buying the continental varieties which already have apple and spices in; I then just add a little more of this and that flavouring and heat it through.

Ingredients *Serves 4–6*

1–1½ lb (450–675 g) red cabbage, thinly sliced	3 tbs Spiced Grape, Rowan or redcurrant jelly (pp. 199–200)
1–2 tbs tasty fat, butter or oil	pinch ground cardamom
1–2 onions, diced	¼ teasp ground cinnamon
1–2 apples, peeled, cored and diced	potato flour for thickening
3–4 tbs wine vinegar, preferably spiced vinegar	salt and pepper

Melt the fat in a heavy casserole, add the onions and soften without browning. Stir in the red cabbage and apple and toss until glistening with fat; then add all the remaining ingredients and toss again. Cover and cook, either gently on the stove or in a slow oven (300°F/150°C/ Gas 2) for about 1½–2 hours until tender.

Adjust the seasoning and sweet-sour flavour and, if there is too much liquid, either boil it away or thicken with a tiny bit of potato flour, mixed with cold water, stirred in off the stove then brought through the boil.

Caribbean Sweet Potato Purée

Sweet potatoes are now quite widely available and they make a most excellent accompaniment for game, especially with a touch of orange and cinnamon. Good with roast birds, especially duck, goose or wild boar and to accompany roast venison and casseroles.

Ingredients *Serves 4–6*

1½–2 lb (675–900 g) sweet potatoes	pinch cinnamon
2–3 oz (50–75 g) butter	a little milk
grated rind ½ orange	salt and pepper
1–2 tbs brown sugar	

Peel the sweet potatoes, cut into chunks and boil in lightly salted water (you can boil then peel them if you wish). Mash the sweet potatoes, while heating over the stove to drive off excess moisture, and add the butter and orange rind, sugar, cinnamon, a little milk, and seasoning to taste.

Fried Potato Rösti

Grated potato, fried into a crisp cake, makes a very good base on which to serve roast birds. You need a good coarse grater, and mine is an inexpensive little *rösti* grater from Switzerland. You also need a good heavy pan; little omelette pans do nicely for individual servings or an 8 inch (20 cm) pan for 4 people.

Ingredients *Serves 4–6*

1–1½ lb (450–675 g) old baking potatoes, peeled	a little chopped onion, tiny dice of smoked bacon, or caraway seeds (all optional)
2–4 tbs tasty dripping or butter	salt and pepper

Heat 2 tbs of the fat in a heavy 8 inch (20 cm) frying pan. Grate the potato on a coarse grater (some potatoes are better boiled rather underdone, then left for a couple of days before grating and frying) and add straight to the pan. Season (add the chopped onion or smoked bacon or caraway seeds if you wish) and pack down in the pan. Cover with a lid and cook over gentlish heat for about 10–15 minutes until golden brown underneath. Turn out on to the underside of a plate, add the remaining fat or butter to the pan and return the cake for a further 10–15 minutes, with the lid off, to brown the other side. Turn out, cut into segments and serve with roast game or casseroles.

Wild Rice Risotto and Little Wild Rice and Spinach Parcels

Wild rice goes especially well with duck or goose as a risotto or stuffing or packed in spinach parcels.

Ingredients *Serves 4–6*

4 oz (100 g) wild rice or wild rice and
   brown rice mixed
2 tbs currants
2 tbs oil
1 onion, finely chopped   *To Parcel*
4 oz (100 g) mushrooms   12–20 fresh spinach or lettuce leaves
2 tbs unblanched almonds   a drop or two of oil
salt and pepper   butter

Risotto. Wash the rices and soak overnight in cold water. Alternatively, toss into plenty of boiling water, simmer for 5 minutes, then draw off the stove and leave for 1 hour. Whichever way you have prepared it, add 1 teasp salt and the currants to the pan and simmer for 20–30 minutes until just tender. Drain into a sieve or colander, cover with a tea towel and steam for 10–15 minutes. Meanwhile heat the oil, add the onion and soften gently until golden; dice and add the mushrooms and sauté briskly. Cut the almonds into lengthways slices and add with the rice. Toss all together and season lightly.

Serve with game or add an egg and use as a stuffing for wild duck, goose or grouse or wrapped as below in spinach or lettuce leaves.

Spinach Parcels. Blanch fresh spinach or lettuce leaves in boiling salted water with a drop of oil added; then drain, refresh with cold water and pat dry. Line well greased timbale moulds or ramekin dishes, with the leaves overhanging the edges. Pack with the rice mixture and fold over the leaves to cover the top. Cover the moulds with buttered paper or tinfoil and pop in a low oven for 10 minutes or, if left aside, steam or microwave to re-heat when ready to serve. You will lose the colour of the spinach if you keep them warm for too long. Turn out and serve.

Green Herb Pudding

Bag or boiled puddings are one of our oldest heritages. Boiled up in a bag in the cauldron with the meat, they were a staple long before potatoes arrived. Now we only have Yorkshire pudding, white pudding and a few others such as Northumberland herb pudding which includes bistort. Sweet and savoury were frequently mixed and this recipe is based on one demonstrated here at Farthinghoe by Glynn Christian, from Fletcher Christian's grand-mother's cookbook; Elinor Fettiplace's Elizabethan recipe book gives an almost identical recipe without the currants. The use of rosewater, currants, nutmeg and plenty of green herbs gives a most attractive flavour and it makes a splendid foil for a number of game dishes such as wild goose, venison, wild boar or wild duck. In winter, spinach, watercress and celery leaf can be included as the green herbs.

Ingredients   *Serves* 4–6

about 6 tbs chopped fresh herbs like
   parsley, winter savory, sorrel, lemon
   thyme, sweet marjoram and watercress
2 eggs
¼ pt (150 ml) cream or milk
about 3–4 oz (75–100 g) brown or white
   coarse breadcrumbs, dryish
2 oz (50 g) currants
1 oz (25 g) sugar

1 oz (25 g) melted butter, chicken or duck
   fat, or good dripping
2 teasp rosewater
some marigold petals, should you have
   them
plenty of grated nutmeg
2–3 tbs self-raising flour
salt and pepper

Whisk the egg and add the cream; add breadcrumbs to take up the liquid and stir in the currants, sugar, butter or fat, rosewater and chopped herbs, including marigold if used. Season and add plenty (¼–½ teasp) of grated nutmeg then just enough flour to make a soft mixture that will just about hold its shape. Turn into a greased loaf tin or bowl and steam for about 1¼ hours. Turn out, slice and serve with game (or any meat of course).

Spätzle

These are little fat Swiss noodles that make a perfect foil for game dishes. I have found a cheaty way of making them using Matzo meal and they are so easy – and so good!

Ingredients   *Serves* 3–4

3 oz (75 g) Rakusen's medium Matzo Meal
4 fl oz (100 ml) boiling water
1 egg, whisked
1 tbs duck fat, chicken fat or melted butter
1 oz (25 g) butter
a little grated nutmeg
salt and pepper

Pour the boiling water over the Matzo meal in a bowl, add the beaten egg and seasoning and stir it all to a stiff paste; leave for about 1 hour in the fridge.

Take little nuggets, large hazelnut size, of the mixture in the palm of your left hand; with the fingers of your right hand roll them down your hand so they form plump little worms, a little fatter in the middle and of pleasingly irregular shape, and drop off on to a board. When they are all made, tip them into a pan of boiling salted water and simmer for about 5–6 minutes (once you get quick you can form them straight into the boiling water). Drain in a colander and turn into a serving dish.

Heat the butter until nutty and brown and dribble it over the spätzle, add a good grating of nutmeg and serve with roast game and game with rich sauces or casseroles. You can fry a few breadcrumbs brown and crisp in the butter and scatter them over the noodles, or even a few chopped almonds, cashew nuts, hazelnuts or sunflower seeds.

Home-Made Noodles

Well-made noodles, from wide-cut noodles with hare (p. 173) to fine noodles with quail, accompany game admirably. Home-made pasta is easy with a food processor and pasta-roller; use 'hard' bread flour or plain flour with fine semolina for best results. I often use up spare yolks making pasta (all yolk pasta is slightly more tender than whole egg), then freeze it ready-rolled and cut. It only needs tipping into boiling water to cook for a moment. Almost any rich left-over game stew can be tossed with pasta and Parmesan or used as a ravioli filling to make a tasty meal.

Ingredients   *Serves 4–6*
10–11 oz (275–300 g) plain 'strong' flour
   or 8 oz (225 g) plain flour and 2 oz (50 g)
   fine semolina
3 eggs, or 2 eggs and 2 yolks, or 6 yolks   *To Serve*
1 tbs oil   butter, nutmeg, herbs, chopped garlic (all
1 teasp salt   optional)

Place the eggs, flour, oil and salt in the food processor in that order. Process until it forms polystyrene-like granules, adding a little water if necessary, or add more flour if it forms a sticky dough. Press into one lump and rest in a plastic bag in the fridge for 1 hour. Alternatively, sieve the flour on to a board, make a well in the middle, add the eggs, salt and oil and work up to a silky and elastic dough; rest.

Roll the pasta, either taking egg-sized lumps and passing them through the pasta-roller or by hand, dividing the dough into two or more pieces and rolling thinly. Cut on the pasta machine or flour and roll up hand-rolled pasta and cut with a very sharp knife into noodles. Shake out on to a floured tray.

Toss the pasta into plenty of boiling salted water with a few drops of added oil and boil for 2–5 minutes only, tasting for it to be *al dente*; drain, not too well, and toss with butter, pepper and nutmeg or perhaps oil and butter, herbs and chopped garlic that you have heated in a little pan or with your rich game sauce. Keep a little cooking water to add if necessary for good pasta will go on absorbing moisture and should not be served dry.

Serve with game dishes or mix with game sauces as a pasta dish.

Skirlie

As a Scottish family we love this traditional Scots dish of oatmeal and onions fried in dripping. It has a lovely nutty flavour and should be considered in place of fried breadcrumbs or as an accompaniment for saucy dishes of pigeon, venison or hare. A tasty bit of bacon fat, pork fat or suet is traditional but butter, goose or duck fat are sublime. Use fresh oatmeal because old stuff can get a slightly bitter flavour.

Ingredients   *Serves 4–6*
2 oz (50 g) medium oatmeal
1 oz (25 g) fat
1 small onion, finely diced
salt and pepper

Melt the fat in a heavy frying pan, add the onion and cook gently until soft and tender; then add the oatmeal, seasoning and maybe a little more fat; keep turning the skirlie in the pan until it all looks golden and the onions are browned. Re-heat in the pan when ready to use.

Burghal Pilau

This cooked cracked wheat from the Middle East must not be confused with grains of wheat crushed or cracked. It makes a lovely bland accompaniment to many game dishes and it also makes a very versatile stuffing (see p. 63).

Ingredients   *Serves 4–6*
8 oz (225 g) burghal (bulgar or pourgouri
    coarse-ground cracked wheat available
    from delicatessen and health food shops)
1 pt (600 ml) boiling water or stock
2–4 oz (50–100 g) butter or oil
1 small onion, finely chopped
salt

Wash the burghal several times until the water is clear then drain very well. Melt the butter in a heavy casserole and fry the onion until soft; add the burghal and fry over high heat for 5 minutes stirring all the time. Add 1 pt (600 ml) boiling water or stock and salt and boil hard for 5 minutes. Reduce heat and cook, uncovered, for 6–8 minutes until all the water has been absorbed (the cooking time may vary with different wheats). Then cover with a folded tea towel and clamp on the lid; stand on the side of the stove for 15–20 minutes or more before serving. Toss lightly with a fork to separate the grains.

WINE WITH GAME by Simon Cox MW

> When I demanded of my friend what viands he preferred,
> He quoth 'A large cold bottle and a small hot bird'.
> Eugene Field

I had to read these lines twice to make sure I understood them correctly because they are open to very different interpretations. The more I looked at them, the more I realised how precisely they fitted my philosophy about wine and food which is, in a nut, that you should drink what you fancy and what you have to hand while keeping your eye on the more obvious rules. The choice of a magnum of Chablis to match the snipe would mark Mr Field as somewhat idiosyncratic but he may have been inexperienced at the time. My point is that if you like Claret with poached salmon or Muscadet with the guineafowl, go to it, even if it's not the classic answer, though in time your palate may become more conventional. Nicola remembers, as a grass widow when I was in Cyprus with the United Nations, and before she knew much about wine, how difficult it was to choose the right bottle for her dinner parties and to show the wine at its best. So here are a few ideas.

My first thought is what sort of party? Is it a supper party for 12 in the kitchen where the glass of apéritif Alsace will do well with the smoked mackerel pâté and plenty of a decent Côtes-du-Rhône will match the venison stew, to be finished off with the cheese? Or is it a couple of gourmet friends for whom you go to the trouble of making a feast of Kippered Salmon and a last-minute Venison Kebab who will appreciate an old Chablis and that mature Châteauneuf-du-Pape you've been longing to open? Or perhaps it's your big dinner party and you want a more elaborate scene with the perfect apéritif, crisp Chablis with the smoked salmon, your finest Claret with the pheasant and a fashionable dessert wine with the crème brûlée: and then, of course, port! The secret is to suit the occasion, the guests and the dishes, match quality with quality and build up from overture to crescendo.

My own views on matching wine to food are simple but if you want more, glance at Hugh Johnson's *Pocket Wine Book* (Mitchell Beazley) which will give you his precise ideas for trout (Mosel) or wild duck (big-scale red). But don't get too worried if you can't find the exact bottle in your cellar because something else at the same level will probably do just as well; it's largely a matter of common sense if you know a little about the character of the wine. For example, good Muscadet (and they aren't all good) is a perfect match for the oyster; both are very clean, Muscadet almost smells of the nearby sea and the matching liquids are light, almost thin: the same wine with a rich poach of salmon would be overborne and here I would choose a rounder, more full-flavoured wine like fine white Burgundy or an Alsace such as Pinot Gris, Gewürztraminer or an older Riesling – all dry but with the character to cope. With meat it is critically important to balance quality *and* strength of flavour: finest red Burgundy would be overpowered by a roast grouse but would be lovely with a delicate quail, both dishes of quality but with such contrasting strength; similarly, a great Barolo, Italy's proud boast, would knock roast guineafowl to pieces yet be perfect with venison. Dessert wines are equally contrasting in their sheer power or elegant simplicity; Muscat de Beaumes de Venise is a match for plum pudding but slaughters a nectarine which seems to me to be better paired off with one of those delectable Loires, whose northern acidity make a gorgeous balance with their honeyed sweetness; but drink nothing with the chocolate soufflé! Most cheeses (except blue cheeses which, though I love them, cannot really be matched with wine) are suited to the last glass of red wine *before* you address the sweet, as they do in France; port and big reds are classic with Cheddar though I love good Beaujolais with most cheeses, especially the creamier ones, and this is an excuse to open a different bottle. Eminent wine buffs have written whole books on the subject but it might be useful if I listed a few ideas in the simplest possible way at the end; don't be cross with me if I've had to miss out your regular choice.

Apéritifs

The heyday of my favourite Dry Martini is past though it makes a just plausible excuse to go to New York! Our guests welcome a glass of wine and my favourites are few and simple. Fine Champagne is unbeatable but don't bother unless it's good; lightly chilled fino Sherry or any crisp dry white wine is delicious or offer a Kir, the apéritif of Burgundy made of Liqueur de Cassis and, correctly, Bourgogne Aligoté, though any decent dry light wine, not too acidic, will do cheaply and admirably. The other thoughts are a wine, such as many Alsaces, that combine crisp dryness with enough body for you to carry on with them during dinner or a clean Mosel of Kabinett quality.

Dry White Wines

If your pocket is long, you may not need to go further than white Burgundy: Muscadet should be *sur lie* (wine matured on its sediment for extra flavour and which will have these words on the label) and don't buy the cheapest: Sancerre and Pouilly Fumé have country cousins in Reuilly, Quincy and Menetou-Salon and, once removed, in the decent Sauvignons of Haut Poitou and Touraine. Ordinary dry white Bordeaux is, well, ordinary but the best are increasingly good and need 4–5 years in bottle: fine white Rhône is powerful and will score you brownie points and if you choose Alsace you will certainly please any wine merchant at your table. The favourite Italian trio of Frascati, Soave and Verdicchio can be good, though I have most enjoyed Frascati in Frascati and Soave in Verona; look out for the word *classico* on the label which means the best district. There are also some interesting German and French lookalikes from the north east of Italy such as Rhein Riesling and Pinot Grigio. There are some good Hungarian wines (very old and honourable wine traditions), Portuguese Vinho Verde is increasingly popular but I find traditionally made white Rioja a little potent: some of the finest whites now made are the Chardonnays (the grape of white Burgundy) from California and Australia, the latter particularly in vogue and excellent value. I have yet to visit New Zealand but they are now pretty good, getting better and are wines to look for.

Red Wines

The important thing about Burgundy is the winemaker; one vineyard may have fifty or more owners and some will be good, some less so; growers' wine is considered more interesting (not necessarily better) than négociants' wine. Claret is simpler; Château de Fieuzal, for instance, is in one ownership and all bottles, subject to the way they are kept, will be to all intents identical. It pays to understand, not necessarily to memorise, the categories and hierarchy of the Bordeaux classifications so that you can judge the relative *placement* of, say, Château Palmer (a 3ième Cru Classé from Margaux) with Château Siran (Grand Cru Exceptionnel also from Margaux); the former will cost more than twice the latter.

The finest red Rhônes are wonderful wines; drink those from the southern Rhône after four or five years but wait longer for Hermitage and Côte Rotie from the north. Beaujolais is the other major French area; the wines in general are drunk very young though some of the ten Cru Beaujolais (villages such as Fleurie) take a year or three to mature, especially in fine years; Beaujolais Villages is way above simple Beaujolais in quality but only a little dearer. The regional wines of France such as Madiran, Fitou, Bergerac and the good red Loires are sound, often good (especially *in situ*) and usually good value.

Never ignore Barolo and Barbaresco from Piedmont or Chianti Classico from Tuscany and delightful wine comes from the Veneto where good examples of Valpolicellas and Bardolinos offer charming value for money, but look for the word *classico* on the label. Spain is a vast lake of increasingly good wine, readily available and good value, much of the best coming from the Rioja area and from Navarra. Of the rest, California (and elsewhere in the States, especially Oregon which makes some goodish Pinot Noirs in Burgundian style) and Australia make fine, sometimes very fine, quite robust reds, notably from the Cabernet Sauvignon and Shiraz grapes; South Africa and Chile also have good quality and value and so do some of the Eastern Europeans, notably Bulgaria.

Dessert Wines

Sweet German wine is delicate enough to be drunk on its own, with conversation, back in the drawing room after dinner. The others make a lovely finale and a bottle does eight. You won't drink any more, just more interestingly, and the only penalty is eight more glasses to wash up.

Port

The 'Englishman's Wine' and a superficially confusing subject, easily clarified. Ruby and tawny ports are matured in wood and are ready to drink when you buy them; the rest are matured in bottle. Ruby port is a bit ordinary: Vintage Character is a superior Ruby and will suit many occasions: cheap Tawny is also rather ordinary; but 10-year-old is good, 20 is excellent and 40 is superb (but very expensive): Late Bottled Vintage is wine of a single year and can be intended (like Taylor) to be drunk from the bottle or (like Warre) to be treated as Vintage Port and decanted; it was aged longer in barrel before bottling and is therefore more mature at bottling than true vintage port and drunk rather sooner. Crusting (maturing) and then Crusted (mature) Port is good, non-vintage wine that matures in bottle like vintage port and needs decanting to remove from the sediment: Vintage Port is the real McCoy, needs time to mature and must be decanted; the 1975 was drinkable after ten years; the finer vintage of 1977 will need twenty.

Ringing the Changes

It's fun to play tunes. Try some iced vodka in tiny glasses with the Fresh Pickled Trout Fillet or dry Sercial Madeira, a nearly lost classic, with the Game Soup. German gourmets enjoy a sweetish Rheinpfalz wine with rich game dishes while Sweet Champagne or Asti Spumante with the peach is out of fashion but a stunning combination.

Cellaring

If you're lucky enough to have a cellar, keep it cool and free from all smells and you should have no problems unless it floods; in this case a submersible electric pump in a sump should sort the problem. If you make do with a cupboard or the garage, avoid light (throw a blanket over the racks), vibration (from a deep-freezer or boiler) and extremes of temperature change. Wine can cope with most other problems.

Temperature

Start your white a *little* too cool as it soon warms in the glass but do not overchill or you will miss the fragrance and some of the taste; *in extremis*, the deep-freeze can be used but beware. Rosé is served a little less cool and reds should be brought to a comfortable cool room temperature (about 58°–64°F/15°–18°C) as slowly as possible, standing up and preferably over a day or so; do not over-warm. This amply repays your trouble and deposits any sediment at the bottom.

Decanting

This both separates wine from sediment and allows it, if necessary, to breathe and 'come on'; it looks nice in a decanter (I sometimes decant big white wines as well) unless you wish your guests to see the label. The classic method is to decant through a clean funnel with a steady hand and a strong light behind the bottle so that you can watch the sediment. An absolutely clean bit of fine muslin can also be used or, if absolutely necessary, a coffee filter though some consider this affects the aroma and flavour of the wine.

Glasses

Leave your blue Bristol in the cabinet and have clear, preferably uncut, glasses, closed in a little at the top to concentrate the aroma to your nose. Have the glass big enough (nothing is more frustrating than claret in a sherry glass) and only half fill to let the wine breathe and develop.

Style of Wines

Crisp Whites	Muscadet; Sancerre and Pouilly Fumé; young Chablis; Muscat d'Alsace and young Alsace Riesling; dry (sec) Champagne; Vinho Verde.
Best Whites	Good Burgundy; Californian and Australian Chardonnays; fine Bordeaux; good Alsace Gewürztraminer and Riesling; vintage Champagne.
Big Whites	Old Burgundy; Rhône; Rioja; Dão; good Orvieto.
Modest Whites	Alsace Pinot Blanc and Edelzwicker; modest Bordeaux and Burgundy; Soave, Verdicchio and Italian Pinot Grigio and Riesling.
Light Reds	Beaujolais; modest Bordeaux and Burgundy, Valpolicella and Bardolino; California and Oregon Pinot Noirs.
Rosé	Dry or medium sweet from Anjou; dry very light Pinot Noir reds from Alsace; fine dry Lirac and Tavel from the Rhône; Marsannay from Burgundy; Pradel from Provence (a brand); Mateus Rosé (a brand).
Best Reds	Finest Burgundy, Bordeaux and fine old Rhône; best mature Californian and Australian Cabernet Sauvignons; top-class old Barolo or Barbaresco and Chianti Classico; Rioja Reserva and Gran Reserva.
Big Reds	Younger Rhône; Barolo, Barbaresco and Gattinara; Young Rioja; Dão; Californian, South African, Australian, Chilean and Bulgarian Cabernet Sauvignon; Californian Zinfandel; South African Pinotage and Australian Shiraz.
French Provincial Reds	Bourgueil and Chinon; Saint Pourçain; Madiran and Côtes de Buzet; Bergerac and Pécharmant; Corbières, Fitou and Minervois and many Vins de Pays.
Table Wines	Up to a point you get what you pay for but it does *not* usually pay to buy the cheapest. The wines should be attractively fruity and not harsh or too alcoholic. There are some very good Italian wines that can only be sold as Vini da Tavola because they use good French grapes like Chardonnay and Cabernet Sauvignon that are not allowed in traditional Italian wines.
Dessert Wines	Sauternes, Barsac and other sweet Bordeaux; Monbazillac; Sweet Loire; Muscat de Beaumes de Venise; sweet (doux) Champagne; Hungarian Tokay Aszu.

Conversion Tables

Weights			Liquid Measures	
Imperial	*Metric*		*Imperial*	*Metric*
¼ oz	6g		1 fl oz	25ml
½ oz	12g		2 fl oz	50ml
¾ oz	20g		3 fl oz	75ml
1 oz	25g		4 fl oz	100ml
1½ oz	35g		5 fl oz (¼ pt/1 gill)	150ml
2 oz	50g		6 fl oz	175ml
3 oz	75g		7 fl oz (⅓ pt)	200ml
4 oz (¼ lb)	100g		8 fl oz	225ml
5 oz	125g		9 fl oz	250ml
6 oz	175g		10 fl oz (½ pt)	300ml
7 oz	200g		11 fl oz	325ml
8 oz (½ lb)	225g		12 fl oz	350ml
9 oz	250g		13 fl oz	400ml
10 oz	275g		14 fl oz	425ml
11 oz	300g		15 fl oz (¾ pt)	450ml
12 oz (¾ lb)	350g		16 fl oz	475ml
13 oz	375g		17 fl oz	500ml
14 oz	400g		18 fl oz	550ml
15 oz	425g		19 fl oz	575ml
16 oz (1 lb)	450g		20 fl oz (1 pt)	600ml
1½ lb	675g		1½ pts	900ml
2 lb	900g		1¾ pts	1l
2½ lb	1.15kg		2 pts	1.2l
3 lb	1.35kg		2½ pts	1.5l
3½ lb	1.6kg		3 pts	1.7l
4 lb	1.8kg		4 pts	2.25l
5 lb	2.25kg		5 pts	2.8l
6 lb	2.7kg			
7 lb	3.2kg			
8 lb	3.6kg			
9 lb	4.0kg			
10 lb	4.5kg			

Oven Temperature Chart

Resting meat	170°F	75°C	–
Very Very Slow	180°F	80°C	'S'
Very Slow	225°F	110°C	Gas ¼
	250°F	120°C	Gas ½
	275°F	140°C	Gas 1
Slow	300°F	150°C	Gas 2
Very Moderate	325°F	170°C	Gas 3
Moderate	350°F	180°C	Gas 4
Moderately Hot	375°F	190°C	Gas 5
Hot	400°F	200°C	Gas 6
	425°F	220°C	Gas 7
Very Hot	450°F	230°C	Gas 8
	475°F	240°C	Gas 9
Very Very Hot	500°F	250°C	–

INDEX

Page numbers in *italics* refer to illustrations